Gotthold Ephraim Lessing.

Heath's Modern Language Series

Lessings

Nathan der Weise

EDITED WITH INTRODUCTION AND NOTES

BY

SYLVESTER PRIMER, PH. D.

LATE PROFESSOR OF TEUTONIC LANGUAGES, UNIVERSITY OF TEXAS

D. C. HEATH & CO., PUBLISHERS

BOSTON NEW YORK CHICAGO

1 D 8

PREFACE.

THE prominence given to this drama in German literature, the deep philosophical and religious nature of the work, the bitter controversy which was the immediate cause of its publication, the many critical treatises and dissertations which it has called forth, and the profound interest we all feel in the questions discussed, make it desirable to include this work in any course of readings in German literature. It is an extremely suitable book for advanced students, as it contains problems having an especial bearing upon every-day life; it is in fact a drama of life, ennobling, uplifting, elevating above sordid interests, and leading imperceptibly to that higher education of the intellect and soul which belongs to modern advanced civilization. None can read it and understand it without being inspired with nobler views of life, purer views of his duty to God and man, and clearer views of faith, love, charity, and tolerance. As a study of literature it is a gem of the first water, and should become a part of the education of every well-informed German scholar. To the student of language also it offers great inducements for a careful study. For Lessing has put excellent work in this drama, which is a model of perspicuity, originality, and naturalness. The verse is not as polished as that of later writers, but is forcible, energetic, and manly. Goethe declares that Lessing „wurde nach und nach ganz epigrammatisch in seinen Gedichten, knapp in der Minna, lakonisch in Emilia Galotti; später kehrte er erst zu einer heiteren Naivetät zurück, die ihn so wohl kleidet im Nathan." It may well be called the last note of the dying swan, for it was Lessing's last words to the public.

The Introduction contains nothing original, as the eminent critics have left but little to be said on the subject. It simply collects and arranges the information necessary to a proper understanding of the situation of the author and the problem of the drama. Acknowledgment is here given for the aid derived from those whose works are mentioned in the Bibliography on p. 299. Special mention is also made in the body of the work wherever necessary.

The text is based on that of Dr. Robert Boxberger in Joseph Kürschner's *Deutsche National-Litteratur*, Band 6c. Some changes have been made after a careful collation with the excellent text of Lachmann-Maltzahn.

The Notes are critical and explanatory, though the literary side has not been forgotten. The aim has been to bring out all the beauties of the play and show the poet and dramatic critic in his work. For the critic produced masterpieces according to his own high standard proclaimed in his Dramaturgy.

The Bibliography contains only those works treating of the *Nathan*. For general works on Lessing see the Bibliography to *Minna von Barnhelm* in this same series.

For helpful suggestions, thanks are due Professor Calvin Thomas, Dr. Walter Lefevre and Dr. Morgan Callaway, Jr.

SYLVESTER PRIMER.

AUSTIN, TEXAS, May 30, 1894.

INTRODUCTION.

„Lessing's Nathan ist neben Goethe's Faust das Eigenthümlichste und Deutscheste, was unsere Poesie geschaffen hat." — Gervinus.

I. LESSING AND RELIGIOUS PHILOSOPHY.

RELIGION, philosophy, the problem of life, all receive a careful consideration in Lessing's Nathan the Wise, and we cannot fully understand it in its bearing upon the burning questions of that day and our own without at least a general knowledge of the religious questions which the author attempts to solve by his drama and some slight examination of the influence which the philosophy of the period exerted upon the discussions of its religious and social problems. It is the child of the Age of Enlightenment, that age in which the minds of men were deeply moved, in which there was such a revolution of opinions and feelings as had not been since the great Reformation. In fact, the Age of Enlightenment really resumes the prematurely interrupted work of the Reformation and carries it to its logical conclusion. The movement of the Reformation is theological, that of the Age of Enlightenment is philosophical; with the former revelation remains intact; the latter denies divine revelation, and lets religious knowledge consist merely in human thought and feeling.

After Luther the Bible became the norm of faith; but who was to guide the believer in discovering its truth? Was he to be a law unto himself, or should there be a third person, or principle, that should be authority to him? Here the Reformers took two courses diametrically opposed to each other. The one party, who did not wish to trust to subjective reason, to human intellect, interpreted the truth contained in the Bible according to the public confessions and symbols of their own church; a course not very different from that of the Roman Catholic Church. Others, without regard to the confessions of faith in their particular churches, explained the Scriptures according to the dictum of their own subjective reason, thus endangering the truth as a whole, the real body of religious faith; for only when there is some generally recognized principle which will enable us to determine what truth the Scriptures do teach, and to distinguish the true from the false, can the freedom demanded by the Reformers, independent of every mere outer authority, be brought into unison with the objective divine truth.

Soon, however, the spiritual life of the Protestant movement yielded to doctrinal soundness, and the piety of the emotions was underrated. Dogmatism now usurped all authority, which was naturally not at all pleasing to the more devout; hence we find mysticism and pietism rapidly gaining ground. But the real attack on the Lutheran faith came from a quarter hitherto little heeded, and with weapons which had not been used for a long time. It threatened to subvert the entire fabric. Reason in religion was the mighty force which now came to the front and began that destructive Biblical criticism which is still raging. The authority which the Reformers, when contesting the infallibility of the Church, had placed in the Holy Scriptures, had yielded to that criticism which subjected the Bible to the same tests as were applied to classic authors. It was the Age of Enlightenment which made reason the norm by which the truth of revelation was to be judged. Belief became doubt; doubt, rationalism. The bonds of the narrow point of view were rent asunder by the free intellect of a general civilization. German theological rationalism endeavored to test thoroughly the underlying principles of the various beliefs, sift the good from the bad, and elevate the moral standard. The clear and sensible doctrine of morality proclaimed by the rationalists, and moral philosophers spread good morals, freedom of thought and religious tolerance. An attempt was made to reconcile philosophy and religion. Many theologians, who believed that the real orthodox faith harmonized with philosophy, confidently asserted that the union between reason and revelation had been sealed forever. But the attempt at such union proved abortive.

It must not be supposed that this new movement was entirely successful in suppressing the adherents of the old faith. This was not accomplished till the last two decades of the century, when Kant's philosophy transformed the essential doctrines of the Christian belief into general expressions of morality; however, the conflict in which Lessing took such an important part was advanced to another stage by Kant's Philosophy of Pure Reason. The representatives of orthodoxy, who insisted upon the authority of the Bible and the symbols, and also claimed the power of the temporal authorities for themselves, strove with all the means at their command to overcome this enemy who was threatening to overthrow the very foundation of the present theological system.

Early in life Lessing showed a deep interest in everything pertaining to the religious nature of man. In the fragment entitled *Thoughts on the Moravians* he sought to free religious truth from all adulteration, and guard it against the caprice of the opinions, subtilties and sophisms of reason. There he maintained that poverty of knowledge is superior to the arrogance of hollow thinking. Cardan (1501–1576) had represented in his *De Subtilitate* (1552) the four religions of the world, Heathenism, Judaism, Christianity, and Islamism, in a dialogue in which each representative defended his own belief and sought to refute the others. Since Cardan showed indifference as to which was victor in the controversy he was accused of hostility to Christianity. Lessing undertook his defence and easily proved that Cardan was really guilty of favoring Christianity, because he had given to the Christian the strongest, to his opponents the weakest arguments. The Jew and the Mussulman, said Lessing, could have defended themselves against the unjust attacks of the Christian far better than Cardan lets them. Then Lessing took up the cause of the Jew and Mussulman and showed how both could and should have answered. In the defence of the Mussulman he used the arguments of the Deists to prove the superiority of Islamism to Christianity. This religious feature reminds us vividly of *Nathan*, and perhaps Danzel is not far wrong when he says that Lessing's first thought of *Nathan* arose here.

What, then, was Lessing's position on the religious questions of the day? A difficult problem to solve. He certainly was not strictly orthodox, and yet he did not wholly reject orthodoxy and pass over to the so-called school of rationalism which seemed to wish to make *tabula rasa* of the past and leave the future to wild speculation. Lessing preferred to leave the old, bad as it was, till something better could be found to take its place. The trend of Lessing's thoughts was on the side of the movement of Enlightenment. But he was by nature an investigator and needed to examine everything carefully, and to consider thoroughly every possible phase of a question before he decided. In his opinion the final object of religion was not absolute salvation, no matter how, but salvation through enlightenment, for enlightenment to him meant salvation. The bent of his mind was toward historical researches, which distinguished him from the popular philosophers of the day. This led him to his favorite idea of a graded and regular historical development of the religious nature of man. He hated dogmatism of whatever kind, whether of old tradition, of authoritative faith, or of Enlightenment itself, and fought it wherever he found it. That combination of philosophy and religion so popular in his day he opposed. He regretted that the natural partition between the two had been torn down; for "under the pretext of making us reasonable Christians they (these tinkers) make us most unreasonable philosophers."

His controversy with Goeze* gave him the desired opportunity to explain and establish more fully his idea of religion and Christianity. He there makes the true distinction between religion *per se* and the form in which it is clothed at any definite time and by any definite sect. Whether religion with him means anything more than morality still remains an unsolved problem. He certainly understood the distinction between the religion of Christ and the Christian religion, that is, the religion of piety and love of mankind, and the worship of Christ as a supernatural being. This is the central thought of the *Nathan*. "The *Nathan* is the poetic glorification of the idea which considers the human side of the question of more importance than the positive, the moral more important than the dogmatic, which judges man, not by what he believes, but by what he is" (Zeller, *Deutsche Philosophie*, 304 ff.). Lessing did not accept the orthodox doctrines of faith without questioning them; he was too independent for that. He certainly showed that he was a thinker on theological questions who understood the speculative depth inherent in the dogmas of Christianity, and took the field against the Socinians and Deists who ignored that depth. And yet, though often a defendant of Lutheran orthodoxy, the time came when Lessing was considered its greatest opponent, and with much justice, though he was forced into this attitude against his own wish and in self-defense.

II. THE ANTI-GOEZE CONTROVERSY.

While in Hamburg Lessing probably made the acquaintance of the writings of Professor H. S. Reimarus (1768†); for he was well acquainted with the children of the professor, and undoubt-

* Pastor J. M. Goeze of Hamburg, with whom Lessing had his celebrated controversy about the Wolfenbüttel Fragments.

edly received a copy of the manuscript from them. Under the title of *Fragments from an Unknown* he published parts of this manuscript while at Wolfenbüttel in his *Contributions to History and Literature*. Their publication was accompanied by Lessing's notes, in which he called attention to the weakness of the author's arguments, and often suggested how they might best be answered. These fragments excited little interest at first; a mere accident drew public attention to them. The Hamburg Pastor Goeze was then engaged in writing the history of the Low Saxon Bibles, and had written to Lessing to collate a Bible found in the library for a certain passage. Lessing was then in great anxiety about the life of his wife, who lay at the point of death, and either neglected or forgot to attend to the matter. This won him the bitter enmity of Goeze, who considered himself misused. Goeze now took up the subject of the *Fragments* with fanatical rage and declared Lessing's running comments on them to be a hostile attack upon the Christian religion. When outdone by Lessing in this literary passage-at-arms he resorted to the Consistory at Brunswick. The *Fragments* were confiscated and Lessing was strictly forbidden for the future to publish anything on religious matters, either at home or abroad, either with or without his name, without the express sanction of the government. But Lessing was not intimidated, and in 1776 he directed another scathing article at his foe entitled, *Necessary Answer to an Unnecessary Question*. It was the last word of the whole controversy. Thus the affair took a different turn from that which Lessing had at first thought to give it. He now found himself obliged to shake the very foundations of the Orthodox-Lutheran system, and to call forth a battle between the spirit and the letter which has been left to us as an inheritance.

Lessing's Anti-Goeze writings which this controversy called forth have ever been admired for their wit and brilliancy. The genius of this great critic is here shown in its full power. If the wit, even where it plays with the person of Goeze, who was by no means to be despised, produces an elevating feeling in us, the reason of this elevation can only be found in the fact that it is the force of the truth by which we feel ourselves imperceptibly drawn on. His first and greatest contributions are his *Axiomata*, of which the first reads thus: "The letter is not the spirit, and the Bible is not religion. The Bible contains more than belongs to religion, and it is a mere hypothesis that the Bible is as infallible in this *more* as in the rest." Lessing thus distinguishes between the spirit, or the absolute principle from which religion proceeds, and the holy Scriptures, that document in which religion is contained, but in which more appears than belongs to religion. He does not deny, therefore, that that part of the Bible which contains real religious principles was inspired by the Holy Ghost. Consequently objections to the letter and the Bible are not likewise objections to the spirit and religion. His second axiom runs thus: "Religion also existed before the Bible. Christianity existed before the evangelists and apostles wrote. Some time passed before the first of these wrote, and a very considerable time before the whole canon was produced. However much we may depend on these writings, the whole truth of the Christian religion cannot possibly rest upon them. If there was indeed a period in which it had already taken possession of so many souls, and in which assuredly no letter of that which has come to us was written, it must be possible that all that the evangelists and apostles wrote was lost and yet the religion taught by them maintained itself." Lessing could easily prove that the teaching of the first apostles was oral and that tradition was more important than the Scriptures. The *Rule of Faith* existed before any book of the New Testament, and it became the test of the writings of the apostles by which the present canon was made, and many other epistles, though bearing the names of apostles, were rejected. He maintained that it was not possible to show that the apostles and evangelists wrote their works for the express purpose of having the Christian religion completely and wholly deduced and proved by them. Ages passed before the Scriptures acquired any authority, and without the *Rule of Faith* it would be impossible to prove the present Christian religion. This was playing into the hands of the Catholics, but whether intentionally or rather to point out a real defect of the Protestant doctrines, is left ambiguous; it is certainly the weighty point in the contest. Lessing feared that he might be misunderstood and therefore sought to forestall hostile criticism in his third axiom, where he says: "Religion is not true because the evangelists and apostles taught it, but they taught it because it is true. From its inner truth the written traditions must be explained, and all written traditions can give it no inner truth when it has none." In other words, religion does not receive its truth from those who proclaim it, nor does the document in which it is contained lend it a truth it does not possess itself. Religion, then, is independent of the Bible.

The enunciation of this principle caused great discontent among those who could not see any difference between religion *par excellence* and the Bible, its promulgator. Our historical knowledge of revealed religion comes to us immediately from the Bible, but the real knowledge of truth is to be found in independent inner signs which are no more dependent on the Bible than the truth of a geometrical problem is dependent on the book in which it is found. Lessing distinguishes in the Bible the spirit from the letter, the eternal from the temporal. Lessing's contemporaries were not able to comprehend nor fully to appreciate the truth which forms the basis of his polemic against his opponents. In his *Education of the Human Race* he advances to a grander truth, viz., that "what Education is to the individual man, Revelation is to the Human Race. Education is Revelation which comes to the individual man. Revelation is Education which has come to the Human Race, and is the theologians a greater joke than with ten more fragments." In another letter he gives the additional information that "it will be anything but a satirical piece which will enable me tc leave the battle-field with sarcastic laughter. It will be as pathetic a piece as I have ever written, and Mr. Moses (Mendelssohn) has judged correctly that mockery and laughter would not be in harmory with the note I struck in my last paper [*Necessary Answer*, etc.] (which you will also find vibrating in this after-piece), unless I wished to give up the whole controversy. But I do not yet have the least desire to abandon it, and he (Moses) shall indeed see that I am not going to injure my own cause by this dramatic digression." On another occasion he adds: "My piece has nothing to do with our present blackcoats (clericals), and I will not block the way for its final appearance on the theatre, if a hundred years must first pass. The theologians of all revealed religions will indeed silently curse it, but they will be careful not to take sides against it openly." In other words *Nathan* represents his third stage.

The soul of our drama, the leading thought in it, is that piety of the heart, justice, and love first impart the genuine consecration to the confession of the definite, positive faith, such consecration as we see in the centurion of Capernaum, in Nicodemus, in Nathanael the Israelite without guile, in the Samaritan, in Cornelius the centurion, who all received God's approbation. For true religion possesses the power of making one's self well-pleasing to God and man. It may not produce its true effect in everyone; for it requires one condition, namely, faith or confidence, and only he who possesses this faith, this confidence, can make himself well pleasing to God and man. Therefore Lessing was not comparing Islamism, Judaism, and Christianity in *Nathan* and judging the three religions according to their respective merits. The very fact that Saladin is a Muhammedan, Nathan a Jew, and the Patriarch a Christian, but neither of them a true representative of his religion, contradicts this view. There is a good reason why Lessing makes the Patriarch a Christian and Nathan a Jew, as we shall see later on.

The gospel of Christian love is taught in the parable of the Good Samaritan and is found in the words of Christ: "Love your enemies, bless them that curse you, do good to them that hate you, and pray for them which despitefully use you, and persecute you; that ye may be the children of your father which is in heaven; for he maketh his sun to rise on the evil and on the good, and sendeth rain on the just and on the unjust" (Mat. v, 44-45). This unegoistic, disinterested love proceeding from resignation to God forms the kernel of Christianity; we see that Lessing acknowledges this as the vital essence of the Christian religion in his beautiful fragment, *The Testament of John*, who repeated constantly to his disciples the words, "Little Children, love ye one another," and when asked why, answered, "because it is the Lord's command and because when ye do that alone, ye do all." Moreover it is not a comparison of religions, but of men. For religion is not an outer garment, but a living, animating principle which makes its possessor well-pleasing to God and man. And yet every religion which does not confine itself to one individual, but is to take root in a nation, must be expressed in a certain form of divine service, in certain customs and rites. Every nation has its peculiar form of religion. Only when a religion is adapted to the nation which possesses it, can it fulfil its mission and educate the people to true religion. Sometimes the mere outward form covers up the real kernel of religion, but as long as the real kernel is there it has some vitalizing power. True tolerance is quite opposed to mere indifference and proceeds from a firm conviction of the truth of one's own faith; it consists in the fact that we recognize in others the moral principle of their convictions and the historical right of certain symbols and rites. But he who thinks that the true essence of religion inheres in these symbols and rites alone will be just as intolerant as he who denies their origin, their significance, and their justification. Lessing cannot therefore be justly reproached with having made Christianity inferior to Islamism and Judaism, nor does any blame attach to him for having left it undecided which of the three religions is in possession of the true ring. "By their fruits ye shall know them," and has he not made it evident in his *Education of the Human Race* and other writings which of the three he considers highest? And do we not know which produces the best fruits? Let modern civilization answer those who still doubt. Although it is Christianity in which the spirit of Christ reveals the truths of God most perfectly, it is not true of all individuals in it, and no one has the right to draw conclusions about the essence of Christianity from isolated examples. For there is a vast difference between the real, vivifying power of the gospel and sporadic distortions produced by crippled, mis-shapen growth; between the truth of an idea itself and individual appearances of the same; between its effect in universal history and its subjective existence in the souls of individual men.

But why, we may justly ask, did Lessing make a Jew (Nathan), a Saracen (Saladin), the representatives of his higher religion, and make of the Patriarch a true pattern of priestly arrogance and all that is most abhorrent in human nature? It has been well answered that Lessing "wished to preach to the Christians, wished to make them conscious of the foolishness and badness of their intolerant views and shame them; for this purpose distortions from their own faith and noble examples from the non-Christian world served him better. For Christ himself held the Good Samaritan as an example to the hard-hearted Pharisees and stiff-necked scribes; but he did not wish to place Samaritanism above Judaism for all that." (Pabst, p. 148.) We repeat that Lessing did not choose the persons of his drama as representatives of their special religions. For if the Christians of the drama are to represent Christianity, then the Jews and Muhammedans must likewise represent their religions. But neither Nathan nor Saladin, nor Sittah, nor Al-Hafi represents at all his religion; but one is forced to believe that Lessing had just the opposite in view in sketching their characters and actions. For he has either completely suppressed, or at least weakened and placed in the background, the peculiar, innate marks of different faiths by the compensating power of their religion of humanity and reason. No one would be able to extract the true doctrine of Christ from the characters and acts of the Patriarch, of Daja, of the Templar, of the Friar. The only reason which induced Lessing to take his best characters from other faiths and to make the Christians the worst is the lesson he wished to teach. He wished to "hold the mirror up to nature, to show virtue her own features, scorn her own image, and the very age and body of the time his form and pressure." And all for the instruction of the Christians. For he wished to rebuke those who put the letter above the spirit, which results in arrogance, hypocrisy, intolerance, and fanatical persecutions. This was the answer to Goeze and his clan and was the continuation of his controversy by which he hoped to defeat his opponents. Therefore he could not take his dramatic characters in which he intended to show the distortions of the Christian religion from among the Jews and Muhammedans, but must choose them from among the Christians. For his drama was intended for effect upon Christians, as he had his motive from them. Had Lessing been a Jew or Mussulman and wished to give them a lesson, he would have chosen a Christian for his model character.

But the real, deep, underlying reason for choosing a Jew as model lies in the fact that the best criterion of strength and skill in a warrior is the degree of strength and skill shown by his opponent over whom he wins the victory. None of the three religions under discussion offers such a contrast with the idea of the *Nathan* as the Jewish; therefore none of them makes it so difficult for its professor to realize this idea and so interweave it into his character as to make it a living principle of life as the Jewish; none but the Jewish offers so many obstacles for overcoming contradictory errors and vices. The belief in Jehovah as the jealous, angry God of punishment rather nourishes hate than the common love of mankind; the belief in Jehovah and in the Jewish nation as his chosen people leads to national and religious arrogance; to contempt for the Gentiles: it obstructs, or at least renders difficult, the germination of the idea of humanitarianism and cosmopolitanism. The history of the Jews confirms this statement. Even the Templar, who had risen above nationality and positive religion, cherishes such prejudice against the Jews that at first he will have nothing to do with Recha and Nathan: "A Jew's a Jew, and I am rude and bearish." The power of reason and love is all the more magnificent when it triumphs over such prejudices; here is the profound reason why Nathan, who so far surpassed all other characters in goodness and wisdom, is made the principal character of the drama. We must not look for his prototype either in the spirit of the time, which indeed in its tendency to Enlightenment was favorable to the Jews, nor in the personal friendship of Lessing with Moses Mendelssohn, who himself says of *Nathan:* "After the appearance of *Nathan* the cabal whispered into the ear of every friend and acquaintance that Lessing had abused Christianity, though he has only ventured to reproach some Christians and at most Christianity. In very truth, however, his *Nathan*, as we must confess, redounds to the honor of Christianity. Upon what high plane of enlightenment and civilization must a people be in which a man can rise to this height of sentiment, can educate himself to this excellent knowledge of divine and human things. At least posterity must think so, it seems to me; but Lessing's contemporaries did not think so." It is safe to assume that the *Nathan* represents Lessing's third stage in the *Education of the Human Race*, the period of "Peace on earth and good will to men," the reign of universal peace where men shall do right because it is right and govern themselves without law or rulers, as each one will prefer another's interest to his own.

IV. THE THREE RINGS.

The setting of Lessing's conception of a perfect religion is the tale of the three rings, to which we now turn our attention. In the times of the crusades the belief obtained to a considerable extent that Christians, Jews and heathen all serve one God; or, as some stated it, God possesses three kinds of children in Christians, Jews and heathen. The decision of rank for the children of the house rests only with the father. The order of Knights Templars favored these liberal views, and even the foremost thinkers among the Jews believed that Judaism and Christianity were two true religions coming from God and that neither was tainted with deceit. One of their wise rabbis (it must have originated in the eastern country which is so full of metaphorical language) clothed this thought in a parable, afterwards known as the parable of the rings. About the year 1100 a Spanish Jew put it in its earliest and simplest Jewish form. Don Pedro of Arragon once asked a rich Jew, who had the reputation of great wisdom, which of the two laws (Mosaic or Christian) he considered the better, in order to have an excuse for appropriating his money, no matter what answer he might give to the question. The Jew took three days' time for thought, at the end of which he came back to the king in apparent confusion and related the following incident: A month ago his neighbor, a jeweler, on the point of making a long journey, had comforted his two sons by giving each a precious stone. This morning they had asked him, the Jew, about the worth of the two treasures, and, on his explanation that they must wait for the return of the father who alone was competent to decide the question, they had abused him and beaten him. Pedro said that this mean conduct of the sons deserved punishment.

"Let thy ear hear what thy mouth speaks," replied the Jew. "The brothers Esau and Jacob have each a precious stone, and, if you wish to know who has the better, send a messenger to the great Jeweler above who alone knows the difference." Pedro, satisfied with the answer, sent the Jew away in peace.

Between this simplest parable of the precious stones and the richest in every way (Lessing's version in *Nathan*) many members and variations appear, full of pride of faith and spiritual freedom, of exclusive confidence and unsparing skepticism, of universal love of man and narrow hate. The moral lesson contained in all these different versions is the teaching of brotherly love, humanity, and mutual tolerance, — which forms the essence and basis of the Christian religion. And this is the same lesson which Lessing had been trying to teach in his controversy with Goeze, in the *Education of the Human Race*, and the other writings of that period, so that *Nathan* only embodies in poetic form what he had already said elsewhere. In Spain, probably, a third religion was added, the Moorish. The indecision remains, but the early Christian transformation clouded the clearness of the Spanish-Jewish anecdote. According to Wünsche (*Origin of the Parable of the Three Rings*) the next earliest account is found in the *Cento Novelle Antiche*, a well-known collection of Italian stories. In number 72 is the parable of the rings which is nearly like the Arragonian, but we have here a Sultan and three rings, one genuine and two false, the father alone knowing the true one. From here the story passed into the *Gesta Romanorum*, where in one of its three versions we have one additional trait which Lessing has made use of. Here the true ring has the power of making its wearer beloved by God and man. Whether Busone da Gabbio (1311) in his novel *Avventuroso Siciliano* took his version of the parable from the *Cento Novelle* or elsewhere is still doubtful, but it is certain that Boccaccio drew from him. Busone made but few changes: only one ring is genuine, but it is not left to the father to decide which religion is the true one; that still remains undecided With Boccaccio it is no longer an indefinite sultan, but the warlike and heroic Saladin who in his need of money calls the rich and usurious Jew Melchisedec from Alexandria to Jerusalem in order to force a loan from him by means of the vexatious question which of the three religions he considers the true one. The Jew is soon resolved and recounts to Saladin as if by sudden inspiration the story of the three rings. This is essentially the same as that given in *Nathan*, Act 3, sc. 7, to which we refer the reader. The story of Boccaccio varies very little from the other Italian accounts. He does not tell us, as the others did, for what purpose the Sultan needed money. Busone also gives the reason why the Sultan seeks to rob the Jew. Jews are hated, therefore they can conscientiously be robbed of their money. For the tolerant Boccaccio this was wrong, so he changes his Jew into a rich, avaricious usurer instead of leaving him a noble and wise person.

Lessing has made several changes. Besides the fact that the ring has been received from "dear hands" it has the power of making its wearer, who should have confidence in its virtue, well-pleasing before God and man. In order to prevent the son who should possess the ring from alone becoming the head and prince of the house, the father had two others made so like the original that he could not distinguish the true from the false. Rejoicing that he could now show each of his sons the same marks of love he calls each one to him separately and gives each of them a blessing and the ring. After the father's death there arose the same controversy about the genuine ring as in the other versions, and the judge before whom all appeared could give no verdict. Boccaccio closes with the remark: "Each of the three nations believes its religion to be the real, divine revelation; but which has the true one can no more be decided than which is the true ring." Lessing does not stop there. After the judge has dismissed the three wrangling sons from his tribunal on account of lack of proof to form any decision, it occurs to him that there is a key to this seeming riddle. The true ring possesses a magic virtue which cannot fail to manifest itself in the one who has it and wears it in this confidence. As none of the three possesses the power to make himself beloved by the others, so none has the true ring; this must be lost and those they have are false; the father would not bear the tyranny of one ring any longer in his house; each may now think he has the true one, and let each strive to show the virtue of his ring.

The magic virtue is the moral effect of religion. When the judge asks the sons to help the virtue of the ring by meekness, by hearty docility, by well-doing, by inner resignation to the will of God, he shows that these virtues are the moral effects of religion meant by the magic virtue of the ring. In them, and not in the outer, historical symbols and rites, lies the infallible proof of the truth of religion. That religion is the true one which produces the best men. Whether Islamism, Judaism, or Christianity is best adapted to effect this result Lessing does not say, but only implies that it is not impossible in all three. We cannot, however, deny that the way in which the principal character of the drama throws doubt on every positive religion which lays claim to objective truth has something dazzling for the great mass of mankind. It would almost appear as if the story in its comprehensive, graceful form, was well suited to spread that Enlightenment which desires to resolve religion into complete agnosticism. The story is highly poetical, however, and does not completely conform to the real thought. Whether only two of the possessors of the rings, or, as the judge seems to think, all three have been deceived, cannot be decided under the circumstances. But this is only a story intended to inculcate a truth, and must be judged as the parables of the Lord. As parables they may be excellent, even for the special purpose used; but if taken as truths they may be complete or incomplete, true or false in themselves, though quite proper to exemplify the truth which the one employing them wished to teach. It cannot be expected that Nathan, who, according to his own confession, does not wish to give the truth as such, but rather by means of the story which he tells the sultan, thinks himself dispensed from the solution of the problem, will really state the principle which distinguishes the truth of the three religions and and their relation to one another. When Saladin objects that the religions named by him can be distinguished from one another, Nathan replies that they are all based on tradition and history, and adds that it is quite natural that we all, Muhammedans, Jews, Christians, should doubt least of all the words of those whose blood flows in our veins, of those who have given us proof of their love from our childhood.

This mode of reasoning is truly such that the conscience, which does not enter into the inner reasons upon which real knowledge rests, is satisfied. But it does not enter into the greater, profounder depths of the question where knowledge alone can guide. It is true that all religions with any real life to them have an historical background and that children accept the religion of their fathers as something from those who are nearest and dearest to them. But this is only belief founded on authority and is to be distinguished from the real religious belief founded on more perfect knowledge and the inner witness of the Spirit. This is why Lessing insists on the fact that the truth of religion is to be recognized in itself, in its inner characteristics, thus rising to an ideal sphere to which Nathan does not attain. While denying that for him who would gain the knowledge, the characteristics of the truth are already present in the three religions, Nathan gives voice to the sentiment that it is the moral life, love, through which the truth of our inherited religion manifests itself. The manner in which the owners of the three rings quarrel with one another tends to show us that that miraculous force inherent in the true religion is active in none of the three religions whose symbols are the rings. Hence they are urged to emulate this love, so that, perhaps, later the truth might be revealed to their descendants. This love we know is the touchstone of real religion.

Having announced the doctrine of love in the story, the poet shows the moral force springing from pure love in his *dénouement*. Characters separated by nationality, but obeying the purely human feelings, appear before us at the close of the drama in a real union. The powerful sultan Saladin, Nathan, the rich Jew living in Jerusalem, a German Templar, prisoner of the Saracens, Sittah, Daja, Recha, are drawn to one another by similar sentiments, and the ties of blood and the benevolence of the Jew seal the bond. As in nature night yields to the rising sun, so here delusion and hate disappear from the consciences of men as soon as love appears. Oriental and Occidental, Muhammedan, Jew, Christian, rise above particular interests, feel drawn to one another as man to man, even love one another as members of one family. This is the same high standard that we saw in the *Education of the Human Race*. The conclusion of "*Nathan*," moreover, is intended to let us see, imperfectly to be sure, the realization of that ideal claimed only for the future. These characters have advanced far enough to accept the new eternal gospel. But this makes them true Christians, in whose religion alone all the conditions for such a development are found.

V. SOURCES OF THE PLAY.

Besides the novel in the Decamerone of Boccaccio already mentioned, two others have an important bearing on the plot of our drama. The family history, some features in Nathan himself, and, in a certain measure, the character of the Templar are undoubtedly due to Lessing's study of this Italian author. The story related in Giorn. V,V, throws light on the family relations of our characters. It is an account of a lost child like Recha who is reared by a kind-hearted old gentleman, Giacomino, as his own daughter. Here, however, two young men fall in love with her, one of whom turns out to be her brother and the other marries her. All the features of the Templar and Recha are present. The two servants are combined in Daja; and Bernabuccio, the father of the lost girl, is Wolf von Filneck, the father of the Templar and Recha. The lovely characteristic of Boccaccio's Giacomino, "who in his time had experienced much, who was a good-natured man," has passed over to Nathan, while the violent impetuosity of Giannole, the brother, is reflected in the Templar.

Lessing is still further indebted to Boccaccio, Giorn. X, Nov. III. Here we have a man named Nathan who is exceedingly wealthy, benevolent, hospitable, of noble sentiments, giving thirty-two times to the same beggar woman without letting her see that she is recognized by him, going about in modest attire, calm and composed when a rival in wealth and goodness comes and tells him that he is going to kill him because he outdoes him in goodness and benevolence, prudent, noble minded and selfdenying in every way. Had he talked and been a Jew he would have been Lessing's Nathan. How much the Nathan in the Novel reminds of the Nathan in the Drama and yet how skilfully Lessing has transformed and remodelled his characters to suit his own idea to be represented in his drama! For the trend, the idea of the drama is profounder, more consistent, more according to the dictates of reason, than any Boccaccio ever even imagined.

Critics say that Boccaccio was not the only source of Lessing's drama. That absurd story that Dean Swift and Esther Johnson, or Stella, were both the natural children of Sir William Temple, the English diplomatist and political writer, is cited as a source. Moreover Swift wrote the *Tale of a Tub*, a parabolical comparison of the three confessions, Catholicism, Lutheranism, and Calvinism, showing that all three had departed so far from the true spirit of Christianity that there was no more life in any of them. The parable of the Three Rings is certainly more elevated than that of the *Tale of the Tub*, though there is a certain resemblance in the subject-matter and trend of the latter to the drama. Lessing was well acquainted with this story and also with Swift's work. But Caro (p. 74 ff) probably goes too far when he says that Lessing here found that inner association of ideas so necessary for the unity of his drama. For there is no more inner connection between the *Tale of a Tub* and Swift's supposed love to a sister (then considered true, but now known to be false) than there is between the three novels of Boccaccio (I, III; Giorn. X, III; Giorn. V, V). For inner connection is not a personal element, but a natural cause and effect. The complete idea contained in Nathan had long been lying in the poet's mind; its external form was a mere secondary thought which Boccaccio's novels were as likely, and even more so, to put into definite shape as Swift's story and work.

Caro's conceit that the name of Swift's supposed father, *Temple*, led Lessing to call the sister's brother a Templar is a clever one, but has no force. For the historical background naturally brought the Templars into action, and it was only to be expected that they would play a prominent part in the drama. It may be possible that the Swift incident had an unconscious influence upon Lessing. For when Voltaire returned from England he brought the *Tale of a Tub* with him, asserting that this notorious *Tale of a Tub* was an imitation of the three undistinguishable rings which the father left to his three children; and we know that Lessing eagerly read and admired Voltaire before their rupture. But no one now contends that it was the veritable source; for Boccaccio stood nearer in thought to the poet's idea than the Swift source.

VI. TIME AND PLACE OF ACTION.

Had Lessing wished to employ dramatic poetry to represent certain general phenomena of the psychological life he could have chosen no better period or locality for his purpose than Palestine during the third crusade. The East and the West met here, and Palestine formed the center of all the historical life of the age. Richard the Lion-hearted of England, Philip Augustus of France, Leopold of Austria, the most powerful rulers of the West accompanied by the greatest and noblest vassals of their kingdoms, the king of Jerusalem with his barons, the bloom of knighthood in the priestly orders of the Templars and Knights of Malta, and a high clergy; Saladin, the victorious warrior of the East, who ruled from the Nile to the Euphrates and Tigris with his Emirs and Pashas were present. Intermingled with these were the clever merchants from the great commercial cities of the Mediterranean; Jews, experienced and educated by their journeyings in all lands, so that, as Lessing says (3, 10), "all the world flocks together here." This congregation of all mankind in both a friendly and hostile manner, must necessarily have exerted a peculiar influence upon the general culture, must have produced a peculiar sentiment and intellectual development, must have made a peculiar impression upon the views taken of the whole world and of life by the more enlightened individuals, especially upon the religious views, as well of the Jews as of the Christian and Mussulmans. Boccaccio had placed his Jew in Alexandria and had him called to Saladin. For his place of action Lessing chose Jerusalem at a time when Saladin had captured the holy city from the crusaders. Here that people, which called itself the chosen people of God, had assembled for worship. Christ, by his glorious death on the cross, had made the city sacred and had promulgated a universal religion. But during the Middle Ages Jerusalem became the seat of the fanatical rage of both Christians and Muhammedans, who there committed execrable deeds of violence and blood. The spirit of humanity displayed by noble men formed a striking contrast with most frightful intolerance, and thus set off the truths announced by our drama; this very contrast makes the ideal part of our poem more real and the real part more ideal. Lessing wished to exhibit the evils of religious fanaticism, and the reign of Saladin was best suited for that. Time and place were admirably adapted to bring the representation of the three religions into close connection. For at this time the spirit of adventure reigned supreme and rumors of strange incidents and curious events filled the air.

From the historical allusions in the play the exact time, as near as that can be determined, was probably between the first of September, 1192, and the fifth of March, 1193, that is, after the conclusion of the truce with Richard the Lion-hearted, and before the death of Saladin. Though Lessing paid no great attention to strict chronological order, he certainly paints a vivid historical picture, and the local coloring is produced in a truly masterly manner.

VII. ANALYSIS OF CHARACTERS.

As *Nathan the Wise* represents the conflict of tolerance with prejudice, we can on this principle divide the characters into certain groups. Nathan, Saladin and the Templar represent the cosmopolitan and humanitarian idea, while the Patriarch, and, in a certain degree, Daja also, stands for narrow-mindedness and intolerance. The friar and Al-Hafi have a leaning to nature-life, and are representatives of noble Naturalism. Nathan himself properly leads the first group. Lessing is said to have glorified in him his life-long friend, Moses Mendelssohn, but there is not a single trait in Nathan bearing any resemblance whatever to Moses Mendelssohn. Most of the features are taken from Melchisedec and that Nathan of Boccaccio already mentioned, though they have been idealized. Nathan possesses endurance, wisdom, calmness, and affability, and is above all narrowness of nationality and religious difference. As merchant he has visited many lands, and gathered experience as well as gold. He is generous and benevolent towards all. The true religion for him is the one which teaches love to God and man. He is in every way the opposite to Shakespeare's Shylock, and is, in fact, the possessor of the true ring, in that he understands how to make himself well-pleasing to God and man. And yet we have something of the Jew in Nathan; the cunning observable in all his dealings with his fellowmen, his deference to others in order to attain his ends (which, indeed, are always the purest and noblest), a fondness for metaphor and parable, these are all Oriental-Jewish traits. He is the ideal hero who has undergone struggles that excite our interest, and we cannot help loving and honoring him.

The historic Saladin was a strict Mussulman who looked upon war against the Crusaders as his life-mission. For these, his natural foes, he cherished an implacable hatred. He was ever true to his word, ever kept faith with the Christians, though they betrayed him again and again. Brave and intrepid by nature, he was yet a peace-loving man, who rose above his environment and showed himself magnanimous alike to friend and foe. His self-abnegation was great, for at the height of power he felt no desire for mere show and magnificence, but was plain and simple in his daily life. Boccaccio had already made him a traditional hero, and the Middle Ages crowned him with a halo of glory. But little was left for Lessing to do. He has idealized in him imperial greatness, noble sentiments, magnanimity and liberality.

Sittah, the sister of Saladin, is not so tolerant as he, and perhaps for that very reason sees Christians and Jews in a truer light, though not unmixed with prejudice. She takes an important part in the action of the drama, especially in the intrigues. Prudence and cunning are her virtues, and we miss in her the individual truth of a real poetic character. Like her brother she is historical, though history barely mentions her.

By birth and name only does the Templar appear as a Christian. The child of Saladin's brother Assad and a Stauffen lady; brought up by his uncle, a Templar; aroused to action by the latter's tales and the information that his father was an Oriental who had returned home with his mother, he enlists in the Crusades in the order of the Templars, though little convinced of the truth of Christianity. The contradictions in his character are so striking that it will require much reflection to bring the special features into harmony. The predominant trait is the vein of deep melancholy which gives a serious earnestness to his every act. The disharmony in his character and his discontent spring partly from his early training and partly from his recent experiences among the Templars, as Christian and as prisoner in the hands of Saladin. He represents the transition state on his passage from a belief in a positive religion, through disbelief, to Lessing's third stage, to Nathan's standard. He has found that no one belief is infallible, but has not yet discovered that there is always wheat in the chaff, none so bad as to be utterly condemned. At the very end of the drama he still appears distrustful and has to pass through a struggle to renounce his passionate love and accept Recha as a sister. Even then the disharmony fermenting in his inner and outer life is but slowly removed. His striking physical resemblance to Assad, his father, is deepened by his striking resemblance in all the qualities of his character. Nathan represents wise old age, Saladin matured manhood, Curd (the Templar) immature youth, which, like fresh *must* must ferment and foam and by long fermentation become purified.

The most fragrant flower of German literature is Recha. In her simple, cheerful nature all the virtues of a maiden's pure heart blossom. How tenderly she loves her father, what thankful love she bears for Daja! Many features of Recha are taken from Malchen König, Lessing's stepdaughter, who had a deep love for her stepfather, and who was educated by him as carefully as Recha by Nathan. The latter is what Nathan made of her, a susceptible and pure soul which a wise and just education has taught self-abnegation and love. She lived in her father; he was her world, her faith, her home. She is tender without being weakly sentimental, intellectual and cultivated without being a bluestocking. Nathan, however, is not her only instructor. Daja, the Christian widow, the nurse, planted many seeds in her receptive mind, and they also brought forth fruit of another kind. On the one hand we find philosophy and reason, on the other wild fancy and belief in angels, legends, the fanciful side of life. She belongs to the poetic figures of German literature, whose presence can be felt rather than described. Like Goethe's Mignon in *Wilhelm Meister* and Schiller's Thekla in *Wallenstein*, she is a concrete though idealized form of flesh and blood. But nevertheless she is as it were surrounded by a glamour, and seems to us a friendly fairy form which enchants us all the more. Rarely do we catch glimpses of such beings in the world's literature, and yet Germany has given us three, Recha, Mignon, Thekla. As sister of the Templar and niece of Saladin, adopted and brought up by Nathan, she forms a convenient center about which all the separate interests of race and religion converge, being of all three, and yet belonging exclusively to neither of the three races or religions.

Of our second group the Patriarch naturally stands at the head and is an excellent pattern of priestly thirst for power; he has also departed farthest from the doctrines which Christ came on earth to preach, not having the least trace of that meekness and gentleness which forms an essential element of a Christian character. He enjoys life in the fullest, but believes in the dogmatic infallibility of the Church. It has been said that Pastor Goezė, Lessing's bitter opponent in his controversy occasioned by the publication of the *Fragments*, is intended to be represented by the Patriarch, but nothing could be farther from the mark. There may be a few thrusts at Goeze, but the character as a whole is far different, too opposite to be modelled after him. It is the portrait of what a true Christian should not be. Instead of self-abnegation we have self-aggrandizement with all its worldly lusts. No feeling of humanity reigns in his breast. While demanding blind submission from others he seeks to draw profit from everything. Faith is for him a subservient means of power, a pliant tool for satisfying his ambition to rule. Though by nature intolerant and fanatical he is himself only a too willing subject, yielding servilely to every dangerous power, even when it is repugnant to him; creeping where he thinks it will advance his interests.

The character is historical. At the time when Saladin captured Jerusalem the reigning Patriarch was Heraclius, though he left the city instead of remaining as represented in our drama. This Heraclius was a notorious character and very much worse than Lessing has painted him in the drama. He thinks of everything else rather than of the welfare of the souls entrusted to him. He was a politician of the worst stamp. Treason and murder are not only legitimate means with him, but become a duty when the priest says that it is for the honor of God. It was no matter to him how kind the Jew may have been to his adopted daughter Recha; if he had taught her no dogma nor positive religion, then he must burn at the stake. Rather a false belief than no belief. He will show how dangerous it is to the state when anyone may have no belief. So preached Goeze in the controversy. He is a priest and ecclesiastical prince, but not a Christian. He represents rather the office of High Priest, or Egyptian Hierophant, or the priests of the Middle Ages, who were mostly opponents of humanity and pure religion. He is bigoted, and the interests of humanity are subordinate to those of his Church and hierarchy. Without this character Lessing could not have done justice to the fundamental idea of his poem. Fr. Theo. Vischer (*Aesth.* III, 1,433) says: "The Patriarch should have gone to extremes, the Templar should have appeared at the most exciting moment of the danger to rescue Nathan and thus have completed his own elevation above the darkness of prejudice; then the drama might have ended well, only not in the discovery that the lovers were brother and sister." But this would have been contrary to the whole tone of the drama, which is intended to show true tolerance triumphing over intolerance and arrogance by quiet, peaceful means.

In Daja we have an example of *sancta simplicitas*, that narrow piety which becomes dangerous in cunning hands. Firm in her belief, she overlooks the genuine kernel of religion in the form which excites her imagination and produces the frenzy of fanaticism. She is the widow of a noble Swiss squire, drowned with the emperor Frederick Barbarossa on the 10th of June, 1190. Nathan took her as companion to Recha, probably because the old nurse had sickened. Soon after Daja's arrival the latter died, but not before she had disclosed the secret of Recha's birth, though it is a mystery where the nurse could have found it out. According to this account Daja could not have been more than two years in the house of Nathan when our drama opens; and yet the references to her indicate a longer service in Nathan's family. There is no way of reconciling these discrepancies without assuming that Lessing intended to discard the old nurse and make Daja's service with him extend over the whole eighteen years of Recha's life, or else he forgot to distinguish between the two persons, and applied words to Daja which belong to the nurse.

Anxious for the welfare of her fosterchild's soul, she is constantly urging Nathan to make good his great sin of keeping his daughter from the true faith. She does not consider what a noble woman Recha has become under the instruction of Nathan; she only sees a Christian child in the hands of a Jew. Nathan had been led to his high standard of faith by the loss of his family, had blessed the chance which had brought him Recha as a charge, and now the intrigues of the well-intentioned Daja were to put to the truest test what reason and long contemplation had ripened in his mind and made a part of his being. One object of the drama is to show us principles in action ; and thus Daja in a sense becomes the motive principle in it, as she, by intrigue, by confusiug the Templar, and arousing his dormant distrust and setting in action his impetuous nature, applies the power that moves the whole action. She plays also the effective part of an exquisitely comical dueña, and "could ill be spared in the economy of the drama."

In the naturalistic group we have two characters which show different phases of that simple, natural worship of God. The friar came to the East as squire, but after serving many masters he finally left the tumult of war for the cloister, devoting him self entirely to the worship of God, to which his pious nature inclined him. Robbed and taken prisoner by Arabian marauders, he managed to escape and fled to Jerusalem into the cloister of the Patriarch, who promised him the first free hermit's cell on Mt. Tabor. Everything unworthy or wrong was repugnant to his upright soul. Though ever obedient to his oath, he realizes that there are bounds to his obedience, and he keeps back the knowledge that Nathan has a Christian child. What he really lacks is the knowledge of the world. Like the Dervish, his leaning is to the religion of Nature, which drives him out of the world ; but the Dervish easily gives himself up to pure contemplation ; with the latter it is pure, simple, joyous renunciation in which the soul feels the full force of its freedom from worldly care, while with the former it is chiefly humility and the feeling that he is too weak to cope with the complex difficulties of the world. Instead of self-abnegation we find self-disparagement, though he is by no means stupid, and knows how to carry out the dishonest commands so honestly that they never do any harm. He sees a brother in everybody and represents the Publican in Christ's parable, while the Patriarch represents the Pharisee; in the parable of the Good Samaritan he represents the good Samaritan, and the Patriarch, the priest and levite. He is one of the poor in spirit to whom the kingdom of heaven belongs. By some he is called the true representative of Christianity in the drama, and probably comes nearer the standard than any of the other representatives. He certainly has childlike simplicity, and all the qualities which go to make up a true Christian character. It is one of the most lovely personages Lessing has sketched for us; and yet the childlike simplicity, the childlike cunning, forms a comical contrast to the priestly, Jesuitical Patriarch.

The Dervish is so little an adherent of the doctrine of Muhammed that he has been a follower of Parsees. He appears to us as the son of pure, unmixed nature, which, as it is manifested in this character, forms a remarkable contrast to those artificial relations on which the social system actually rests. In the awkward cynic Al-Hafi, Lessing's friends recognized the free copy of a Berlin eccentricity, Abram Wulff, the secretary of Aaron Meyer. He was considered the greatest mathematical genius of the day, who, however, had no idea of the world and its relations. He was also an excellent chess-player, and this characteristic has been skillfully brought out in the drama. Lessing had great respect for him on account of his piety and natural cynicism. The temptation was too great; he was introduced into the drama in the person of the Dervish as the unfortunate treasurer and chess-critic, where he cuts a most wonderful figure. He has free entrance to his friend Nathan's house and preaches undisturbed his principles of cynic philosophy in grotesque words.

VIII. FORM, VERSIFICATION, STYLE AND ESTIMATION OF THE POEM.

Considered from an aesthetical point of view and from the philosophical purpose pervading the whole poem, it has by some been denied the name of drama in the usual acceptance of the word. But there was no lack of material as inducement to a real drama, and this fact undoubtedly aided the poet greatly in giving true, independent life to the action. The general historical situation furnished an excellent foundation upon which Lessing could build with his own inventions. A. W. Schlegel, in his *Lectures on Art and Literature*, remarks: "It is strange that of all Lessing's dramatic works, the last, *Nathan the Wise*, conforms best to the rules of art." "The form is freer, more comprehensive than in the other pieces of Lessing; it is almost like a Shakesperian drama." Usually the philosophical features of the *Nathan* receive so much attention that the high artistic qualities of the work are neglected. The action is slower because the development of the truths Lessing wished to inculcate demanded a more quiet movement, but it bears the indelible stamp of classic beauty, whether we call it a drama or didactic poem.

The *Nathan* is the first complete drama that Lessing wrote in verse, not in the usual Alexandrine verse, but in the English iambic pentameter, in imitation of Shakespeare and Milton, which, since the *Nathan*, has become the usual form in real drama. The length of the verse varies from eight to thirteen syllables and, though the pentameters are far more numerous than other measures, still Lessing did not trouble himself much about the matter. The liberties he had taken with the meter deprive the drama of a symmetrical beauty of form, so that the verse often appears harsh and unmusical.

His style is simple, natural, and original. Each character uses the language peculiarly suited to it, and this changes to suit the scene. Not unfrequently Lessing went into the street and picked up the most expressive phrases, and legalized their use by adopting them. Lessing portrays the very spirit of the Orient, and the first Oriental scholars could not do better; the parabolical teachings remind us of the East.

Perhaps no German poem, except *Faust*, has received so much special study as the *Nathan*, and none has certainly rewarded it so well. It has, therefore, held a prominent place in German literature, and will always claim a large share of interest for itself.

J. A. Froude acknowledges Lessing's *Nathan* to be the finest didactic work produced in modern times, but adds "that it will pass away with the mode of thought which gave it birth." And yet the world is over a hundred years older and seems as far from the ideal set up in the *Nathan* as when Lessing wrote his piece, though there has evidently been an advance in many ways. It is true that this drama has here served the poet in making a special plea, but all who love art for art's sake must perceive that the feat is achieved with true power, even if we are forced to admit that Lessing's conceptions are rather those of the understanding than of the imagination and passion. The drama, however has those qualities which will stand the buffets and shocks of time.

Nathan der Weise

Ein dramatisches Gedicht in fünf Aufzügen

Introite, nam et heic Dii sunt.
Apud Gellium.

[1779]

Personen.

Sultan Saladin.

Sittah, dessen Schwester.

Nathan, ein reicher Jude in Jerusalem.

Recha, dessen angenommene Tochter.

Daja, eine Christin, aber im Hause des Juden, als Gesellschafterin der Recha.

Ein junger Tempelherr.

Ein Derwisch.

Der Patriarch von Jerusalem.

Ein Klosterbruder.

Ein Emir nebst verschiedenen Mameluken des Saladin.

Die Scene ist in Jerusalem.

Erster Aufzug.

Erster Auftritt.

Scene: Flur in Nathans Hause.

Nathan von der Reise kommend. Daja ihm entgegen.

Daja.

Er ist es! Nathan! — Gott sei ewig Dank,
Daß Ihr doch endlich einmal wiederkommt.

Nathan.

Ja, Daja, Gott sei Dank! Doch warum endlich?
Hab' ich denn eher wiederkommen wollen?
5 Und wiederkommen können? Babylon
Ist von Jerusalem, wie ich den Weg,
Seitab bald rechts, bald links, zu nehmen bin
Genötigt worden, gut zweihundert Meilen;
Und Schulden einkassieren ist gewiß
10 Auch kein Geschäft, das merklich fördert, das
So von der Hand sich schlagen läßt.

Daja.

O Nathan,
Wie elend, elend hättet Ihr indeß
Hier werden können! Euer Haus . . .

Nathan.

Das brannte.
So hab' ich schon vernommen. — Gebe Gott,
15 Daß ich nur alles schon vernommen habe!

Daja.

Und wäre leicht von Grund aus abgebrannt.

Nathan.

Dann, Daja, hätten wir ein neues uns
Gebaut, und ein bequemeres.

Daja.

Schon wahr! —
Doch Recha wär' bei einem Haare mit
20 Verbrannt.

Nathan.

Verbrannt? Wer? meine Recha? sie? —
Das hab' ich nicht gehört. — Nun dann! So hätte
Ich keines Hauses mehr bedurft. — Verbrannt
Bei einem Haare! — Ha! sie ist es wohl!
Ist wirklich wohl verbrannt! — Sag nur heraus!
25 Heraus nur! — Töte mich: und martre mich
Nicht länger. — Ja, sie ist verbrannt.

Daja.

Wenn sie
Es wäre, würdet Ihr von mir es hören?

Nathan.

Warum erschreckest du mich denn? — O Recha!
O meine Recha!

Daja.

Eure? Eure Recha?

Nathan.

30 Wenn ich mich wieder je entwöhnen müßte,
Dies Kind mein Kind zu nennen!

Daja.

Nennt Ihr alles,
Was Ihr besitzt, mit eben soviel Rechte
Das Eure?

Nathan.

Nichts mit größerm! Alles, was
Ich sonst besitze, hat Natur und Glück
35 Mir zugeteilt. Dies Eigentum allein
Dank' ich der Tugend.

Daja.

O, wie teuer laßt
Ihr Eure Güte, Nathan, mich bezahlen!
Wenn Güt', in solcher Absicht ausgeübt,
Noch Güte heißen kann!

Nathan.

In solcher Absicht?
40 In welcher?

Daja.

Mein Gewissen . . .

Nathan.

Daja, laß
Vor allen Dingen dir erzählen . . .

Daja.

Mein
Gewissen, sag' ich . . .

Nathan.

Was in Babylon
Für einen schönen Stoff ich dir gekauft.
45 So reich, und mit Geschmack so reich! Ich bringe
Für Recha selbst kaum einen schönern mit.

Daja.

Was hilft's? Denn mein Gewissen, muß ich Euch
Nur sagen, läßt sich länger nicht betäuben.

Nathan.

Und wie die Spangen, wie die Ohrgehenke,
Wie Ring und Kette dir gefallen werden,
50 Die in Damaskus ich dir ausgesucht:
Verlanget mich zu sehn.

Daja.

So seid Ihr nun!
Wenn Ihr nur schenken könnt! nur schenken könnt!

Nathan.

Nimm du so gern, als ich dir geb': — und schweig!

Daja.

Und schweig! — Wer zweifelt, Nathan, daß Ihr nicht
55 Die Ehrlichkeit, die Großmut selber seid?
Und doch . . .

Nathan.

Doch bin ich nur ein Jude. — Gelt,
Das willst du sagen?

Daja.

Was ich sagen will,
Das wißt Ihr besser.

Nathan.

Nun so schweig!

Daja.

Ich schweige.
Was Sträfliches vor Gott hierbei geschieht
60 Und ich nicht hindern kann, nicht ändern kann, —
Nicht kann, — komm' über Euch!

Nathan.

Komm' über mich! —
Wo aber ist sie denn? wo bleibt sie? — Daja,

Wenn du mich hintergehst! — Weiß sie es denn,
Daß ich gekommen bin?

Daja.

Das frag' ich Euch!

65 Noch zittert ihr der Schreck durch jede Nerve.
Noch malet Feuer ihre Phantasie
Zu allem, was sie malt. Im Schlafe wacht,
Im Wachen schläft ihr Geist: bald weniger
Als Tier, bald mehr als Engel.

Nathan.

Armes Kind!

70 Was sind wir Menschen!

Daja.

Diesen Morgen lag
Sie lange mit verschloßnem Aug' und war
Wie tot. Schnell fuhr sie auf und rief: „Horch! horch!
Da kommen die Kamele meines Vaters!
Horch! seine sanfte Stimme selbst!" — Indem
75 Brach sich ihr Auge wieder, und ihr Haupt,
Dem seines Armes Stütze sich entzog,
Stürzt' auf das Kissen. — Ich zur Pfort' hinaus!
Und sieh, da kommt Ihr wahrlich! kommt Ihr wahrlich! —
Was Wunder! Ihre ganze Seele war
80 Die Zeit her nur bei Euch — und ihm. —

Nathan.

Bei ihm?

Bei welchem Ihm?

Daja.

Bei ihm, der aus dem Feuer
Sie rettete.

Nathan.

Wer war das? wer? — Wo ist **er?**
Wer rettete mir meine Recha? wer?

Daja.

Ein junger Tempelherr, den, wenig Tage
85 Zuvor, man hier gefangen eingebracht,
Und Saladin begnadigt hatte.

Nathan.

Wie?
Ein Tempelherr, dem Sultan Saladin
Das Leben ließ? Durch ein gering'res Wunder
War Recha nicht zu retten? Gott!

Daja.

Ohn' ihn,
90 Der seinen unvermuteten Gewinst
Frisch wieder wagte, war es aus mit ihr.

Nathan.

Wo ist er, Daja, dieser edle Mann? —
Wo ist er? Führe mich zu seinen Füßen.
Ihr gabt ihm doch vors erste, was an Schätzen
95 Ich euch gelassen hatte? gabt ihm alles?
Verspracht ihm mehr? weit mehr?

Daja.

Wie konnten wir?

Nathan.

Nicht? nicht?

Daja.

Er kam, und niemand weiß woher.
Er ging, und niemand weiß wohin. — Ohn' alle
Des Hauses Kundschaft, nur von seinem Ohr
100 Geleitet, drang mit vorgespreiztem Mantel

Er kühn durch Flamm' und Rauch der Stimme nach,
Die uns um Hilfe rief. Schon hielten wir
Ihn für verloren, als aus Rauch und Flamme
Mit eins er vor uns stand, im starken Arm
105 Empor sie tragend. Kalt und ungerührt
Vom Jauchzen unsers Danks, setzt seine Beute
Er nieder, drängt sich unters Volk und ist —
Verschwunden!

Nathan.

Nicht auf immer, will ich hoffen.

Daja.

Nachher die ersten Tage sahen wir
110 Ihn untern Palmen auf und nieder wandeln,
Die dort des Auferstandnen Grab umschatten.
Ich nahte mich ihm mit Entzücken, dankte,
Erhob, entbot, beschwor, — nur einmal noch
Die fromme Kreatur zu sehen, die
115 Nicht ruhen könne, bis sie ihren Dank
Zu seinen Füßen ausgeweinet.

Nathan.

Nun?

Daja.

Umsonst! Er war zu unsrer Bitte taub
Und goß so bittern Spott auf mich besonders . .

Nathan.

Bis dadurch abgeschreckt . . .

Daja.

Nichts weniger!
120 Ich trat ihn jeden Tag von neuem an,
Ließ jeden Tag von neuem mich verhöhnen.

Was litt ich nicht von ihm! Was hätt' ich nicht
Noch gern ertragen! — Aber lange schon
Kommt er nicht mehr, die Palmen zu besuchen,
125 Die unsers Auferstandnen Grab umschatten,
Und niemand weiß, wo er geblieben ist. —
Ihr staunt? Ihr sinnt?

Nathan.

Ich überdenke mir,
Was das auf einen Geist, wie Rechas, wohl
Für Eindruck machen muß. Sich so verschmäht
130 Von dem zu finden, den man hochzuschätzen
Sich so gezwungen fühlt; so weggestoßen
Und doch so angezogen werden — traun,
Da müssen Herz und Kopf sich lange zanken,
Ob Menschenhaß, ob Schwermut siegen soll.
135 Oft siegt auch keines, und die Phantasie,
Die in den Streit sich mengt, macht Schwärmer,
Bei welchen bald der Kopf das Herz, und bald
Das Herz den Kopf muß spielen. — Schlimmer Tausch! —
Der letztere, verkenn' ich Recha nicht,
140 Ist Rechas Fall: sie schwärmt.

Daja.

Allein so fromm,
So liebenswürdig!

Nathan.

Ist doch auch geschwärmt!

Daja.

Vornehmlich eine — Grille, wenn Ihr wollt,
Ist ihr sehr wert. Es sei ihr Tempelherr
Kein Irdischer und keines Irdischen;

145 Der Engel einer, deren Schutze sich
Ihr kleines Herz von Kindheit auf so gern
Vertrauet glaubte, sei aus seiner Wolke,
In die er sonst verhüllt, auch noch im Feuer,
Um sie geschwebt, mit eins als Tempelherr
150 Hervorgetreten. — Lächelt nicht! — Wer weiß?
Laßt lächelnd wenigstens ihr einen Wahn,
In dem sich Jud' und Christ und Muselmann
Vereinigen, — so einen süßen Wahn!

Nathan.

Auch mir so süß! — Geh, wackre Daja, geh;
155 Sieh, was sie macht, ob ich sie sprechen kann. —
Sodann such' ich den wilden, launigen
Schutzengel auf. Und wenn ihm noch beliebt,
Hiernieden unter uns zu wallen, noch
Beliebt, so ungesittet Ritterschaft
160 Zu treiben: find' ich ihn gewiß und bring'
Ihn her.

Daja.

Ihr unternehmet viel.

Nathan.

Macht dann
Der süße Wahn der süßern Wahrheit Platz: —
Denn, Daja, glaube mir, dem Menschen ist
Ein Mensch noch immer lieber als ein Engel —
165 So wirst du doch auf mich, auf mich nicht zürnen,
Die Engelschwärmerin geheilt zu sehn?

Daja.

Ihr seid so gut und seid zugleich so schlimm!
Ich geh'! — Doch hört! — doch seht! — Da kommt
[sie selbst.

Zweiter Auftritt.

Recha und die Vorigen.

Recha.

So seid Ihr es doch ganz und gar, mein Vater?
170 Ich glaubt', Ihr hättet Eure Stimme nur
Vorausgeschickt. Wo bleibt Ihr? Was für Berge,
Für Wüsten, was für Ströme trennen uns
Denn noch? Ihr atmet Wand an Wand mit ihr
Und eilt nicht, Eure Recha zu umarmen?
175 Die arme Recha, die indeß verbrannte! —
Fast, fast verbrannte! Fast nur. Schaudert nicht!
Es ist ein garst'ger Tod, verbrennen. O!

Nathan.

Mein Kind! mein liebes Kind!

Recha.

Ihr mußtet über
Den Euphrat, Tigris, Jordan, über — wer
180 Weiß was für Wasser all? — Wie oft hab' ich
Um Euch gezittert, eh' das Feuer mir
So nahe kam! Denn seit das Feuer mir
So nahe kam, dünkt mich im Wasser sterben
Erquickung, Labsal, Rettung. — Doch Ihr seid
185 Ja nicht ertrunken; ich, ich bin ja nicht
Verbrannt. Wie wollen wir uns freu'n und Gott,
Gott loben! Er, er trug Euch und den Nachen
Auf Flügeln seiner unsichtbaren Engel
Die ungetreuen Ström' hinüber. Er,
190 Er winkte meinem Engel, daß er sichtbar
Auf seinem weißen Fittiche mich durch
Das Feuer trüge —

Nathan.

(Weißem Fittiche!
Ja, ja! der weiße, vorgespreizte Mantel
Des Tempelherrn.)

Recha.

Er sichtbar, sichtbar mich
195 Durchs Feuer trüg', von seinem Fittiche
Verweht. — Ich also, ich hab' einen Engel
Von Angesicht zu Angesicht gesehn,
Und meinen Engel.

Nathan.

Recha wär' es wert
Und würd' an ihm nichts Schön'res sehn, als er
200 An ihr.

Recha (lächelnd).

Wem schmeichelt Ihr, mein Vater? wem?
Dem Engel oder Euch?

Nathan.

Doch hätt' auch nur
Ein Mensch, — ein Mensch, wie die Natur sie täglich
Gewährt, dir diesen Dienst erzeigt, er müßte
Für dich ein Engel sein. Er müßt' und würde.

Recha.

205 Nicht so ein Engel, nein! ein wirklicher;
Es war gewiß ein wirklicher! — Habt Ihr,
Ihr selbst die Möglichkeit, daß Engel sind,
Daß Gott zum Besten derer, die ihn lieben,
Auch Wunder könne thun, mich nicht gelehrt?
210 Ich lieb' ihn ja.

Nathan.

Und er liebt dich und thut
Für dich und deinesgleichen stündlich Wunder,
Ja, hat sie schon von aller Ewigkeit
Für euch gethan.

Recha.

Das hör' ich gern.

Nathan.

Wie? weil
Es ganz natürlich, ganz alltäglich klänge,
215 Wenn dich ein eigentlicher Tempelherr
Gerettet hätte: sollt' es darum weniger
Ein Wunder sein? — Der Wunder höchstes ist,
Daß uns die wahren, echten Wunder so
Alltäglich werden können, werden sollen.
220 Ohn' dieses allgemeine Wunder hätte
Ein Denkender wohl schwerlich Wunder je
Genannt, was Kindern bloß so heißen müßte,
Die gaffend nur das Ungewöhnlichste,
Das Neuste nur verfolgen.

Daja (zu Nathan).

Wollt Ihr denn
225 Ihr ohnedem schon überspanntes Hirn
Durch solcherlei Subtilitäten ganz
Zersprengen?

Nathan.

Laß mich! — Meiner Recha wär'
Es Wunders nicht genug, daß sie ein Mensch
Gerettet, welchen selbst kein kleines Wunder
230 Erst retten müssen? Ja, kein kleines Wunder!
Denn wer hat schon gehört, daß Saladin

Je eines Tempelherrn verschont? Daß je
Ein Tempelherr von ihm verschont zu werden
Verlangt? gehofft? ihm je für seine Freiheit
235 Mehr als den ledern Gurt geboten, der
Sein Eisen schleppt, und höchstens seinen Dolch?

Recha.

Das schließt für mich, mein Vater. — Darum eben
War das kein Tempelherr; er schien es nur. —
Kommt kein gefangner Tempelherr je anders
240 Als zum gewissen Tode nach Jerusalem;
Geht keiner in Jerusalem so frei
Umher: wie hätte mich des Nachts freiwillig
Denn einer retten können?

Nathan.

Sieh, wie sinnreich!
Jetzt, Daja, nimm das Wort. Ich hab' es ja
245 Von dir, daß er gefangen hergeschickt
Ist worden. Ohne Zweifel weißt du mehr.

Daja.

Nun ja. — So sagt man freilich; — doch man sagt
Zugleich, daß Saladin den Tempelherrn
Begnadigt, weil er seiner Brüder einem,
250 Den er besonders lieb gehabt, so ähnlich sehe.
Doch da es viele zwanzig Jahre her,
Daß dieser Bruder nicht mehr lebt, — er hieß,
Ich weiß nicht wie; — er blieb, ich weiß nicht wo: —
So klingt das ja so gar — so gar unglaublich,
255 Daß an der ganzen Sache wohl nichts ist.

Nathan.

Ei, Daja! Warum wäre denn das so
Unglaublich? Doch wohl nicht — wie's wohl geschieht —

Um lieber etwas noch Unglaublichers
Zu glauben? — Warum hätte Saladin,
260 Der sein Geschwister insgesamt so liebt,
In jüngern Jahren einen Bruder nicht
Noch ganz besonders lieben können? — Pflegen
Sich zwei Gesichter nicht zu ähneln? — Ist
Ein alter Eindruck ein verlorner? — Wirkt
265 Das nämliche nicht mehr das nämliche? —
Seit wenn? — Wo steckt hier das Unglaubliche? —
Ei freilich, weise Daja, wär's für dich
Kein Wunder mehr; und deine Wunder nur
Bedürf . . . verdienen, will ich sagen, Glauben.

Daja.

270 Ihr spottet.

Nathan.

Weil du meiner spottest. — Doch
Auch so noch, Recha, bleibet deine Rettung
Ein Wunder, dem nur möglich, der die strengsten
Entschlüsse, die unbändigsten Entwürfe
Der Könige, sein Spiel, — wenn nicht sein Spott —
275 Gern an den schwächsten Fäden lenkt.

Recha.

Mein Vater!
Mein Vater, wenn ich irr', ihr wißt, ich irre
Nicht gern.

Nathan.

Vielmehr, du läßt dich gern belehren. —
Sieh! eine Stirn, so oder so gewölbt;
Der Rücken einer Nase, so vielmehr
280 Als so geführet; Augenbraunen, die
Auf einem scharfen oder stumpfen Knochen

So oder so sich schlängeln; eine Linie,
Ein Bug, ein Winkel, eine Falt', ein Mal,
Ein Nichts auf eines wilden Europäers
285 Gesicht: — und du entkömmst dem Feu'r, in Asien!
Das wär' kein Wunder, wundersücht'ges Volk?
Warum bemüht Ihr denn noch einen Engel?

Daja.

Was schadet's — Nathan, wenn ich sprechen darf —
Bei alle dem, von einem Engel lieber
290 Als einem Menschen sich gerettet denken?
Fühlt man der ersten unbegreiflichen
Ursache seiner Rettung nicht sich so
Viel näher?

Nathan.

Stolz! und nichts als Stolz! Der Topf
Von Eisen will mit einer silbern Zange
295 Gern aus der Glut gehoben sein, um selbst
Ein Topf von Silber sich zu dünken. — Pah! —
Und was es schadet, fragst du? was es schadet?
Was hilft es? dürft' ich nur hinwieder fragen. —
Denn dein „Sich Gott um so viel näher fühlen"
300 Ist Unsinn oder Gotteslästerung. —
Allein es schadet; ja, es schadet allerdings. —
Kommt! hört mir zu. — Nicht wahr? dem Wesen, das
Dich rettete, — es sei ein Engel oder
Ein Mensch, — dem möchtet ihr, und du besonders,
305 Gern wieder viele große Dienste thun? —
Nicht wahr? — Nun, einem Engel, was für Dienste,
Für große Dienste könnt ihr dem wohl thun?
Ihr könnt ihm danken, zu ihm seufzen, beten;
Könnt in Entzückung über ihn zerschmelzen:

310 Könnt an dem Tage seiner Feier fasten,
Almosen spenden. — Alles nichts. — Denn mich
Deucht immer, daß ihr selbst und euer Nächster
Hierbei weit mehr gewinnt als er. Er wird
Nicht fett durch euer Fasten, wird nicht reich
315 Durch eure Spenden, wird nicht herrlicher
Durch eu'r Entzücken, wird nicht mächtiger
Durch eu'r Vertrau'n. Nicht wahr? Allein ein Mensch!

Daja.

Ei freilich hätt' ein Mensch, etwas für ihn
Zu thun, uns mehr Gelegenheit verschafft.
320 Und Gott weiß, wie bereit wir dazu waren!
Allein er wollte ja, bedurfte ja
So völlig nichts, war in sich, mit sich so
Vergnügsam, als nur Engel sind, nur Engel
Sein können.

Recha.

Endlich, als er gar verschwand ...

Nathan.

325 Verschwand? — Wie denn verschwand? — Sich untern
Nicht ferner sehen ließ? — Wie? oder habt [Palmen
Ihr wirklich schon ihn weiter aufgesucht?

Daja.

Das nun wohl nicht.

Nathan.

Nicht, Daja? nicht? — Da sieh
Nun, was es schad't — Grausame Schwärmerinnen! —
330 Wenn dieser Engel nun — nun krank geworden! ...

Recha.

Krank!

Daja.

Krank! Er wird doch nicht!

Recha.

Welch kalter Schauer
Befällt mich! — Daja! — Meine Stirne, sonst
So warm, fühl! ist auf einmal Eis.

Nathan.

Er ist
Ein Franke, dieses Klimas ungewohnt,
335 Ist jung, der harten Arbeit seines Standes,
Des Hungerns, Wachens ungewohnt.

Recha.

Krank! krank!

Daja.

Das wäre möglich, meint ja Nathan nur.

Nathan.

Nun liegt er da! hat weder Freund, noch Geld,
Sich Freunde zu besolden.

Recha.

Ah, mein Vater!

Nathan.

340 Liegt ohne Wartung, ohne Rat und Zusprach',
Ein Raub der Schmerzen und des Todes da!

Recha.

Wo? wo?

Nathan.

Er, der für eine, die er nie
Gekannt, gesehn — genug, es war ein Mensch —
Ins Feu'r sich stürzte . . .

Daja.

Nathan, schonet ihrer!

Nathan.

345 Der, was er rettete, nicht näher kennen,
Nicht weiter sehen mocht', um ihm den Dank
Zu sparen . . .

Daja.

Schonet ihrer, Nathan!

Nathan.

Weiter
Auch nicht zu sehn verlangt', es wäre denn,
Daß er zum zweitenmal es retten sollte —
350 Denn g'nug, es ist ein Mensch . . .

Daja.

Hört auf und seht!

Nathan.

Der, der hat, sterbend sich zu laben, nichts —
Als das Bewußtsein dieser That!

Daja.

Hört auf!
Ihr tötet sie!

Nathan.

Und du hast ihn getötet! —
Hätt'st so ihn töten können. — Recha! Recha!
355 Es ist Arznei, nicht Gift, was ich dir reiche.
Er lebt! — komm zu dir! — ist auch wohl nicht krank,
Nicht einmal krank!

Recha.

Gewiß? — nicht tot? nicht krank?

Nathan.

Gewiß, nicht tot! Denn Gott lohnt Gutes, hier
Gethan, auch hier noch. — Geh! — Begreifst du aber,
360 Wie viel *andächtig schwärmen* leichter als

Gut handeln ist? Wie gern der schlaffste Mensch
Andächtig schwärmt, um nur — ist er zu Zeiten
Sich schon der Absicht deutlich nicht bewußt —
Um nur gut handeln nicht zu dürfen?

Recha.

Ah,
365 Mein Vater! laßt, laßt Eure Recha doch
Nie wiederum allein! — Nicht wahr, er kann
Auch wohl verreist nur sein? —

Nathan.

Geht! — Allerdings. —
Ich seh', dort mustert mit neugier'gem Blick
Ein Muselmann mir die beladenen
370 Kamele. Kennt ihr ihn?

Daja.

Ha! Euer Derwisch.

Nathan.

Wer?

Daja.

Euer Derwisch, Euer Schachgesell!

Nathan.

Al=Hafi? das Al=Hafi?

Daja.

Jetzt des Sultans
Schatzmeister.

Nathan.

Wie? Al=Hafi? Träumst du wieder? —
Er ist's — wahrhaftig, ist's! — kömmt auf uns zu.
375 Hinein mit euch, geschwind! — Was werd' ich hören!

Dritter Auftritt.

Nathan und der Derwisch.

Derwisch.

Reißt nur die Augen auf, so weit Ihr könnt!

Nathan.

Bist du's? Bist du es nicht? — In dieser Pracht,
Ein Derwisch! . . .

Derwisch.

Nun? Warum denn nicht? Läßt sich
Aus einem Derwisch denn nichts, gar nichts machen?

Nathan.

380 Ei wohl, genug! — Ich dachte mir nur immer,
Der Derwisch — so der rechte Derwisch — woll'
Aus sich nichts machen lassen.

Derwisch.

Beim Propheten!
Daß ich kein rechter bin, mag auch wohl wahr sein.
Zwar wenn man muß —

Nathan.

Muß! Derwisch! — Derwisch muß?
385 Kein Mensch muß müssen, und ein Derwisch müßte?
Was müßt' er denn?

Derwisch.

Warum man ihn recht bittet,
Und er für gut erkennt: das muß ein Derwisch.

Nathan.

Bei unserm Gott! Da sagst du wahr. — Laß dich
Umarmen, Mensch. — Du bist doch noch mein Freund?

Derwisch.

390 Und fragt nicht erst, was ich geworden bin?

Nathan.

Trotz dem, was du geworden!

Derwisch.

Könnt' ich nicht
Ein Kerl im Staat geworden sein, des Freundschaft
Euch ungelegen wäre?

Nathan.

Wenn dein Herz
Noch Derwisch ist, so wag' ich's drauf. Der Kerl
395 Im Staat ist nur dein Kleid.

Derwisch.

Das auch geehrt
Will sein. — Was meint Ihr? ratet! — Was wär' ich
An Eurem Hofe?

Nathan.

Derwisch, weiter nichts.
Doch nebenher wahrscheinlich — Koch.

Derwisch.

Nun ja!
Mein Handwerk bei Euch zu verlernen. — Koch!
400 Nicht Kellner auch? — Gesteht, daß Saladin
Mich besser kennt. — Schatzmeister bin ich bei
Ihm worden.

Nathan.

Du? — bei ihm?

Derwisch.

Versteht:
Des kleinern Schatzes; denn des größern waltet
Sein Vater noch — des Schatzes für sein Haus.

Nathan.

405 Sein Haus ist groß.

Derwisch.

Und größer, als Ihr glaubt;
Denn jeder Bettler ist von seinem Hause.

Nathan.

Doch ist den Bettlern Saladin so feind —

Derwisch.

Daß er mit Strumpf und Stiel sie zu vertilgen
Sich vorgesetzt, — und sollt' er selbst darüber
410 Zum Bettler werden.

Nathan.

Brav! So mein' ich's eben.

Derwisch.

Er ist's auch schon, trotz einem! — Denn sein Schatz
Ist jeden Tag mit Sonnenuntergang
Viel leerer noch als leer. Die Flut, so hoch
Sie Morgens eintritt, ist des Mittags längst
415 Verlaufen —

Nathan.

Weil Kanäle sie zum Teil
Verschlingen, die zu füllen oder zu
Verstopfen, gleich unmöglich ist.

Derwisch.

Getroffen!

Nathan.

Ich kenne das!

Derwisch.

Es taugt nun freilich nichts,
Wenn Fürsten Geier unter Äsern sind.

420 Doch sind sie Äser unter Geiern, taugt's
Noch zehnmal weniger.

Nathan.

O nicht doch, Derwisch!
Nicht doch!

Derwisch.

Ihr habt gut reden, Ihr! — Kommt an;
Was gebt Ihr mir? so tret' ich meine Stell'
Euch ab.

Nathan.

Was bringt dir deine Stelle?

Derwisch.

Mir?
425 Nicht viel. Doch Euch, Euch kann sie trefflich wuchern.
Denn ist es Ebb' im Schatz, — wie öfters ist —
So zieht Ihr Eure Schleusen auf, schießt vor
Und nehmt an Zinsen, was Euch nur gefällt.

Nathan.

Auch Zins vom Zins der Zinsen?

Derwisch.

Freilich!

Nathan.

Bis
430 Mein Kapital zu lauter Zinsen wird.

Derwisch.

Das lockt Euch nicht? So schreibet unsrer Freundschaft
Nur gleich den Scheidebrief! Denn wahrlich hab'
Ich sehr auf Euch gerechnet.

Nathan.

Wahrlich? Wie
Denn so? wie so denn?

Derwisch.

Daß Ihr mir mein Amt
435 Mit Ehren würdet führen helfen; daß
Ich allzeit offne Kasse bei Euch hätte. —
Ihr schüttelt?

Nathan.

Nun, verstehn wir uns nur recht!
Hier giebt's zu unterscheiden. — Du? warum
Nicht du? Al-Hafi Derwisch ist zu allem,
440 Was ich vermag, mir stets willkommen. — Aber
Al-Hafi Defterdar des Saladin,
Der — dem —

Derwisch.

Erriet ich's nicht? Daß Ihr doch immer
So gut als klug, so klug als weise seid! —
Geduld! Was Ihr am Hafi unterscheidet,
445 Soll bald geschieden wieder sein. — Seht da
Das Ehrenkleid, das Saladin mir gab.
Eh' es verschossen ist, eh' es zu Lumpen
Geworden, wie sie einen Derwisch kleiden,
Hängt's in Jerusalem am Nagel, und
450 Ich bin am Ganges, wo ich leicht und barfuß
Den heißen Sand mit meinen Lehrern trete.

Nathan.

Dir ähnlich g'nug!

Derwisch.

Und Schach mit ihnen spiele.

Nathan.

Dein höchstes Gut!

Derwisch.

Denkt nur, was mich verführte! —
Damit ich selbst nicht länger betteln dürfte?

455 Den reichen Mann mit Bettlern spielen könnte?
Vermögend wär', im Hui den reichsten Bettler
In einen armen Reichen zu verwandeln?

Nathan.

Das nun wohl nicht.

Derwisch.

Weit etwas Abgeschmackters!
Ich fühlte mich zum erstenmal geschmeichelt,
460 Durch Saladins gutherz'gen Wahn geschmeichelt —

Nathan.

Der war?

Derwisch.

Ein Bettler wisse nur, wie Bettlern
Zu Mute sei; ein Bettler habe nur
Gelernt, mit guter Weise Bettlern geben.
„Dein Vorfahr," sprach er, „war mir viel zu kalt,
465 Zu rauh. Er gab so unhold, wenn er gab,
Erkundigte so ungestüm sich erst
Nach dem Empfänger; nie zufrieden, daß
Er nur den Mangel kenne, wollt' er auch
Des Mangels Ursach' wissen, um die Gabe
470 Nach dieser Ursach' filzig abzuwägen.
Das wird Al-Hafi nicht! So unmild mild
Wird Saladin im Hafi nicht erscheinen!
Al-Hafi gleicht verstopften Röhren nicht,
Die ihre klar und still empfangnen Wasser
475 So unrein und so sprudelnd wiedergeben.
Al-Hafi denkt, Al-Hafi fühlt wie ich!" —
So lieblich klang des Voglers Pfeife, bis
Der Gimpel in dem Netze war. — Ich Geck!
Ich eines Gecken Geck!

Nathan.

Gemach, mein Derwisch,

480 Gemach!

Derwisch.

Ei was! — Es wär' nicht Geckerei,
Bei Hunderttausenden die Menschen drücken,
Ausmergeln, plündern, martern, würgen und
Ein Menschenfreund an einzeln scheinen wollen?
Es wär' nicht Geckerei, des Höchsten Milde,
485 Die sonder Auswahl über Bös' und Gute
Und Flur und Wüstenei, in Sonnenschein
Und Regen sich verbreitet, — nachzuäffen,
Und nicht des Höchsten immer volle Hand
Zu haben? Was? es wär' nicht Geckerei ...

Nathan.

490 Genug! hör auf!

Derwisch.

Laßt meiner Geckerei
Mich doch nur auch erwähnen! — Was? es wäre
Nicht Geckerei, an solchen Geckereien
Die gute Seite dennoch auszuspüren,
Um Anteil, dieser guten Seite wegen,
495 An dieser Geckerei zu nehmen? He?
Das nicht?

Nathan.

Al-Hafi, mache, daß du bald
In deine Wüste wieder kömmst. Ich fürchte,
Grad' unter Menschen möchtest du ein Mensch
Zu sein verlernen.

Derwisch.

Recht, das fürcht' ich auch.

500 Lebt wohl!

Nathan.

So hastig? — Warte doch, Al-Hafi!
Entläuft dir denn die Wüste? Warte doch! —
Daß er mich hörte! — He, Al-Hafi! hier! —
Weg ist er, und ich hätt' ihn noch so gern
Nach unserm Tempelherrn gefragt. Vermutlich,
505 Daß er ihn kennt.

Vierter Auftritt.

Daja eilig herbei. Nathan.

Daja.

O Nathan, Nathan!

Nathan.

Nun?
Was giebt's?

Daja.

Er läßt sich wieder sehn! Er läßt
Sich wieder sehn!

Nathan.

Wer, Daja? wer?

Daja.

Er! er!

Nathan.

Er? er? — Wann läßt sich der nicht sehn! — Ja so,
Nur euer Er heißt er. — Das sollt' er nicht!
510 Und wenn er auch ein Engel wäre, nicht!

Daja.

Er wandelt untern Palmen wieder auf
Und ab und bricht von Zeit zu Zeit sich Datteln.

Nathan.

Sie essend? — und als Tempelherr?

Daja.

Was quält
Ihr mich? — Ihr gierig Aug' erriet ihn hinter
515 Den dicht verschränkten Palmen schon und folgt
Ihm unverrückt. Sie läßt Euch bitten, — Euch
Beschwören, — ungesäumt ihn anzugehn.
O eilt! Sie wird Euch aus dem Fenster winken,
Ob er hinauf geht oder weiter ab
520 Sich schlägt. O eilt!

Nathan.

So wie ich vom Kamele
Gestiegen? — Schickt sich das? — Geh, eile du
Ihm zu und meld ihm meine Wiederkunft.
Gieb acht, der Biedermann hat nur mein Haus
In meinem Absein nicht betreten wollen,
525 Und kömmt nicht ungern, wenn der Vater selbst
Ihn laden läßt. Geh, sag, ich laß ihn bitten,
Ihn herzlich bitten . . .

Daja.

All umsonst! Er kömmt
Euch nicht. — Denn kurz, er kömmt zu keinen Juden

Nathan.

So geh, geh wenigstens ihn anzuhalten,
530 Ihn wenigstens mit deinen Augen zu
Begleiten. — Geh, ich komme gleich dir nach.

(Nathan eilt hinein und Daja heraus.)

Fünfter Auftritt.

Scene: ein Platz mit Palmen, unter welchen der Tempelherr auf und nieder geht. Ein Klosterbruder folgt ihm in einiger Entfernung von der Seite, immer als ob er ihn anreden wolle.

Tempelherr.

Der folgt mir nicht vor Langerweile! — Sieh,
Wie schielt er nach den Händen! — Guter Bruder, —
Ich kann Euch auch wohl Vater nennen, nicht?

Klosterbruder.

535 Nur Bruder, — Laienbruder nur, zu dienen.

Tempelherr.

Ja, guter Bruder, wer nur selbst was hätte!
Bei Gott! Bei Gott! Ich habe nichts —

Klosterbruder.

Und doch
Recht warmen Dank! Gott geb' Euch tausendfach,
Was Ihr gern geben wolltet. Denn der Wille,
540 Und nicht die Gabe macht den Geber. — Auch
Ward ich dem Herrn Almosens wegen gar
Nicht nachgeschickt.

Tempelherr.

Doch aber nachgeschickt?

Klosterbruder.

Ja, aus dem Kloster.

Tempelherr.

Wo ich eben jetzt
Ein kleines Pilgermahl zu finden hoffte!

Klosterbruder.

545 Die Tische waren schon besetzt; komm' aber
Der Herr nur wieder mit zurück.

Tempelherr.

Wozu?
Ich habe Fleisch wohl lange nicht gegessen,
Allein, was thut's? Die Datteln sind ja reif.

Klosterbruder.

Nehm' sich der Herr in acht mit dieser Frucht.
550 Zu viel genossen taugt sie nicht, verstopft
Die Milz, macht melancholisches Geblüt.

Tempelherr.

Wenn ich nun melancholisch gern mich fühlte? —
Doch dieser Warnung wegen wurdet Ihr
Mir doch nicht nachgeschickt?

Klosterbruder.

O nein! — Ich soll
555 Mich nur nach Euch erkunden, auf den Zahn
Euch fühlen.

Tempelherr.

Und das sagt Ihr mir so selbst?

Klosterbruder.

Warum nicht?

Tempelherr.

Ein verschmitzter Bruder! — Hat
Das Kloster Euresgleichen mehr?

Klosterbruder.

Weiß nicht.
Ich muß gehorchen, lieber Herr.

Tempelherr.

Und da

560 Gehorcht Ihr denn auch, ohne viel zu klügeln?

Klosterbruder.

Wär's sonst gehorchen, lieber Herr?

Tempelherr.

Daß doch

Die Einfalt immer recht behält! — Ihr dürft
Mir doch auch wohl vertrauen, wer mich gern
Genauer kennen möchte? — Daß Ihr's selbst
565 Nicht seid, will ich wohl schwören.

Klosterbruder.

Ziemte mir's?

Und frommte mir's?

Tempelherr.

Wem ziemt und frommt es denn,
Daß er so neubegierig ist? Wem denn?

Klosterbruder.

Dem Patriarchen, muß ich glauben; — denn
Der sandte mich Euch nach.

Tempelherr.

Der Patriarch!

570 Kennt der das rote Kreuz auf weißem Mantel
Nicht besser?

Klosterbruder.

Kenn' ja ich's!

Tempelherr.

Nun, Bruder? Nun? —

Ich bin ein Tempelherr, und ein gefangner —

Setz' ich hinzu: gefangen bei Tebnin,
Der Burg, die mit des Stillstands letzter Stunde
575 Wir gern erstiegen hätten, um sodann
Auf Sidon loszugehn; — setz' ich hinzu:
Selbzwanzigster gefangen und allein
Vom Saladin begnadiget: so weiß
Der Patriarch, was er zu wissen braucht —
580 Mehr als er braucht.

Klosterbruder.

Wohl aber schwerlich mehr,
Als er schon weiß. — Er wüßt' auch gern, warum
Der Herr vom Saladin begnadigt worden,
Er ganz allein.

Tempelherr.

Weiß ich das selber? — Schon
Den Hals entblößt, kniet' ich auf meinem Mantel,
585 Den Streich erwartend, als mich schärfer Saladin
Ins Auge faßt, mir näher springt und winkt.
Man hebt mich auf; ich bin entfesselt, will
Ihm danken, seh' sein Aug' in Thränen: stumm
Ist er, bin ich; er geht, ich bleibe. — Wie
590 Nun das zusammenhängt, enträtsle sich
Der Patriarche selbst.

Klosterbruder.

Er schließt daraus,
Daß Gott zu großen, großen Dingen Euch
Müß' aufbehalten haben.

Tempelherr.

Ja, zu großen!
Ein Judenmädchen aus dem Feu'r zu retten,

595 Auf Sinai neugier'ge Pilger zu
Geleiten, und dergleichen mehr.

Klosterbruder.

Wird schon
Noch kommen! — Ist inzwischen auch nicht übel. —
Vielleicht hat selbst der Patriarch bereits
Weit wicht'gere Geschäfte für den Herrn.

Tempelherr.

600 So? meint Ihr, Bruder? Hat er gar Euch schon
Was merken lassen?

Klosterbruder.

Ei, ja wohl! — Ich soll
Den Herrn nur erst ergründen, ob er so
Der Mann wohl ist.

Tempelherr.

Nun ja; ergründet nur!
(Ich will doch sehn, wie der ergründet!) — Nun?

Klosterbruder.

605 Das Kürz'ste wird wohl sein, daß ich dem Herrn
Ganz gradezu des Patriarchen Wunsch
Eröffne.

Tempelherr.

Wohl!

Klosterbruder.

Er hätte durch den Herrn
Ein Briefchen gern bestellt.

Tempelherr.

Durch mich? Ich bin
Kein Bote. — Das, das wäre das Geschäft,
610 Das weit glorreicher sei, als Judenmädchen
Dem Feu'r entreißen?

Klosterbruder.

Muß doch wohl! — Denn — sagt
Der Patriarch — an diesem Briefchen sei
Der ganzen Christenheit sehr viel gelegen.
Dies Briefchen wohl bestellt zu haben, — sagt
615 Der Patriarch — werd' einst im Himmel Gott
Mit einer ganz besondern Krone lohnen.
Und dieser Krone — sagt der Patriarch —
Sei niemand würd'ger als mein Herr.

Tempelherr.

Als ich?

Klosterbruder.

Denn diese Krone zu verdienen, sagt
620 Der Patriarch — sei schwerlich jemand auch
Geschickter als mein Herr.

Tempelherr.

Als ich?

Klosterbruder.

Er sei
Hier frei; könn' überall sich hier besehn;
Versteh', wie eine Stadt zu stürmen und
Zu schirmen; könne — sagt der Patriarch —
625 Die Stärk' und Schwäche der von Saladin
Neu aufgeführten, innern, zweiten Mauer
Am besten schätzen, sie am deutlichsten
Den Streitern Gottes, sagt der Patriarch,
Beschreiben.

Tempelherr.

Guter Bruder, wenn ich doch
630 Nun auch des Briefchens nähern Inhalt wüßte.

Klosterbruder.

Ja den, — den weiß ich nun wohl nicht so recht.
Das Briefchen aber ist an König Philipp. —
Der Patriarch . . . Ich hab' mich oft gewundert,
Wie doch ein Heiliger, der sonst so ganz
635 Im Himmel lebt, zugleich so unterrichtet
Von Dingen dieser Welt zu sein herab
Sich lassen kann. Es muß ihm sauer werden.

Tempelherr.

Nun dann? Der Patriarch? —

Klosterbruder.

Weiß ganz genau
Ganz zuverlässig, wie und wo, wie stark,
640 Von welcher Seite Saladin, im Fall
Es völlig wieder losgeht, seinen Feldzug
Eröffnen wird.

Tempelherr.

Das weiß er?

Klosterbruder.

Ja, und möcht'
Es gern dem König Philipp wissen lassen,
Damit der ungefähr ermessen könne,
645 Ob die Gefahr denn gar so schrecklich, um
Mit Saladin den Waffenstillestand,
Den Euer Orden schon so brav gebrochen,
Es koste was es wolle, wieder her
Zu stellen.

Tempelherr.

Welch ein Patriarch! — Ja so!
650 Der liebe, tapfre Mann will mich zu keinem
Gemeinen Boten, will mich zum Spion. —

Sagt Euerm Patriarchen, guter Bruder,
Soviel Ihr mich ergründen können, wär'
Das meine Sache nicht. — Ich müsse mich
655 Noch als Gefangenen betrachten, und
Der Tempelherren einziger Beruf
Sei, mit dem Schwerte drein zu schlagen, nicht
Kundschafterei zu treiben.

Klosterbruder.

Dacht' ich's doch! —
Will's auch dem Herrn nicht eben sehr verübeln. —
660 Zwar kömmt das Beste noch. — Der Patriarch
Hiernächst hat ausgegattert, wie die Feste
Sich nennt, und wo auf Libanon sie liegt,
In der die ungeheuren Summen stecken,
Mit welchen Saladins vorsicht'ger Vater
665 Das Heer besoldet und die Zurüstungen
Des Kriegs bestreitet. Saladin verfügt
Von Zeit zu Zeit auf abgelegnen Wegen
Nach dieser Feste sich, nur kaum begleitet. —
Ihr merkt doch?

Tempelherr.

Nimmermehr!

Klosterbruder.

Was wäre da
670 Wohl leichter, als des Saladins sich zu
Bemächtigen? den Garaus ihm zu machen? —
Ihr schaudert? — O, es haben schon ein Paar
Gottsfürcht'ge Maroniten sich erboten,
Wenn nur ein wackrer Mann sie führen wolle,
675 Das Stück zu wagen.

Tempelherr.

Und der Patriarch
Hätt' auch zu diesem wackern Manne mich
Ersehn?

Klosterbruder.

Er glaubt, daß König Philipp wohl
Von Ptolemais aus die Hand hierzu
Am besten bieten könne.

Tempelherr.

Mir? mir, Bruder?
580 Mir? Habt Ihr nicht gehört? nur erst gehört,
Was für Verbindlichkeit dem Saladin
Ich habe?

Klosterbruder.

Wohl hab' ich's gehört.

Tempelherr.

Und doch?

Klosterbruder.

Ja, — meint der Patriarch — das wär' schon gut:
Gott aber und der Orden . . .

Tempelherr.

Ändern nichts!
685 Gebieten mir kein Bubenstück!

Klosterbruder.

Gewiß nicht! —
Nur — meint der Patriarch — sei Bubenstück
Vor Menschen nicht auch Bubenstück vor Gott.

Tempelherr.

Ich wär' dem Saladin mein Leben schuldig:
Und raubt' ihm seines?

Klosterbruder.

Pfui! — Doch bliebe — meint
690 Der Patriarch — noch immer Saladin
Ein Feind der Christenheit, der Euer Freund
Zu sein, kein Recht erwerben könne.

Tempelherr.

Freund?
An dem ich bloß nicht will zum Schurken werden,
Zum undankbaren Schurken?

Klosterbruder.

Allerdings! —
695 Zwar — meint der Patriarch — des Dankes sei
Man quitt, vor Gott und Menschen quitt, wenn uns
Der Dienst um unsertwillen nicht geschehen.
Und da verlauten wolle, — meint der Patriarch —
Daß Euch nur darum Saladin begnadet,
700 Weil ihm in Eurer Mien', in Euerm Wesen
So was von seinem Bruder eingeleuchtet . . .

Tempelherr.

Auch dieses weiß der Patriarch, und doch? —
Ah! wäre das gewiß! Ah, Saladin! —
Wie? die Natur hätt' auch nur Einen Zug
705 Von mir in deines Bruders Form gebildet,
Und dem entspräche nichts in meiner Seele?
Was dem entspräche, könnt' ich unterdrücken,
Um einem Patriarchen zu gefallen? —
Natur, so lügst du nicht! So widerspricht
710 Sich Gott in seinen Werken nicht! — Geht, Bruder! —
Erregt mir meine Galle nicht! — Geht! geht!

Klosterbruder.

Ich geh', und geh' vergnügter, als ich kam.
Verzeihe mir der Herr. Wir Klosterleute
Sind schuldig, unsern Obern zu gehorchen.

Sechster Auftritt.

Der Tempelherr und Daja, die den Tempelherrn schon eine Zeitlang von weitem beobachtet hatte und sich nun ihm nähert.

Daja.

715 Der Klosterbruder, wie mich dünkt, ließ in
Der besten Laun' ihn nicht. — Doch muß ich mein
Paket nur wagen.

Tempelherr.

Nun, vortrefflich! — Lügt
Das Sprichwort wohl, daß Mönch und Weib, und Weib
Und Mönch des Teufels beide Krallen sind?
720 Er wirft mich heut' aus einer in die andre.

Daja.

Was seh' ich? — Edler Ritter, Euch? — Gott Dank!
Gott tausend Dank! — Wo habt Ihr denn
Die ganze Zeit gesteckt? — Ihr seid doch wohl
Nicht krank gewesen?

Tempelherr.

Nein.

Daja.

Gesund doch?

Tempelherr.

Ja.

Daja.

725 Wir waren Euretwegen wahrlich ganz
Bekümmert.

Tempelherr.

So?

Daja.

Ihr wart gewiß verreist?

Tempelherr.

Erraten!

Daja.

Und kamt heut' erst wieder?

Tempelherr.

Gestern.

Daja.

Auch Rechas Vater ist heut' angekommen.
Und nun darf Recha doch wohl hoffen?

Tempelherr.

Was?

Daja.

730 Warum sie Euch so öfters bitten lassen.
Ihr Vater ladet Euch nun selber bald
Aufs dringlichste. Er kömmt von Babylon
Mit zwanzig hochbeladenen Kamelen
Und allem, was an edeln Spezereien,
735 An Steinen und an Stoffen Indien
Und Persien und Syrien, gar Sina
Kostbares nur gewähren.

Tempelherr.

Kaufe nichts.

Daja.

Sein Volk verehret ihn als einen Fürsten.
Doch daß es ihn den weisen Nathan nennt

740 Und nicht vielmehr den Reichen, hat mich oft
Gewundert.

Tempelherr.

Seinem Volk ist reich und weise
Vielleicht das nämliche.

Daja.

Vor allem aber
Hätt's ihn den Guten nennen müssen. Denn
Ihr stellt Euch gar nicht vor, wie gut er ist.
745 Als er erfuhr, wie viel Euch Recha schuldig,
Was hätt' in diesem Augenblicke nicht
Er alles Euch gethan, gegeben!

Tempelherr.

Ei!

Daja.

Versucht's und kommt und seht!

Tempelherr.

Was denn? wie schnell
Ein Augenblick vorüber ist?

Daja.

Hätt' ich,
750 Wenn er so gut nicht wär', es mir so lange
Bei ihm gefallen lassen? Meint Ihr etwa,
Ich fühle meinen Wert als Christin nicht?
Auch mir ward's vor der Wiege nicht gesungen,
Daß ich nur darum meinem Eh'gemahl
755 Nach Palästina folgen würd', um da
Ein Judenmädchen zu erziehn. Es war
Mein lieber Eh'gemahl ein edler Knecht
In Kaiser Friedrichs Heere —

Tempelherr.

Von Geburt
Ein Schweizer, dem die Ehr' und Gnade ward,
760 Mit Seiner Kaiserlichen Majestät
In einem Flusse zu ersaufen. — Weib!
Wie vielmal habt Ihr mir das schon erzählt?
Hört Ihr denn gar nicht auf, mich zu verfolgen?

Daja.

Verfolgen! lieber Gott!

Tempelherr.

Ja, ja, verfolgen.
765 Ich will nun einmal Euch nicht weiter sehn!
Nicht hören! Will von Euch an eine That
Nicht fort und fort erinnert sein, bei der
Ich nichts gedacht, die, wenn ich drüber denke,
Zum Rätsel von mir selbst mir wird. Zwar möcht'
770 Ich sie nicht gern bereuen. Aber seht,
Ereignet so ein Fall sich wieder: Ihr
Seid schuld, wenn ich so rasch nicht handle; wenn
Ich mich vorher erkund' — und brennen lasse,
Was brennt.

Daja.

Bewahre Gott!

Tempelherr.

Von heut' an thut
775 Mir den Gefallen wenigstens, und kennt
Mich weiter nicht. Ich bitt' Euch drum. Auch laßt
Den Vater mir vom Halse. Jud' ist Jude.
Ich bin ein plumper Schwab. Des Mädchens Bild
Ist längst aus meiner Seele, wenn es je
780 Da war.

Daja.

Doch Eures ist aus ihrer nicht.

Tempelherr.

Was soll's nun aber da? was soll's?

Daja.

Wer weiß!

Die Menschen sind nicht immer, was sie scheinen.

Tempelherr.

Doch selten etwas Bessers.

(Er geht.)

Daja.

Wartet doch!

Was eilt Ihr?

Tempelherr.

Weib, macht mir die Palmen nicht

185 Verhaßt, worunter ich so gern sonst wandle

Daja.

So geh, du deutscher Bär! so geh! — Und doch
Muß ich die Spur des Tieres nicht verlieren.

(Sie geht ihm von weitem nach.)

Zweiter Aufzug.

Erster Auftritt.

Scene: des Sultans Palast.

Saladin und Sittah spielen Schach.

Sittah.

Wo bist du, Saladin? Wie spielst du heut'?

Saladin.

Nicht gut? Ich dächte doch.

Sittah.

Für mich, und kaum.

190 Nimm diesen Zug zurück.

Saladin.

Warum?

Sittah.

Der Springer

Wird unbedeckt.

Saladin.

Ist wahr. Nun so!

Sittah.

So zieh'

Ich in die Gabel.

Saladin.

Wieder wahr. — Schach dann!

Sittah.

Was hilft dir das? Ich setze vor, und du
Bist, wie du warst.

Saladin.

Aus dieser Klemme, seh'
795 Ich wohl, ist ohne Buße nicht zu kommen.
Mag's! nimm den Springer nur.

Sittah.

Ich will ihn nicht.
Ich geh' vorbei.

Saladin.

Du schenkst mir nichts. Dir liegt
An diesem Platze mehr als an dem Springer.

Sittah.

Kann sein.

Saladin.

Mach deine Rechnung nur nicht ohne
800 Den Wirt. Denn sieh! Was gilt's, das warst du nicht
Vermuten?

Sittah.

Freilich nicht. Wie konnt' ich auch
Vermuten, daß du deiner Königin
So müde wärst?

Saladin.

Ich meiner Königin?

Sittah.

Ich seh' nun schon, ich soll heut' meine tausend
805 Dinar', kein Naserinchen mehr gewinnen.

Saladin.

Wie so?

Sittah.

Frag noch! — Weil du mit Fleiß, mit aller
Gewalt verlieren willst. — Doch dabei find'
Ich meine Rechnung nicht. Denn außer, daß
Ein solches Spiel das unterhaltendste
810 Nicht ist, gewann ich immer nicht am meisten
Mit dir, wenn ich verlor? Wenn hast du mir
Den Satz, mich des verlornen Spieles wegen
Zu trösten, doppelt nicht hernach geschenkt?

Saladin.

Ei sieh! so hättest du ja wohl, wenn du
815 Verlorst, mit Fleiß verloren, Schwesterchen?

Sittah.

Zum wenigsten kann gar wohl sein, daß deine
Freigebigkeit, mein liebes Brüderchen,
Schuld ist, daß ich nicht besser spielen lernen.

Saladin.

Wir kommen ab vom Spiele. Mach ein Ende!

Sittah.

820 So bleibt es? Nun denn: Schach! und doppelt Schach!

Saladin.

Nun freilich, dieses Abschach hab' ich nicht
Gesehn, das meine Königin zugleich
Mit niederwirft.

Sittah.

War dem noch abzuhelfen?
Laß sehn.

Saladin.

Nein, nein; nimm nur die Königin.
825 Ich war mit diesem Steine nie recht glücklich.

Sittah.

Bloß mit dem Steine?

Saladin.

Fort damit! — Das thut
Mir nichts. Denn so ist alles wiederum
Geschützt.

Sittah.

Wie höflich man mit Königinnen
Verfahren müsse, hat mein Bruder mich
830 Zu wohl gelehrt.

(Sie läßt sie stehen.)

Saladin.

Nimm oder nimm sie nicht!
Ich habe keine mehr.

Sittah.

Wozu sie nehmen?
Schach! — Schach!

Saladin.

Nur weiter.

Sittah.

Schach! — und Schach! — und Schach! —

Saladin.

Und matt!

Sittah.

Nicht ganz; du ziehst den Springer noch
Dazwischen, oder was du machen willst.
835 Gleichviel!

Saladin.

Ganz recht! — Du hast gewonnen, und
Al-Hafi zahlt. Man lass' ihn rufen! gleich! —

Du hattest, Sittah, nicht so unrecht; ich
War nicht so ganz beim Spiele, war zerstreut.
Und dann: wer giebt uns denn die glatten Steine
840 Beständig? die an nichts erinnern, nichts
Bezeichnen. Hab' ich mit dem Iman denn
Gespielt? — Doch was? Verlust will Vorwand. Nicht
Die ungeformten Steine, Sittah, sind's,
Die mich verlieren machten: deine Kunst,
845 Dein ruhiger und schneller Blick . . .

Sittah.

Auch so
Willst du den Stachel des Verlusts nur stumpfen.
Genug, du warst zerstreut, und mehr als ich.

Saladin.

Als du? Was hätte dich zerstreuet?

Sittah.

Deine
Zerstreuung freilich nicht! — O Saladin,
850 Wann werden wir so fleißig wieder spielen!

Saladin.

So spielen wir um so viel gieriger! —
Ah! weil es wieder losgeht, meinst du? — Mag's! —
Nur zu! — Ich habe nicht zuerst gezogen;
Ich hätte gern den Stillestand aufs neue
855 Verlängert; hätte meiner Sittah gern,
Gern einen guten Mann zugleich verschafft.
Und das muß Richards Bruder sein; er ist
Ja Richards Bruder.

Sittah.

Wenn du deinen Richard
Nur loben kannst!

Saladin.

Wenn unserm Bruder Melek
860 Dann Richards Schwester wär' zu Teile worden:
Ha! welch ein Haus zusammen! Ha, der ersten,
Der besten Häuser in der Welt das beste! —
Du hörst, ich bin mich selbst zu loben auch
Nicht faul. Ich dünk' mich meiner Freunde wert. —
865 Das hätte Menschen geben sollen! das!

Sittah.

Hab' ich des schönen Traums nicht gleich gelacht?
Du kennst die Christen nicht, willst sie nicht kennen.
Ihr Stolz ist: Christen sein, nicht Menschen. Denn
Selbst das, was noch von ihrem Stifter her
870 Mit Menschlichkeit den Aberglauben würzt,
Das lieben sie, nicht weil es menschlich ist:
Weil's Christus lehrt, weil's Christus hat gethan. —
Wohl ihnen, daß er so ein guter Mensch
Noch war! Wohl ihnen, daß sie seine Tugend
875 Auf Treu' und Glauben nehmen können! — Doch
Was Tugend? — Seine Tugend nicht, sein Name
Soll überall verbreitet werden, soll
Die Namen aller guten Menschen schänden,
Verschlingen. Um den Namen, um den Namen
880 Ist ihnen nur zu thun.

Saladin.

Du meinst, warum
Sie sonst verlangen würden, daß auch ihr,
Auch du und Melek, Christen hießet, eh'
Als Eh'gemahl ihr Christen lieben wolltet?

Sittah.

Ja wohl! Als wär' von Christen nur, als Christen,

885 Die Liebe zu gewärtigen, womit
Der Schöpfer Mann und Männin ausgestattet!

Saladin.

Die Christen glauben mehr Armseligkeiten,
Als daß sie die nicht auch noch glauben könnten! —
Und gleichwohl irrst du dich. — Die Tempelherren,
890 Die Christen nicht, sind schuld, sind, nicht als Christen,
Als Tempelherren schuld. Durch die allein
Wird aus der Sache nichts. Sie wollen Acca,
Das Richards Schwester unserm Bruder Melek
Zum Brautschatz bringen müßte, schlechterdings
895 Nicht fahren lassen. Daß des Ritters Vorteil
Gefahr nicht laufe, spielen sie den Mönch,
Den albern Mönch. Und ob vielleicht im Fluge
Ein guter Streich gelänge, haben sie
Des Waffenstillestandes Ablauf kaum
900 Erwarten können. — Lustig! Nur so weiter!
Ihr Herren, nur so weiter! — Mir schon recht! —
Wär' alles sonst nur, wie es müßte.

Sittah.

Nun?
Was irrte dich denn sonst? Was könnte sonst
Dich aus der Fassung bringen?

Saladin.

Was von je
905 Mich immer aus der Fassung hat gebracht. —
Ich war auf Libanon, bei unserm Vater.
Er unterliegt den Sorgen noch . . .

Sittah.

O weh!

Saladin.

Er kann nicht durch; es klemmt sich aller Orten;
Es fehlt bald da, bald dort —

Sittah.

Was klemmt? was fehlt?

Saladin.

910 Was sonst, als was ich kaum zu nennen würd'ge?
Was, wenn ich's habe, mir so überflüssig,
Und hab' ich's nicht, so unentbehrlich scheint. —
Wo bleibt Al-Hafi denn? Ist niemand nach
Ihm aus? — Das leidige, verwünschte Geld! —
915 Gut, Hafi, daß du kömmst.

Zweiter Auftritt.

Der Derwisch Al-Hafi. Saladin. Sittah.

Al-Hafi.

Die Gelder aus
Ägypten sind vermutlich angelangt.
Wenn's nur fein viel ist.

Saladin.

Hast du Nachricht?

Al-Hafi.

Ich?
Ich nicht. Ich denke, daß ich hier sie in
Empfang soll nehmen.

Saladin.

Zahl an Sittah tausend
920 Dinare!

(In Gedanken hin- und hergehend.)

Al-Hafi.

Zahl! anstatt empfang! O schön!
Das ist für was noch weniger als nichts. —
An Sittah? — wiederum an Sittah? Und
Verloren? — wiederum im Schach verloren? —
Da steht es noch, das Spiel!

Sittah.

Du gönnst mir doch
925 Mein Glück?

Al-Hafi
(das Spiel betrachtend).

Was gönnen? Wenn — Ihr wißt ja wohl.

Sittah (ihm winkend).

Bst! Hafi! bst!

Al-Hafi
(noch auf das Spiel gerichtet).

Gönnt's Euch nur selber erst!

Sittah.

Al-Hafi, bst!

Al-Hafi (zu Sittah).

Die Weißen waren Euer?
Ihr bietet Schach?

Sittah.

Gut, daß er nichts gehört!

Al-Hafi.

Nun ist der Zug an ihm?

Sittah (ihm näher tretend).

So sage doch,
930 Daß ich mein Geld bekommen kann.

Al-Hafi
(noch auf das Spiel geheftet).

Nun ja,
Ihr sollt's bekommen, wie Ihr's stets bekommen.

Sittah.

Wie? bist du toll?

Al-Hafi.

Das Spiel ist ja nicht aus.
Ihr habt ja nicht verloren, Saladin.

Saladin (kaum hinhörend).

Doch! doch! Bezahl! bezahl!

Al-Hafi.

Bezahl! bezahl!
935 Da steht ja Eure Königin.

Saladin (noch so).

Gilt nicht;
Gehört nicht mehr ins Spiel.

Sittah.

So mach und sag,
Daß ich das Geld mir nur kann holen lassen.

Al-Hafi
(noch immer in das Spiel vertieft).

Versteht sich, so wie immer. — Wenn auch schon,
Wenn auch die Königin nichts gilt: Ihr seid
940 Doch darum noch nicht matt.

Saladin
(tritt hinzu und wirft das Spiel um).

Ich bin es, will
Es sein.

Al-Hafi.

Ja so! — Spiel wie Gewinst! So wie
Gewonnen, so bezahlt.

Saladin (zu Sittah).

Was sagt er? was?

Sittah

(von Zeit zu Zeit dem Hafi winkend).

Du kennst ihn ja. Er sträubt sich gern, läßt gern
Sich bitten, ist wohl gar ein wenig neidisch. —

Saladin.

945 Auf dich doch nicht? Auf meine Schwester nicht? —
Was hör' ich, Hafi? Neidisch? Du?

Al-Hafi.

Kann sein!
Kann sein! — Ich hätt' ihr Hirn wohl lieber selbst,
Wär' lieber selbst so gut als sie.

Sittah.

Indeß
Hat er doch immer richtig noch bezahlt,
950 Und wird auch heut' bezahlen. Laß ihn nur! —
Geh nur, Al-Hafi, geh! Ich will das Geld
Schon holen lassen.

Al-Hafi.

Nein, ich spiele länger
Die Mummerei nicht mit. Er muß es doch
Einmal erfahren.

Saladin.

Wer? und was?

Sittah.

Al-Hafi!

955 Ist dieses dein Versprechen? Hältst du so
Mir Wort?

Al-Hafi.

Wie konnt' ich glauben, daß es so
Weit gehen würde.

Saladin.

Nun? erfahr' ich nichts?

Sittah.

Ich bitte dich, Al-Hafi, sei bescheiden.

Saladin.

Das ist doch sonderbar! Was könnte Sittah
960 So feierlich, so warm bei einem Fremden,
Bei einem Derwisch lieber als bei mir,
Bei ihrem Bruder, sich verbitten wollen.
Al-Hafi, nun befehl' ich. — Rede, Derwisch!

Sittah.

Laß eine Kleinigkeit, mein Bruder, dir
965 Nicht näher treten, als sie würdig ist.
Du weißt, ich habe zu verschiednen Malen
Dieselbe Summ' im Schach von dir gewonnen.
Und weil ich jetzt das Geld nicht nötig habe,
Weil jetzt in Hafis Kasse doch das Geld
970 Nicht eben allzu häufig ist, so sind
Die Posten stehn geblieben. Aber sorgt
Nur nicht! Ich will sie weder dir, mein Bruder
Noch Hafi, noch der Kasse schenken.

Al-Hafi.

Ja,

Wenn's das nur wäre! das!

Sittah.

Und mehr dergleichen. —

975 Auch das ist in der Kasse stehn geblieben,
Was du mir einmal ausgeworfen, ist
Seit wenig Monden stehn geblieben.

Al-Hafi.

Noch
Nicht alles.

Saladin.

Noch nicht? — Wirst du reden?

Al-Hafi.

Seit aus Ägypten wir das Geld erwarten,
980 Hat sie . . .

Sittah (zu Saladin).

Wozu ihn hören?

Al-Hafi.

Nicht nur nichts
Bekommen . . .

Saladin.

Gutes Mädchen! — Auch beiher
Mit vorgeschossen. Nicht?

Al-Hafi.

Den ganzen Hof
Erhalten; Euern Aufwand ganz allein
Bestritten.

Saladin.

Ha! das, das ist meine Schwester!
(Sie umarmend.)

Sittah.

985 Wer hatte, dies zu können, mich so reich
Gemacht als du, mein Bruder?

Al-Hafi.

Wird schon auch
So bettelarm sie wieder machen, als
Er selber ist.

Saladin.

Ich arm? der Bruder arm?
Wenn hab' ich mehr? wenn weniger gehabt? –
990 Ein Kleid, Ein Schwert, Ein Pferd — und Einen Gott!
Was brauch' ich mehr? Wenn kann's an dem mir fehlen?
Und doch, Al-Hafi, könnt' ich mit dir schelten.

Sittah.

Schilt nicht, mein Bruder. Wenn ich unserm Vater
Auch seine Sorgen so erleichtern könnte!

Saladin.

995 Ah! Ah! Nun schlägst du meine Freudigkeit
Auf einmal wieder nieder! — Mir, für mich
Fehlt nichts, und kann nichts fehlen. Aber ihm,
Ihm fehlet, und in ihm uns allen. — Sagt,
Was soll ich machen? — Aus Ägypten kommt
1000 Vielleicht noch lange nichts. Woran das liegt,
Weiß Gott. Es ist doch da noch alles ruhig. —
Abbrechen, einziehn, sparen will ich gern,
Mir gern gefallen lassen, wenn es mich,
Bloß mich betrifft, bloß mich, und niemand sonst
1005 Darunter leidet. — Doch was kann das machen?
Ein Pferd, Ein Kleid, Ein Schwert muß ich doch haben.
Und meinem Gott ist auch nichts abzudingen.
Ihm g'nügt schon so mit wenigem genug,
Mit meinem Herzen. — Auf den Überschuß
1010 Von deiner Kasse, Hafi, hatt' ich sehr
Gerechnet.

Al-Hafi.

Überschuß? — Sagt selber, ob
Ihr mich nicht hättet spießen, wenigstens
Mich drosseln lassen, wenn auf Überschuß
Ich von Euch wär' ergriffen worden. Ja,
1015 Auf Unterschleif! das war zu wagen.

Saladin.

Nun,
Was machen wir denn aber? — Konntest du
Vorerst bei niemand andern borgen als
Bei Sittah?

Sittah.

Würd' ich dieses Vorrecht, Bruder,
Mir haben nehmen lassen? Mir von ihm?
1020 Auch noch besteh' ich drauf. Noch bin ich auf
Dem Trocknen völlig nicht.

Saladin.

Nur völlig nicht!
Das fehlte noch! — Geh gleich, mach Anstalt, Hafi!
Nimm auf, bei wem du kannst! und wie du kannst!
Geh, borg, versprich. — Nur, Hafi, borge nicht
1025 Bei denen, die ich reich gemacht. Denn borgen
Von diesen, möchte wiederfordern heißen.
Geh zu den Geizigsten; die werden mir
Am liebsten leihen. Denn sie wissen wohl,
Wie gut ihr Geld in meinen Händen wuchert.

Al-Hafi.

1030 Ich kenne deren keine.

Sittah.

Eben fällt
Mir ein, gehört zu haben, Hafi, daß
Dein Freund zurückgekommen.

Al-Hafi (betroffen).

Freund? mein Freund?

Wer wär' denn das?

Sittah.

Dein hochgepries'ner Jude.

Al-Hafi.

Gepries'ner Jude? hoch von mir?

Sittah.

Dem Gott, —

1035 Mich denkt des Ausdrucks noch recht wohl, des einst
Du selber dich von ihm bedientest, — dem
Sein Gott von allen Gütern dieser Welt
Das kleinst' und größte so in vollem Maß
Erteilet habe. —

Al-Hafi.

Sagt' ich so? — Was meint'

1040 Ich denn damit?

Sittah.

Das kleinste: Reichtum. Und
Das größte: Weisheit.

Al-Hafi.

Wie? von einem Juden?
Von einem Juden hätt' ich das gesagt?

Sittah.

Das hättest du von deinem Nathan nicht
Gesagt?

Al-Hafi.

Ja so! von dem! vom Nathan! — Fiel
1045 Mir der doch gar nicht bei. — Wahrhaftig? Der

Ist endlich wieder heim gekommen? Ei!
So mag's doch gar so schlecht mit ihm nicht stehn. —
Ganz recht: den nannt' einmal das Volk den Weisen!
Den Reichen auch.

Sittah.

Den Reichen nennt es ihn
1050 Jetzt mehr als je. Die ganze Stadt erschallt,
Was er für Kostbarkeiten, was für Schätze
Er mitgebracht.

Al-Hafi.

Nun, ist's der Reiche wieder,
So wird's auch wohl der Weise wieder sein.

Sittah.

Was meinst du, Hafi, wenn du diesen angingst?

Al-Hafi.

1055 Und was bei ihm? — Doch wohl nicht borgen? — Ja,
Da kennt Ihr ihn. — Er borgen! — Seine Weisheit
Ist eben, daß er niemand borgt.

Sittah.

Du hast
Mir sonst doch ganz ein ander Bild von ihm
Gemacht.

Al-Hafi.

Zur Not wird er Euch Waren borgen.
1060 Geld aber, Geld? Geld nimmermehr. — Es ist
Ein Jude freilich übrigens, wie's nicht
Viel Juden giebt. Er hat Verstand; er weiß
Zu leben, spielt gut Schach. Doch zeichnet er
Im Schlechten sich nicht minder als im Guten
1065 Von allen andern Juden aus. — Auf den,

Auf den nur rechnet nicht. — Den Armen giebt
Er zwar, und giebt vielleicht trotz Saladin,
Wenn schon nicht ganz so viel, doch ganz so gern,
Doch ganz so sonder Ansehn. Jud' und Christ
1070 Und Muselmann und Parsi, alles ist
Ihm eins.

Sittah.

Und so ein Mann . . .

Saladin.

Wie kommt es denn,
Daß ich von diesem Manne nie gehört? . . .

Sittah.

Der sollte Saladin nicht borgen? nicht
Dem Saladin, der nur für andre braucht,
1075 Nicht sich?

Al-Hafi.

Da seht nun gleich den Juden wieder,
Den ganz gemeinen Juden! — Glaubt mir's doch! —
Er ist aufs Geben euch so eifersüchtig,
So neidisch! Jedes Lohn von Gott, das in
Der Welt gesagt wird, zög' er lieber ganz
1080 Allein. Nur darum eben leiht er keinem,
Damit er stets zu geben habe. Weil
Die Mild' ihm im Gesetz geboten, die
Gefälligkeit ihm aber nicht geboten, macht
Die Mild' ihn zu dem ungefälligsten
1085 Gesellen auf der Welt. Zwar bin ich seit
Geraumer Zeit ein wenig übern Fuß
Mit ihm gespannt; doch denkt nur nicht, daß ich
Ihm darum nicht Gerechtigkeit erzeige.
Er ist zu allem gut, bloß dazu nicht,

1090 Bloß dazu wahrlich nicht. Ich will auch gleich
Nur gehn, an andre Thüren klopfen . . . Da
Besinn' ich mich soeben eines Mohren,
Der reich und geizig ist. — Ich geh', ich geh'.

Sittah.

Was eilst du, Hafi?

Saladin.

Laß ihn! laß ihn!

Dritter Auftritt.

Sittah. Saladin.

Sittah.

Eilt
1095 Er doch, als ob er mir nur gern entkäme! —
Was heißt das? — Hat er wirklich sich in ihm
Betrogen, oder — möcht' er uns nur gern
Betriegen?

Saladin.

Wie? das fragst du mich? Ich weiß
Ja kaum, von wem die Rede war, und höre
1100 Von euerm Juden, euerm Nathan heut'
Zum erstenmal.

Sittah.

Ist's möglich? daß ein Mann
Dir so verborgen blieb, von dem es heißt,
Er habe Salomons und Davids Gräber
Erforscht und wisse deren Siegel durch
1105 Ein mächtiges, geheimes Wort zu lösen?

Aus ihnen bring' er dann von Zeit zu Zeit
Die unermeßlichen Reichtümer an
Den Tag, die keinen mindern Quell verrieten.

Saladin.

Hat seinen Reichtum dieser Mann aus Gräbern,
1110 So waren's sicherlich nicht Salomons,
Nicht Davids Gräber. Narren lagen da
Begraben!

Sittah.

Oder Bösewichter! — Auch
Ist seines Reichtums Quelle weit ergiebiger,
Weit unerschöpflicher als so ein Grab
1115 Voll Mammon.

Saladin.

Denn er handelt, wie ich hörte.

Sittah.

Sein Saumtier treibt auf allen Straßen, zieht
Durch alle Wüsten; seine Schiffe liegen
In allen Häfen. Das hat mir wohl eh
Al-Hafi selbst gesagt und voll Entzücken
1120 Hinzugefügt, wie groß, wie edel dieser
Sein Freund anwende, was so klug und emsig
Er zu erwerben für zu klein nicht achte;
Hinzugefügt, wie frei von Vorurteilen
Sein Geist, sein Herz wie offen jeder Tugend,
1125 Wie eingestimmt mit jeder Schönheit sei.

Saladin.

Und jetzt sprach Hafi doch so ungewiß,
So kalt von ihm.

Sittah.

Kalt nun wohl nicht; verlegen
Als halt' er's für gefährlich, ihn zu loben,

Und woll' ihn unverdient doch auch nicht tadeln. —
1130 Wie? oder wär' es wirklich so, daß selbst
Der Beste seines Volkes seinem Volke
Nicht ganz entfliehen kann? daß wirklich sich
Al-Hafi seines Freunds von dieser Seite
Zu schämen hätte? — Sei dem, wie ihm wolle! —
1135 Der Jud', sei mehr oder weniger
Als Jud', ist er nur reich: genug für uns!

Saladin.

Du willst ihm aber doch das Seine mit
Gewalt nicht nehmen, Schwester?

Sittah.

Ja, was heißt
Bei dir Gewalt? Mit Feu'r und Schwert? Nein, nein,
1140 Was braucht es bei den Schwachen für Gewalt
Als ihre Schwäche? — Komm für jetzt nur mit
In meinen Haram, eine Sängerin
Zu hören, die ich gestern erst gekauft.
Es reift indeß bei mir vielleicht ein Anschlag,
1145 Den ich auf diesen Nathan habe. — Komm!

Vierter Auftritt.

Scene: vor dem Hause des Nathan, wo es an die Palmen stößt.

Recha und Nathan kommen heraus. Zu ihnen Daja.

Recha.

Ihr habt Euch sehr verweilt, mein Vater. Er
Wird kaum noch mehr zu treffen sein.

Nathan.

Nun, nun;
Wenn hier, hier untern Palmen schon nicht mehr,

Doch anderwärts. — Sei jetzt nur ruhig. — Sieh!
1150 Kommt dort nicht Daja auf uns zu?

Recha.

Sie wird
Ihn ganz gewiß verloren haben.

Nathan.

Auch
Wohl nicht.

Recha.

Sie würde sonst geschwinder kommen.

Nathan.

Sie hat uns wohl noch nicht gesehn . . .

Recha.

Nun sieht
Sie uns.

Nathan.

Und doppelt ihre Schritte. Sieh! —
1155 Sei doch nur ruhig! ruhig!

Recha.

Wolltet Ihr
Wohl eine Tochter, die hier ruhig wäre?
Sich unbekümmert ließe, wessen Wohlthat
Ihr Leben sei? Ihr Leben, — das ihr nur
So lieb, weil sie es Euch zuerst verdanket.

Nathan.

1160 Ich möchte dich nicht anders, als du bist,
Auch wenn ich wüßte, daß in deiner Seele
Ganz etwas andres noch sich rege.

Recha.

Was,
Mein Vater?

Nathan.

Fragst du mich? so schüchtern mich?
Was auch in deinem Innern vorgeht, ist
1165 Natur und Unschuld. Laß es keine Sorge
Dir machen. Mir, mir macht es keine. Nur
Versprich mir: wenn dein Herz vernehmlicher
Sich einst erklärt, mir seiner Wünsche keinen
Zu bergen.

Recha.

Schon die Möglichkeit, mein Herz
1170 Euch lieber zu verhüllen, macht mich zittern.

Nathan.

Nichts mehr hiervon! Das ein= für allemal
Ist abgethan. — Da ist ja Daja. — Nun?

Daja.

Noch wandelt er hier untern Palmen und
Wird gleich um jene Mauer kommen. — Seht,
1175 Da kömmt er!

Recha.

Ah! und scheinet unentschlossen,
Wohin? ob weiter? ob hinab? ob rechts?
Ob links?

Daja.

Nein, nein; er macht den Weg ums Kloster
Gewiß noch öfter, und dann muß er hier
Vorbei. — Was gilt's?

Recha.

Recht! recht! — Hast du ihn schon
1180 Gesprochen? Und wie ist er heut'?

Daja.

Wie immer.

Nathan.

So macht nur, daß er euch hier nicht gewahr
Wird. Tretet mehr zurück. Geht lieber ganz
Hinein.

Recha.

Nur einen Blick noch! — Ah! die Hecke,
Die mir ihn stiehlt.

Daja.

Kommt! kommt! Der Vater hat
1185 Ganz recht. Ihr lauft Gefahr, wenn er Euch sieht,
Daß auf der Stell' er umkehrt.

Recha.

Ah! die Hecke!

Nathan.

Und kömmt er plötzlich dort aus ihr hervor,
So kann er anders nicht, er muß euch sehn.
Drum geht doch nur!

Daja.

Kommt! kommt! Ich weiß ein Fenster,
1190 Aus dem wir sie bemerken können.

Recha.

Ja?

(Beide hinein.)

Fünfter Auftritt.

Nathan und bald darauf der Tempelherr.

Nathan.

Fast scheu' ich mich des Sonderlings. Fast macht
Mich seine rauhe Tugend stutzen. Daß
Ein Mensch doch einen Menschen so verlegen
Soll machen können! — Ha! er kömmt. — Bei Gott!

1195 Ein Jüngling wie ein Mann. Ich mag ihn wohl,
Den guten, trotz'gen Blick! den drallen Gang!
Die Schale kann nur bitter sein, der Kern
Ist's sicher nicht. — Wo sah ich doch dergleichen? —
Verzeihet, edler Franke . . .

Tempelherr.

Was?

Nathan.

Erlaubt . . .

Tempelherr.

1200 Was, Jude? was?

Nathan.

Daß ich mich untersteh',
Euch anzureden.

Tempelherr.

Kann ich's wehren? Doch
Nur kurz.

Nathan.

Verzieht, und eilet nicht so stolz,
Nicht so verächtlich einem Mann vorüber,
Den Ihr auf ewig Euch verbunden habt.

Tempelherr.

1205 Wie das? Ah, fast errat' ich's. Nicht? Ihr seid . . .

Nathan.

Ich heiße Nathan, bin des Mädchens Vater,
Das Eure Großmut aus dem Feu'r gerettet,
Und komme . . .

Tempelherr.

Wenn zu danken, — spart's! Ich hab'
Um diese Kleinigkeit des Dankes schon

1210 Zu viel erdulden müssen. — Vollends Ihr,
Ihr seid mir gar nichts schuldig. Wußt' ich denn,
Daß dieses Mädchen Eure Tochter war?
Es ist der Tempelherren Pflicht, dem ersten,
Dem besten beizuspringen, dessen Not
1215 Sie sehn. Mein Leben war mir ohnedem
In diesem Augenblicke lästig. Gern,
Sehr gern ergriff ich die Gelegenheit,
Es für ein andres Leben in die Schanze
Zu schlagen, für ein andres, — wenn's auch nur
1220 Das Leben einer Jüdin wäre.

Nathan.

Groß!
Groß und abscheulich! — Doch die Wendung läßt
Sich denken. Die bescheidne Größe flüchtet
Sich hinter das Abscheuliche, um der
Bewund'rung auszuweichen. — Aber wenn
1225 Sie so das Opfer der Bewunderung
Verschmäht, was für ein Opfer denn verschmäht
Sie minder? — Ritter, wenn Ihr hier nicht fremd
Und nicht gefangen wäret, würd' ich Euch
So dreist nicht fragen. Sagt, befehlt, womit
1230 Kann man Euch dienen?

Tempelherr.

Ihr? Mit nichts.

Nathan.

Ich bin
Ein reicher Mann.

Tempelherr.

Der reiche Jude war
Mir nie der beſſ're Jude.

Nathan.

Dürft Ihr denn
Darum nicht nützen, was demungeachtet
Er Bess'res hat? nicht seinen Reichtum nützen?

Tempelherr.

1235 Nun gut, das will ich auch nicht ganz verreden;
Um meines Mantels willen nicht. Sobald
Der ganz und gar verschlissen, weder Stich
Noch Fetze länger halten will, komm' ich
Und borge mir bei Euch zu einem neuen
1240 Tuch oder Geld. — Seht nicht mit eins so finster!
Noch seid Ihr sicher; noch ist's nicht so weit
Mit ihm. Ihr seht, er ist so ziemlich noch
Im Stande. Nur der eine Zipfel da
Hat einen garst'gen Fleck; er ist versengt.
1245 Und das bekam er, als ich Eure Tochter
Durchs Feuer trug.

Nathan
(der nach dem Zipfel greift und ihn betrachtet).

Es ist doch sonderbar,
Daß so ein böser Fleck, daß so ein Brandmal
Dem Mann ein bess'res Zeugnis redet als
Sein eigner Mund. Ich möcht' ihn küssen gleich —
1250 Den Flecken! — Ah, verzeiht! — Ich that es ungern.

Tempelherr.

Was?

Nathan.

Eine Thräne fiel darauf.

Tempelherr.

Thut nichts!
Er hat der Tropfen mehr. — (Bald aber fängt
Mich dieser Jud' an zu verwirren.)

Nathan.

Wär't
Ihr wohl so gut und schicktet Euern Mantel
1255 Auch einmal meinem Mädchen?

Tempelherr.

Was damit?

Nathan.

Auch ihren Mund auf diesen Fleck zu drücken.
Denn Eure Kniee selber zu umfassen,
Wünscht sie nun wohl vergebens.

Tempelherr.

Aber, Jude —
Ihr heißet Nathan? — Aber, Nathan — Ihr
1260 Setzt Eure Worte sehr — sehr gut — sehr spitz —
Ich bin betreten — Allerdings — ich hätte . . .

Nathan.

Stellt und verstellt Euch, wie Ihr wollt. Ich find'
Auch hier Euch aus. — Ihr war't zu gut, zu bieder,
Um höflicher zu sein. — Das Mädchen ganz
1265 Gefühl, der weibliche Gesandte ganz
Dienstfertigkeit, der Vater weit entfernt —
Ihr trugt für ihren guten Namen Sorge,
Floht ihre Prüfung, floht, um nicht zu siegen.
Auch dafür dank' ich Euch —

Tempelherr.

Ich muß gestehn,
1270 Ihr wißt, wie Tempelherren denken sollten.

Nathan.

Nur Tempelherren? *sollten* bloß? und bloß
Weil es die Ordensregeln so gebieten?

Ich weiß, wie gute Menschen denken, weiß,
Daß alle Länder gute Menschen tragen.

Tempelherr.

1275 Mit Unterschied, doch hoffentlich?

Nathan.

Ja wohl;
An Farb', an Kleidung, an Gestalt verschieden.

Tempelherr.

Auch hier bald mehr, bald weniger als dort.

Nathan.

Mit diesem Unterschied ist's nicht weit her.
Der große Mann braucht überall viel Boden,
1280 Und mehrere, zu nah gepflanzt, zerschlagen
Sich nur die Äste. Mittelgut, wie wir,
Find't sich hingegen überall in Menge.
Nur muß der eine nicht den andern mäkeln;
Nur muß der Knorr den Knubben hübsch vertragen;
1285 Nur muß ein Gipfelchen sich nicht vermessen,
Daß es allein der Erde nicht entschossen.

Tempelherr.

Sehr wohl gesagt! — Doch kennt Ihr auch das Volk,
Das diese Menschenmäkelei zuerst
Getrieben? Wißt Ihr, Nathan, welches Volk
1290 Zuerst das auserwählte Volk sich nannte?
Wie? wenn ich dieses Volk nun, zwar nicht haßte,
Doch wegen seines Stolzes zu verachten
Mich nicht entbrechen könnte? Seines Stolzes,
Den es auf Christ und Muselmann vererbte,
1295 Nur sein Gott sei der rechte Gott! — Ihr stutzt,
Daß ich, ein Christ, ein Tempelherr so rede?

Wenn hat, und wo die fromme Raserei,
Den bessern Gott zu haben, diesen bessern
Der ganzen Welt als besten aufzudringen,
1300 In ihrer schwärzesten Gestalt sich mehr
Gezeigt als hier, als jetzt? Wem hier, wem jetzt
Die Schuppen nicht vom Auge fallen ... Doch
Sei blind, wer will! — Vergeßt, was ich gesagt,
Und laßt mich! (Will gehen.)

Nathan.

Ha! Ihr wißt nicht, wie viel fester
1305 Ich nun mich an Euch drängen werde. — Kommt,
Wir müssen, müssen Freunde sein! — Verachtet
Mein Volk, so sehr Ihr wollt. Wir haben beide
Uns unser Volk nicht auserlesen. Sind
Wir unser Volk? Was heißt denn Volk?
1310 Sind Christ und Jude eher Christ und Jude
Als Mensch? Ah! wenn ich einen mehr in Euch
Gefunden hätte, dem es g'nügt, ein Mensch
Zu heißen!

Tempelherr.

Ja, bei Gott, das habt Ihr, Nathan!
Das habt Ihr! — Eure Hand! — Ich schäme mich,
1315 Euch einen Augenblick verkannt zu haben.

Nathan.

Und ich bin stolz darauf. Nur das Gemeine
Verkennt man selten.

Tempelherr.

Und das Seltene
Vergißt man schwerlich. — Nathan, ja;
Wir müssen, müssen Freunde werden.

Nathan.

Sind
1320 Es schon. — Wie wird sich meine Recha freuen! —
Und ah! welch eine heitre Ferne schließt
Sich meinen Blicken auf! — Kennt sie nur erst!

Tempelherr.

Ich brenne vor Verlangen. — Wer stürzt dort
Aus Euerm Hause? Ist's nicht ihre Daja?

Nathan.

1325 Ja wohl. So ängstlich?

Tempelherr.

Unsrer Recha ist
Doch nichts begegnet?

Sechster Auftritt.

Die Vorigen und Daja eilig.

Daja.

Nathan! Nathan!

Nathan.

Nun?

Daja.

Verzeihet, edler Ritter, daß ich Euch
Muß unterbrechen.

Nathan.

Nun, was ist's?

Tempelherr.

Was ist's?

Daja.

Der Sultan hat geschickt. Der Sultan will
1330 Euch sprechen. Gott, der Sultan!

Nathan.

Mich? der Sultan?
Er wird begierig sein, zu sehen, was
Ich Neues mitgebracht. Sag nur, es sei
Noch wenig oder gar nichts ausgepackt.

Daja.

Nein, nein; er will nichts sehen, will Euch sprechen,
1335 Euch in Person, und bald, sobald Ihr könnt.

Nathan.

Ich werde kommen. — Geh nur wieder, geh!

Daja.

Nehmt ja nicht übel auf, gestrenger Ritter —
Gott, wir sind so bekümmert, was der Sultan
Doch will.

Nathan.

Das wird sich zeigen. Geh nur, geh!

Siebenter Auftritt.

Nathan und der Tempelherr.

Tempelherr.

1340 So kennt Ihr ihn noch nicht? — ich meine, von
Person.

Nathan.

Den Saladin? Noch nicht. Ich habe
Ihn nicht vermieden, nicht gesucht zu kennen.

Der allgemeine Ruf sprach viel zu gut
Von ihm, daß ich nicht lieber glauben wollte
1345 Als sehn. Doch nun — wenn anders dem so ist —
Hat er durch Sparung Eures Lebens . . .

Tempelherr.

Ja,
Dem allerdings ist so. Das Leben, das
Ich leb', ist sein Geschenk.

Nathan.

Durch das er mir
Ein doppelt, dreifach Leben schenkte. Dies
1350 Hat alles zwischen uns verändert, hat
Mit eins ein Seil mir umgeworfen, das
Mich seinem Dienst auf ewig fesselt. Kaum,
Und kaum, kann ich es nun erwarten, was
Er mir zuerst befehlen wird. Ich bin
1355 Bereit zu allem, bin bereit, ihm zu
Gestehn, daß ich es Euretwegen bin.

Tempelherr.

Noch hab' ich selber ihm nicht danken können,
So oft ich auch ihm in den Weg getreten.
Der Eindruck, den ich auf ihn machte, kam
1360 So schnell, als schnell er wiederum verschwunden.
Wer weiß, ob er sich meiner gar erinnert.
Und dennoch muß er, einmal wenigstens,
Sich meiner noch erinnern, um mein Schicksal
Ganz zu entscheiden. Nicht genug, daß ich
1365 Auf sein Geheiß noch bin, mit seinem Willen
Noch leb': ich muß nun auch von ihm erwarten,
Nach wessen Willen ich zu leben habe.

Nathan.

Nicht anders; um so mehr will ich nicht säumen. —
Es fällt vielleicht ein Wort, das mir, auf Euch
1370 Zu kommen, Anlaß giebt. — Erlaubt, verzeiht —
Ich eile — Wenn, wenn aber sehn wir Euch
Bei uns?

Tempelherr.

Sobald ich darf.

Nathan.

Sobald Ihr wollt.

Tempelherr.

Noch heut'.

Nathan.

Und Euer Name? — muß ich bitten.

Tempelherr.

Mein Name war — ist Curd von Stauffen. — Curd!

Nathan.

1375 Von Stauffen? — Stauffen? — Stauffen?

Tempelherr.

Warum fällt
Euch das so auf?

Nathan.

Von Stauffen? — Des Geschlechts
Sind wohl schon mehrere ...

Tempelherr.

O ja! hier waren,
Hier faulen des Geschlechts schon mehrere.
Mein Oheim selbst, — mein Vater will ich sagen, —

1380 Doch warum schärft sich Euer Blick auf mich
Je mehr und mehr?

Nathan.

O nichts! o nichts! Wie kann
Ich Euch zu sehn ermüden?

Tempelherr.

Drum verlass'
Ich Euch zuerst. Der Blick des Forschers fand
Nicht selten mehr, als er zu finden wünschte.
1385 Ich fürcht' ihn, Nathan. Laßt die Zeit allmählich,
Und nicht die Neugier, unsre Kundschaft machen.

(Er geht.)

Nathan

(der ihm mit Erstaunen nachsieht).

„Der Forscher fand nicht selten mehr, als er
Zu finden wünschte." — Ist es doch, als ob
In meiner Seel' er lese! — Wahrlich ja;
1390 Das könnt' auch mir begegnen. — Nicht allein
Wolfs Wuchs, Wolfs Gang: auch seine Stimme. So,
Vollkommen so warf Wolf sogar den Kopf,
Trug Wolf sogar das Schwert im Arm, strich Wolf
Sogar die Augenbraunen mit der Hand
1395 Gleichsam das Feuer seines Blicks zu bergen. —
Wie solche tiefgeprägte Bilder doch
Zu Zeiten in uns schlafen können, bis
Ein Wort, ein Laut sie weckt. — Von Stauffen! —
Ganz recht, ganz recht, Filnek und Stauffen. —
1400 Ich will das bald genauer wissen; bald.
Nur erst zum Saladin. — Doch wie? lauscht dort
Nicht Daja? — Nun so komm nur näher, Daja.

Achter Auftritt.

Daja. Nathan.

Nathan.

Was gilt's? nun drückt's euch beiden schon das Herz,
Noch ganz was andres zu erfahren, als
1405 Was Saladin mir will.

Daja.

Verdenkt Ihr's ihr?
Ihr fingt soeben an, vertraulicher
Mit ihm zu sprechen, als des Sultans Botschaft
Uns von dem Fenster scheuchte.

Nathan.

Nun, so sag
Ihr nur, daß sie ihn jeden Augenblick
1410 Erwarten darf.

Daja.

Gewiß? gewiß?

Nathan.

Ich kann
Mich doch auf dich verlassen, Daja? Sei
Auf deiner Hut, ich bitte dich. Es soll
Dich nicht gereuen. Dein Gewissen selbst
Soll seine Rechnung dabei finden. Nur
1415 Verdirb mir nichts in meinem Plane. Nur
Erzähl und frage mit Bescheidenheit,
Mit Rückhalt . . .

Daja.

Daß Ihr doch noch erst so was
Erinnern könnt! — Ich geh'; geht Ihr nur auch.
Denn seht! ich glaube gar, da kömmt vom Sultan
1420 Ein zweiter Bot', Al-Hafi, Euer Derwisch.

(Geht ab.)

Neunter Auftritt.

Nathan. Al-Hafi.

Al-Hafi.

Ha! ha! zu Euch wollt' ich nun eben wieder.

Nathan.

Ist's denn so eilig? Was verlangt er denn
Von mir?

Al-Hafi.

Wer?

Nathan.

Saladin. — Ich komm', ich komme.

Al-Hafi.

Zu wem? Zum Saladin?

Nathan.

Schickt Saladin
1425 Dich nicht?

Al-Hafi.

Mich? nein. Hat er denn schon geschickt?

Nathan.

Ja freilich hat er.

Al-Hafi.

Nun, so ist es richtig.

Nathan.

Was? was ist richtig?

Al-Hafi.

Daß — ich bin nicht schuld;
Gott weiß, ich bin nicht schuld. — Was hab' ich nicht
Von Euch gesagt, gelogen, um es abzuwenden!

Nathan.

1430 Was abzuwenden? Was ist richtig?

Al-Hafi.

Daß
Nun Ihr sein Defterdar geworden. Ich
Bedaur' Euch. Doch mit ansehn will ich's nicht.
Ich geh' von Stund an, geh'. Ihr habt es schon
Gehört, wohin, und wißt den Weg. — Habt Ihr
1435 Des Wegs was zu bestellen, sagt; ich bin
Zu Diensten. Freilich muß es mehr nicht sein,
Als was ein Nackter mit sich schleppen kann.
Ich geh', sagt bald.

Nathan.

Besinn dich doch, Al-Hafi.
Besinn dich, daß ich noch von gar nichts weiß.
1440 Was plauderst du denn da?

Al-Hafi.

Ihr bringt sie doch
Gleich mit, die Beutel?

Nathan.

Beutel?

Al-Hafi.

Nun, das Geld,
Das Ihr dem Saladin vorschießen sollt.

Nathan.

Und weiter ist es nichts?

Al-Hafi.

Ich sollt' es wohl
Mit ansehn, wie er Euch von Tag zu Tag

1445 Aushöhlen wird bis auf die Zehen? Sollt'
Es wohl mit ansehn, daß Verschwendung aus
Der weisen Milde sonst nie leeren Scheuern
So lange borgt und borgt und borgt, bis auch
Die armen eingebornen Mäuschen drin
1450 Verhungern? — Bildet Ihr vielleicht Euch ein,
Wer Euers Gelds bedürftig sei, der werde
Doch Euerm Rate wohl auch folgen? — Ja,
Er Rate folgen! Wenn hat Saladin
Sich raten lassen? — Denkt nur, Nathan, was
1455 Mir eben jetzt mit ihm begegnet.

Nathan.

Nun?

Al-Hafi.

Da komm' ich zu ihm, eben daß er Schach
Gespielt mit seiner Schwester. Sittah spielt
Nicht übel, und das Spiel, das Saladin
Verloren glaubte, schon gegeben hatte,
1460 Das stand noch ganz so da. Ich seh' Euch hin
Und sehe, daß das Spiel noch lange nicht
Verloren.

Nathan.

Ei! das war für dich ein Fund!

Al-Hafi.

Er durfte mit dem König an den Bauer
Nur rücken, auf ihr Schach. — Wenn ich's Euch gleich
1465 Nur zeigen könnte!

Nathan.

O, ich traue dir!

Al-Hafi.

Denn so bekam der Roche Feld, und sie

War hin. — Das alles will ich ihm nun weisen
Und ruf' ihn. — Denkt! . . .

Nathan.

Er ist nicht deiner Meinung?

Al-Hafi.

Er hört mich gar nicht an und wirft verächtlich
1470 Das ganze Spiel in Klumpen.

Nathan.

Ist das möglich?

Al-Hafi.

Und sagt: er wolle matt nun einmal sein;
Er wolle! Heißt das spielen?

Nathan.

Schwerlich wohl;
Heißt mit dem Spiele spielen.

Al-Hafi.

Gleichwohl galt
Es keine taube Nuß.

Nathan.

Geld hin, Geld her!
1475 Das ist das wenigste. Allein dich gar
Nicht anzuhören! über einen Punkt
Von solcher Wichtigkeit dich nicht einmal
Zu hören! deinen Adlerblick nicht zu
Bewundern! das, das schreit um Rache; nicht?

Al-Hafi.

1480 Ach was! Ich sag' Euch das nur so, damit
Ihr sehen könnt, was für ein Kopf er ist.
Kurz, ich, ich halt's mit ihm nicht länger aus.
Da lauf' ich nun bei allen schmutz'gen Mohren

Herum und frage, wer ihm borgen will.
1485 Ich, der ich nie für mich gebettelt habe,
Soll nun für andre borgen. Borgen ist
Viel besser nicht als betteln: so wie leihen,
Auf Wucher leihen, nicht viel besser ist
Als stehlen. Unter meinen Ghebern, an
1490 Dem Ganges, brauch' ich beides nicht und brauche
Das Werkzeug beider nicht zu sein. Am Ganges,
Am Ganges nur giebt's Menschen. Hier seid Ihr
Der einzige, der noch so würdig wäre,
Daß er am Ganges lebte. — Wollt Ihr mit? —
1495 Laßt ihm mit eins den Plunder ganz im Stiche,
Um den es ihm zu thun. Er bringt Euch nach
Und nach doch drum. So wär' die Plackerei
Auf einmal aus. Ich schaff' Euch einen Delk.
Kommt! kommt!

Nathan.

Ich dächte zwar, das blieb' uns ja
1500 Noch immer übrig. Doch, Al-Hafi, will
Ich's überlegen. Warte . . .

Al-Hafi.

Überlegen?
Nein, so was überlegt sich nicht.

Nathan.

Nur bis
Ich von dem Sultan wiederkomme, bis
Ich Abschied erst . . .

Al-Hafi.

Wer überlegt, der sucht
1505 Bewegungsgründe, nicht zu dürfen. Wer
Sich Knall und Fall, ihm selbst zu leben, nicht

Entschließen kann, der lebet andrer Sklav'
Auf immer. — Wie Ihr wollt! — Lebt wohl! wie's Euch
Wohl dünkt. — Mein Weg liegt dort, und Eurer da.

Nathan.

1510 Al-Hafi! Du wirst selbst doch erst das Deine
Berichtigen?

Al-Hafi.

Ach Possen! Der Bestand
Von meiner Kass' ist nicht des Zählens wert;
Und meine Rechnung bürgt — Ihr oder Sittah.
Lebt wohl! (Ab.)

Nathan (ihm nachsehend).

Die bürg' ich! — Wilder, guter, edler —
1515 Wie nenn' ich ihn? — Der wahre Bettler ist
Doch einzig und allein der wahre König!

(Von einer andern Seite ab.)

Dritter Aufzug.

Erster Auftritt.

Scene: in Nathans Hause.

Recha und Daja.

Recha.

Wie, Daja, drückte sich mein Vater aus?
„Ich dürf' ihn jeden Augenblick erwarten?"
Das klingt — nicht wahr? — als ob er noch so bald
1520 Erscheinen werde. — Wie viel Augenblicke
Sind aber schon vorbei! — Ah nun, wer denkt
An die verflossenen? — Ich will allein
In jedem nächsten Augenblicke leben.
Er wird doch einmal kommen, der ihn bringt.

Daja.

1525 O der verwünschten Botschaft von dem Sultan!
Denn Nathan hätte sicher ohne sie
Ihn gleich mit hergebracht.

Recha.

Und wenn er nun
Gekommen, dieser Augenblick; wenn denn
Nun meiner Wünsche wärmster, innigster
1530 Erfüllet ist: was dann? — was dann?

Daja.

Was dann?

Dann hoff' ich, daß auch meiner Wünsche wärmster
Soll in Erfüllung gehen.

Recha.

Was wird dann
In meiner Brust an dessen Stelle treten,
Die schon verlernt, ohn' einen herrschenden
1535 Wunsch aller Wünsche sich zu dehnen? — Nichts?
Ah, ich erschrecke! ...

Daja.

Mein, mein Wunsch wird dann
An des erfüllten Stelle treten; meiner.
Mein Wunsch, dich in Europa, dich in Händen
Zu wissen, welche deiner würdig sind.

Recha.

1540 Du irrst. — Was diesen Wunsch zu deinem macht,
Das nämliche verhindert, daß er meiner
Je werden kann. Dich zieht dein Vaterland,
Und meines, meines sollte mich nicht halten?
Ein Bild der Deinen, das in deiner Seele
1545 Noch nicht verloschen, sollte mehr vermögen,
Als die ich sehn und greifen kann und hören,
Die Meinen?

Daja.

Sperre dich, so viel du willst!
Des Himmels Wege sind des Himmels Wege.
Und wenn es nun dein Retter selber wäre,
1550 Durch den sein Gott, für den er kämpft, dich in
Das Land, dich zu dem Volke führen wollte,
Für welche du geboren wurdest?

Recha.

Daja!
Was sprichst du da nun wieder, liebe Daja!
Du hast doch wahrlich deine sonderbaren
1555 Begriffe! „Sein, sein Gott! für den er kämpft!"
Wem eignet Gott? was ist das für ein Gott,
Der einem Menschen eignet? der für sich
Muß kämpfen lassen? — Und wie weiß
Man denn, für welchen Erdkloß man geboren,
1560 Wenn man's für den nicht ist, auf welchem man
Geboren? — Wenn mein Vater dich so hörte! —
Was that er dir, mir immer nur mein Glück
So weit von ihm als möglich vorzuspiegeln?
Was that er dir, den Samen der Vernunft,
1565 Den er so rein in meine Seele streute,
Mit deines Landes Unkraut oder Blumen
So gern zu mischen? — Liebe, liebe Daja,
Er will nun deine bunten Blumen nicht
Auf meinem Boden! — Und ich muß dir sagen,
1570 Ich selber fühle meinen Boden, wenn
Sie noch so schön ihn kleiden, so entkräftet,
So ausgezehrt durch deine Blumen; fühle
In ihrem Dufte, sauersüßem Dufte,
Mich so betäubt, so schwindelnd! — Dein Gehirn
1575 Ist dessen mehr gewohnt. Ich tadle drum
Die stärkern Nerven nicht, die ihn vertragen.
Nur schlägt er mir nicht zu; und schon dein Engel,
Wie wenig fehlte, daß er mich zur Närrin
Gemacht? — Noch schäm' ich mich vor meinem Vater
1580 Der Posse!

Daja.

Posse! — Als ob der Verstand
Nur hier zu Hause wäre! Posse! Posse!
Wenn ich nur reden dürfte!

Recha.

Darfst du nicht?
Wenn war ich nicht ganz Ohr, so oft es dir
Gefiel, von deinen Glaubenshelden mich
1585 Zu unterhalten? Hab' ich ihren Thaten
Nicht stets Bewunderung und ihren Leiden
Nicht immer Thränen gern gezollt? Ihr Glaube
Schien freilich mir das Heldenmäßigste
An ihnen nie. Doch so viel tröstender
1590 War mir die Lehre, daß Ergebenheit
In Gott von unserm Wähnen über Gott
So ganz und gar nicht abhängt. — Liebe Daja,
Das hat mein Vater uns so oft gesagt;
Darüber hast du selbst mit ihm so oft
1595 Dich einverstanden: warum untergräbst
Du denn allein, was du mit ihm zugleich
Gebauet? — Liebe Daja, das ist kein
Gespräch, womit wir unserm Freund am besten
Entgegensehn. Für mich zwar, ja! Denn nur,
1600 Mir liegt daran unendlich, ob auch er . . .
Horch, Daja! — Kommt es nicht an unsre Thüre?
Wenn er es wäre! Horch!

Zweiter Auftritt.

Recha. Daja und der Tempelherr, dem jemand von außen die Thüre öffnet mit den Worten:

Nur hier herein!

Recha
(fährt zusammen, faßt sich und will ihm zu Füßen fallen).

Er ist's! — Mein Retter, ah!

Tempelherr.

Dies zu vermeiden,
Erschien ich bloß so spät; und doch —

Recha.

Ich will
1605 Ja zu den Füßen dieses stolzen Mannes
Nur Gott noch einmal danken, nicht dem Manne.
Der Mann will keinen Dank, will ihn so wenig,
Als ihn der Wassereimer will, der bei
Dem Löschen so geschäftig sich erwiesen.
1610 Der ließ sich füllen, ließ sich leeren, mir
Nichts, dir nichts: also auch der Mann. Auch der
Ward nun so in die Glut hineingestoßen;
Da fiel ich ungefähr ihm in den Arm;
Da blieb ich ungefähr, so wie ein Funken
1615 Auf seinem Mantel, ihm in seinen Armen,
Bis wiederum, ich weiß nicht was, uns beide
Herausschmiß aus der Glut. — Was giebt es da
Zu danken? — In Europa treibt der Wein
Zu noch weit andern Thaten. — Tempelherren,
1620 Die müssen einmal nun so handeln, müssen
Wie etwas besser zugelernte Hunde
Sowohl aus Feuer, als aus Wasser holen.

Tempelherr

(der sie mit Erstaunen und Unruhe die ganze Zeit über betrachtet).

O Daja, Daja! Wenn in Augenblicken
Des Kummers und der Galle meine Laune
1625 Dich übel anließ, warum jede Thorheit,
Die meiner Zung' entfuhr, ihr hinterbringen?
Das hieß sich zu empfindlich rächen, Daja!
Doch wenn du nur von nun an besser mich
Bei ihr vertreten willst.

Daja.

Ich denke, Ritter,
1630 Ich denke nicht, daß diese kleinen Stacheln,
Ihr an das Herz geworfen, Euch da sehr
Geschadet haben.

Recha.

Wie? Ihr hattet Kummer?
Und wart mit Euerm Kummer geiziger
Als Euerm Leben?

Tempelherr.

Gutes, holdes Kind! —
1635 Wie ist doch meine Seele zwischen Auge
Und Ohr geteilt! — Das war das Mädchen nicht,
Nein, nein, das war es nicht, das aus dem Feuer
Ich holte. — Denn wer hätte die gekannt
Und aus dem Feuer nicht geholt? Wer hätte
1640 Auf mich gewartet? — Zwar — verstellt — der Schreck

(Pause, unter der er in Anschauung ihrer sich wie verliert.)

Recha.

Ich aber find' Euch noch den nämlichen. —

(Desgleichen, bis sie fortfährt, um ihn in seinem Anstaunen zu unterbrechen.)

Nun, Ritter, sagt uns doch, wo Ihr so lange
Gewesen? — Fast dürft' ich auch fragen, wo
Ihr jetzo seid?

Tempelherr.

Ich bin, — wo ich vielleicht
1645 Nicht sollte sein. —

Recha.

Wo Ihr gewesen? — Auch
Wo Ihr vielleicht nicht solltet sein gewesen?
Das ist nicht gut.

Tempelherr.

Auf — auf — wie heißt der Berg?
Auf Sinai.

Recha.

Auf Sinai? — Ah schön!
Nun kann ich zuverlässig doch einmal
1650 Erfahren, ob es wahr . . .

Tempelherr.

Was? was? Ob's wahr,
Daß noch daselbst der Ort zu sehn, wo Moses
Vor Gott gestanden, als . . .

Recha.

Nun das wohl nicht;
Denn wo er stand, stand er vor Gott. Und davon
Ist mir zur G'nüge schon bekannt. — Ob's wahr,
1655 Möcht' ich nur gern von Euch erfahren, daß —
Daß es bei weitem nicht so mühsam sei,
Auf diesen Berg hinauf zu steigen als
Herab? — Denn seht, soviel ich Berge noch

Gestiegen bin, war's just das Gegenteil. —
1660 Nun, Ritter? — Was? — Ihr kehrt Euch von mir ab?
Wollt mich nicht sehn?

Tempelherr.

Weil ich Euch hören will.

Recha.

Weil Ihr mich nicht wollt merken lassen, daß
Ihr meiner Einfalt lächelt; daß Ihr lächelt,
Wie ich Euch doch so gar nichts Wichtigers
1665 Von diesem heiligen Berg aller Berge
Zu fragen weiß? Nicht wahr?

Tempelherr.

So muß
Ich doch Euch wieder in die Augen sehn. —
Was? Nun schlagt Ihr sie nieder? nun verbeißt
Das Lächeln Ihr? wie ich noch erst in Mienen,
1670 In zweifelhaften Mienen lesen will,
Was ich so deutlich hör', Ihr so vernehmlich
Mir sagt — verschweigt? — Ah Recha! Recha! Wie
Hat er so wahr gesagt: „Kennt sie nur erst!"

Recha.

Wer hat? — von wem? — Euch das gesagt?

Tempelherr.

„Kennt sie
1675 Nur erst!" hat Euer Vater mir gesagt,
Von Euch gesagt.

Daja.

Und ich nicht etwa auch?
Ich denn nicht auch?

Tempelherr.

Allein wo ist er denn?
Wo ist denn Euer Vater? Ist er noch
Beim Sultan?

Recha.

Ohne Zweifel.

Tempelherr.

Noch, noch da? —
1680 O mich Vergeßlichen! Nein, nein; da ist
Er schwerlich mehr. — Er wird dort unten bei
Dem Kloster meiner warten; ganz gewiß.
So red'ten, mein' ich, wir es ab. Erlaubt!
Ich geh', ich hol' ihn . . .

Daja.

Das ist meine Sache.
1685 Bleibt, Ritter, bleibt. Ich bring' ihn unverzüglich.

Tempelherr.

Nicht so, nicht so! Er sieht mir selbst entgegen;
Nicht Euch. Dazu, er könnte leicht . . . wer weiß? —
Er könnte bei dem Sultan leicht, — Ihr kennt
Den Sultan nicht! — leicht in Verlegenheit
1690 Gekommen sein. — Glaubt mir; es hat Gefahr,
Wenn ich nicht geh'.

Recha.

Gefahr? was für Gefahr?

Tempelherr.

Gefahr für mich, für Euch, für ihn, wenn ich
Nicht schleunig, schleunig geh'. (Ab.)

Dritter Auftritt.

Recha und Daja.

Recha.

Was ist das, Daja? —
So schnell? — Was kömmt ihm an? Was fiel ihm auf?
1695 Was jagt ihn?

Daja.

Laßt nur, laßt. Ich denk', es ist
Kein schlimmes Zeichen.

Recha.

Zeichen? und wovon?

Daja.

Daß etwas vorgeht innerhalb. Es kocht
Und soll nicht überkochen. Laßt ihn nur.
Nun ist's an Euch.

Recha.

Was ist an mir? Du wirst,
1700 Wie er, mir unbegreiflich.

Daja.

Bald nun könnt
Ihr ihm die Unruh' all vergelten, die
Er Euch gemacht hat. Seid nur aber auch
Nicht allzu streng, nicht allzu rachbegierig.

Recha.

Wovon du sprichst, das magst du selber wissen.

Daja.

1705 Und seid denn Ihr bereits so ruhig wieder?

Recha.

Das bin ich; ja, das bin ich . . .

Daja.

Wenigstens
Gesteht, daß Ihr Euch seiner Unruh' freut
Und seiner Unruh' danket, was Ihr jetzt
Von Ruh' genießt.

Recha.

Mir völlig unbewußt!
1710 Denn was ich höchstens dir gestehen könnte,
Wär', daß es mich — mich selbst befremdet, wie
Auf einen solchen Sturm in meinem Herzen
So eine Stille plötzlich folgen können.
Sein voller Anblick, sein Gespräch, sein Ton
1715 Hat mich . . .

Daja.

Gesättigt schon?

Recha.

Gesättigt, will
Ich nun nicht sagen; nein — bei weitem nicht —

Daja.

Den heißen Hunger nur gestillt.

Recha.

Nun ja,
Wenn du so willst.

Daja.

Ich eben nicht.

Recha.

Er wird
Mir ewig wert, mir ewig werter als
1720 Mein Leben bleiben, wenn auch schon mein Puls
Nicht mehr bei seinem bloßen Namen wechselt,
Nicht mehr mein Herz, so oft ich an ihn denke,

Geschwinder, stärker schlägt. — Was schwatz' ich? Komm,
Komm, liebe Daja, wieder an das Fenster,
1725 Das auf die Palmen sieht.

Daja.

So ist er doch
Wohl noch nicht ganz gestillt, der heiße Hunger.

Recha.

Nun werd' ich auch die Palmen wieder sehn,
Nicht ihn bloß untern Palmen.

Daja.

Diese Kälte
Beginnt auch wohl ein neues Fieber nur.

Recha.

1730 Was Kält'? Ich bin nicht kalt. Ich sehe wahrlich
Nicht minder gern, was ich mit Ruhe sehe.

Vierter Auftritt.

Scene: ein Audienzsaal in dem Palaste des Saladin.

Saladin und Sittah.

Saladin
(im Hereintreten, gegen die Thüre).

Hier bringt den Juden her, sobald er kömmt.
Er scheint sich eben nicht zu übereilen.

Sittah.

Er war auch wohl nicht bei der Hand, nicht gleich
1735 Zu finden.

Saladin.

Schwester! Schwester!

Sittah.

Thust du doch,

Als stünde dir ein Treffen vor.

Saladin.

Und das

Mit Waffen, die ich nicht gelernt zu führen.
Ich soll mich stellen, soll besorgen lassen,
Soll Fallen legen, soll auf Glatteis führen.
1740 Wenn hätt' ich das gekonnt? Wo hätt' ich das
Gelernt? — Und soll das alles, ah, wozu?
Wozu? — Um Geld zu fischen! Geld! — Um Geld,
Geld einem Juden abzubangen; Geld!
Zu solchen kleinen Listen wär' ich endlich
1745 Gebracht, der Kleinigkeiten kleinste mir
Zu schaffen?

Sittah.

Jede Kleinigkeit, zu sehr
Verschmäht, die rächt sich, Bruder.

Saladin.

Leider wahr. —
Und wenn nun dieser Jude gar der gute,
Vernünft'ge Mann ist, wie der Derwisch dir
1750 Ihn ehedem beschrieben?

Sittah.

O nun dann!
Was hat es dann für Not! Die Schlinge liegt
Ja nur dem geizigen, besorglichen,
Furchtsamen Juden, nicht dem guten, nicht
Dem weisen Manne. Dieser ist ja so

1755 Schon unser, ohne Schlinge. Das Vergnügen,
Zu hören, wie ein solcher Mann sich ausred't;
Mit welcher dreisten Stärk' entweder er
Die Stricke kurz zerreißet, oder auch
Mit welcher schlauen Vorsicht er die Netze
1760 Vorbei sich windet: dies Vergnügen hast
Du obendrein.

Saladin.

Nun, das ist wahr. Gewiß,
Ich freue mich darauf.

Sittah.

So kann dich ja
Auch weiter nichts verlegen machen. Denn
Ist's einer aus der Menge bloß; ist's bloß
1765 Ein Jude wie ein Jude: gegen den
Wirst du dich doch nicht schämen, so zu scheinen,
Wie er die Menschen all' sich denkt? Vielmehr,
Wer sich ihm besser zeigt, der zeigt sich ihm
Als Geck, als Narr.

Saladin.

So muß ich ja wohl gar
1770 Schlecht handeln, daß von mir der Schlechte nicht
Schlecht denke?

Sittah.

Traun, wenn du schlecht handeln nennst,
Ein jedes Ding nach seiner Art zu brauchen.

Saladin.

Was hätt' ein Weiberkopf erdacht, das er
Nicht zu beschönen wüßte!

Sittah.

Zu beschönen!

Saladin.

1775 Das feine, spitze Ding, besorg' ich nur,
In meiner plumpen Hand zerbricht! — So was
Will ausgeführt sein, wie's erfunden ist,
Mit aller Pfiffigkeit, Gewandtheit. — Doch,
Mag's doch nur, mag's! Ich tanze, wie ich kann;
1780 Und könnt' es freilich lieber — schlechter noch
Als besser.

Sittah.

Trau dir auch nur nicht zu wenig!
Ich stehe dir für dich! Wenn du nur willst. —
Daß uns die Männer deinesgleichen doch
So gern bereden möchten, nur ihr Schwert,
1785 Ihr Schwert nur habe sie so weit gebracht.
Der Löwe schämt sich freilich, wenn er mit
Dem Fuchse jagt: — des Fuchses, nicht der List.

Saladin.

Und daß die Weiber doch so gern den Mann
Zu sich herunter hätten! — Geh nur, geh! —
1790 Ich glaube meine Lektion zu können.

Sittah.

Was? ich soll gehn?

Saladin.

Du wolltest doch nicht bleiben?

Sittah.

Wenn auch nicht bleiben ... im Gesicht euch bleiben —
Doch hier im Nebenzimmer —

Saladin.

Da zu horchen?
Auch das nicht, Schwester, wenn ich soll bestehn. —
1795 Fort, fort! der Vorhang rauscht; er kömmt! — doch daß
Du ja nicht da verweilst! Ich sehe nach.

(Indem sie sich durch die eine Thüre entfernt, tritt Nathan zu der andern herein, und Saladin hat sich gesetzt.)

Fünfter Auftritt.

Saladin und Nathan.

Saladin.

Tritt näher, Jude! — Näher! — Nur ganz her! —
Nur ohne Furcht!

Nathan.

Die bleibe deinem Feinde!

Saladin.

Du nennst dich Nathan?

Nathan.

Ja.

Saladin.

Den weisen Nathan?

Nathan.

1800 Nein.

Saladin.

Wohl! nennst du dich nicht, nennt dich das Volk.

Nathan.

Kann sein, das Volk!

Saladin.

Du glaubst doch nicht, daß ich
Verächtlich von des Volkes Stimme denke? —
Ich habe längst gewünscht, den Mann zu kennen,
Den es den Weisen nennt.

Nathan.

Und wenn es ihn
1805 Zum Spott so nennte? Wenn dem Volke weise
Nichts weiter wär' als klug? und klug nur der,
Der sich auf seinen Vorteil gut versteht?

Saladin.

Auf seinen wahren Vorteil, meinst du doch?

Nathan.

Dann freilich wär' der Eigennützigste
1810 Der Klügste. Dann wär' freilich klug und weise
Nur eins.

Saladin.

Ich höre dich erweisen, was
Du widersprechen willst. — Des Menschen wahre
Vorteile, die das Volk nicht kennt, kennst du.
Hast du zu kennen wenigstens gesucht;
1815 Hast drüber nachgedacht: das auch allein
Macht schon den Weisen.

Nathan.

Der sich jeder dünkt
Zu sein.

Saladin.

Nun der Bescheidenheit genug!
Denn sie nur immerdar zu hören, wo
Man trockene Vernunft erwartet, ekelt.

(Er springt auf.)

1820 Laß uns zur Sache kommen! Aber, aber
Aufrichtig, Jud', aufrichtig!

Nathan.

Sultan, ich
Will sicherlich dich so bedienen, daß
Ich deiner fernern Kundschaft würdig bleibe.

Saladin.

Bedienen? wie?

Nathan.

Du sollst das Beste haben
1825 Von allem; sollst es um den billigsten
Preis haben.

Saladin.

Wovon sprichst du? doch wohl nicht
Von deinen Waren? — Schachern wird mit dir
Schon meine Schwester. (Das der Horcherin!) —
Ich habe mit dem Kaufmann nichts zu thun.

Nathan.

1830 So wirst du ohne Zweifel wissen wollen,
Was ich auf meinem Wege von dem Feinde,
Der allerdings sich wieder reget, etwa
Bemerkt, getroffen? — Wenn ich unverhohlen ..

Saladin.

Auch darauf bin ich eben nicht mit dir
1835 Gesteuert. Davon weiß ich schon, soviel
Ich nötig habe. — Kurz; —

Nathan.

Gebiete, Sultan.

Saladin.

Ich heische deinen Unterricht in ganz
Was anderm, ganz was anderm. — Da du nun

So weise bist, so sage mir doch einmal —
1840 Was für ein Glaube, was für ein Gesetz
Hat dir am meisten eingeleuchtet?

Nathan.

Sultan,

Ich bin ein Jud'.

Saladin.

Und ich ein Muselmann.
Der Christ ist zwischen uns. — Von diesen drei
Religionen kann doch eine nur
1845 Die wahre sein. — Ein Mann wie du bleibt da
Nicht stehen, wo der Zufall der Geburt
Ihn hingeworfen; oder wenn er bleibt,
Bleibt er aus Einsicht, Gründen, Wahl des Bessern.
Wohlan! so teile deine Einsicht mir
1850 Denn mit. Laß mich die Gründe hören, denen
Ich selber nachzugrübeln nicht die Zeit
Gehabt. Laß mich die Wahl, die diese Gründe
Bestimmt, — versteht sich, im Vertrauen — wissen,
Damit ich sie zu meiner mache. Wie?
1855 Du stutzest? wägst mich mit dem Auge? — Kann
Wohl sein, daß ich der erste Sultan bin,
Der eine solche Grille hat, die mich
Doch eines Sultans eben nicht so ganz
Unwürdig dünkt. — Nicht wahr? — So rede doch!
1860 Sprich! — Oder willst du einen Augenblick,
Dich zu bedenken? Gut, ich geb' ihn dir. —
(Ob sie wohl horcht? Ich will sie doch belauschen;
Will hören, ob ich's recht gemacht. —) Denk nach!
Geschwind denk nach! Ich säume nicht, zurück
1865 Zu kommen.

(Er geht in das Nebenzimmer, nach welchem sich Sittah begeben.)

Sechster Auftritt.

Nathan (allein).

Hm! hm! — wunderlich! — Wie ist
Mir denn? — Was will der Sultan? was? — Ich bin
Auf Geld gefaßt, und er will — Wahrheit. Wahrheit!
Und will sie so, — so bar, so blank, — als ob
Die Wahrheit Münze wäre! — Ja, wenn noch
1870 Uralte Münze, die gewogen ward! —
Das ginge noch! Allein so neue Münze,
Die nur der Stempel macht, die man aufs Brett
Nur zählen darf, das ist sie doch nun nicht!
Wie Geld in Sack, so striche man in Kopf
1875 Auch Wahrheit ein? Wer ist denn hier der Jude?
Ich oder er? — Doch wie? Sollt' er auch wohl
Die Wahrheit nicht in Wahrheit fordern? — Zwar,
Zwar der Verdacht, daß er die Wahrheit nur
Als Falle brauche, wär' auch gar zu klein! —
1880 Zu klein? — Was ist für einen Großen denn
Zu klein? — Gewiß, gewiß, er stürzte mit
Der Thüre so ins Haus! Man pocht doch, hört
Doch erst, wenn man als Freund sich naht. — Ich muß
Behutsam gehn! — Und wie? wie das? — So ganz
1885 Stockjude sein zu wollen, geht schon nicht. —
Und ganz und gar nicht Jude, geht noch minder.
Denn, wenn kein Jude, dürft' er mich nur fragen,
Warum kein Muselmann? — Das war's! Das kann
Mich retten! — Nicht die Kinder bloß speist man
1890 Mit Märchen ab. — Er kömmt. Er komme nur!

Siebenter Auftritt.

Saladin und Nathan.

Saladin.

(So ist das Feld hier rein!) — Ich komm' dir doch
Nicht zu geschwind zurück? Du bist zu Rande
Mit deiner Überlegung — Nun so rede!
Es hört uns keine Seele.

Nathan.

Möcht' auch doch
1895 Die ganze Welt uns hören.

Saladin.

So gewiß
Ist Nathan seiner Sache? Ha! das nenn'
Ich einen Weisen! Nie die Wahrheit zu
Verhehlen! für sie alles auf das Spiel
Zu setzen! Leib und Leben! Gut und Blut!

Nathan.

1900 Ja! ja! wenn's nötig ist und nützt.

Saladin.

Von nun
An darf ich hoffen, einen meiner Titel,
Verbesserer der Welt und des Gesetzes,
Mit Recht zu führen.

Nathan.

Traun, ein schöner Titel!
Doch, Sultan, eh' ich mich dir ganz vertraue,
1905 Erlaubst du wohl, dir ein Geschichtchen zu
Erzählen?

Saladin.

Warum das nicht? Ich bin stets
Ein Freund gewesen von Geschichtchen, gut
Erzählt.

Nathan.

Ja, gut erzählen, das ist nun
Wohl eben meine Sache nicht.

Saladin.

Schon wieder
1910 So stolz bescheiden? — Mach! erzähl, erzähle!

Nathan.

Vor grauen Jahren lebt' ein Mann in Osten,
Der einen Ring von unschätzbarem Wert'
Aus lieber Hand besaß. Der Stein war ein
Opal, der hundert schöne Farben spielte,
1915 Und hatte die geheime Kraft, vor Gott
Und Menschen angenehm zu machen, wer
In dieser Zuversicht ihn trug. Was Wunder,
Daß ihn der Mann in Osten darum nie
Vom Finger ließ und die Verfügung traf,
1920 Auf ewig ihn bei seinem Hause zu
Erhalten? Nämlich so. Er ließ den Ring
Von seinen Söhnen dem geliebtesten
Und setzte fest, daß dieser wiederum
Den Ring von seinen Söhnen dem vermache,
1925 Der ihm der liebste sei, und stets der liebste,
Ohn' Ansehn der Geburt, in Kraft allein
Des Rings, das Haupt, der Fürst des Hauses werde. —
Verstehe mich, Sultan.

Saladin.

Ich versteh' dich. Weiter!

Nathan.

So kam nun dieser Ring, von Sohn zu Sohn,
1930 Auf einen Vater endlich von drei Söhnen,
Die alle drei ihm gleich gehorsam waren,
Die alle drei er folglich gleich zu lieben
Sich nicht entbrechen konnte. Nur von Zeit
Zu Zeit schien ihm bald der, bald dieser, bald
1935 Der dritte, — so wie jeder sich mit ihm
Allein befand, und sein ergießend Herz
Die andern zwei nicht teilten, — würdiger
Des Ringes, den er denn auch einem jeden
Die fromme Schwachheit hatte zu versprechen.
1940 Das ging nun so, solang es ging. — Allein
Es kam zum Sterben, und der gute Vater
Kömmt in Verlegenheit. Es schmerzt ihn, zwei
Von seinen Söhnen, die sich auf sein Wort
Verlassen, so zu kränken. — Was zu thun? —
1945 Er sendet in geheim zu einem Künstler,
Bei dem er, nach dem Muster seines Ringes,
Zwei andere bestellt und weder Kosten
Noch Mühe sparen heißt, sie jenem gleich,
Vollkommen gleich zu machen. Das gelingt
1950 Dem Künstler. Da er ihm die Ringe bringt,
Kann selbst der Vater seinen Musterring
Nicht unterscheiden. Froh und freudig ruft
Er seine Söhne, jeden insbesondre,
Giebt jedem insbesondre seinen Segen —
1955 Und seinen Ring — und stirbt. — Du hörst doch, Sultan?

Saladin

(der sich betroffen von ihm gewandt).

Ich hör', ich höre! — Komm mit deinem Märchen
Nur bald zu Ende. — Wird's?

Nathan.

Ich bin zu Ende.
Denn was noch folgt, versteht sich ja von selbst. —
Kaum war der Vater tot, so kommt ein jeder
1960 Mit seinem Ring, und jeder will der Fürst
Des Hauses sein. Man untersucht, man zankt,
Man klagt. Umsonst; der rechte Ring war nicht
Erweislich; —

(Nach einer Pause, in welcher er des Sultans Antwort erwartet.)

Fast so unerweislich als
Uns jetzt — der rechte Glaube.

Saladin.

Wie? das soll
1965 Die Antwort sein auf meine Frage? . .

Nathan.

Soll
Mich bloß entschuldigen, wenn ich die Ringe
Mir nicht getrau' zu unterscheiden, die
Der Vater in der Absicht machen ließ,
Damit sie nicht zu unterscheiden wären.

Saladin.

1970 Die Ringe! — Spiele nicht mit mir! — Ich dächte,
Daß die Religionen, die ich dir
Genannt, doch wohl zu unterscheiden wären.
Bis auf die Kleidung, bis auf Speis' und Trank!

Nathan.

Und nur von seiten ihrer Gründe nicht. —
1975 Denn gründen alle sich nicht auf Geschichte?
Geschrieben oder überliefert! — Und
Geschichte muß doch wohl allein auf Treu'

Und Glauben angenommen werden? — Nicht? —
Nun, wessen Treu' und Glauben zieht man denn
1980 Am wenigsten in Zweifel? Doch der Seinen?
Doch deren Blut wir sind? doch deren, die
Von Kindheit an uns Proben ihrer Liebe
Gegeben? die uns nie getäuscht, als wo
Getäuscht zu werden uns heilsamer war? —
1985 Wie kann ich meinen Vätern weniger
Als du den deinen glauben? Oder umgekehrt.
Kann ich von dir verlangen, daß du deine
Vorfahren Lügen strafst, um meinen nicht
Zu widersprechen? Oder umgekehrt.
1990 Das nämliche gilt von den Christen. Nicht? —

Saladin.

(Bei dem Lebendigen! Der Mann hat recht.
Ich muß verstummen.)

Nathan.

Laß auf unsre Ring'
Uns wieder kommen. Wie gesagt: die Söhne
Verklagten sich, und jeder schwur dem Richter,
1995 Unmittelbar aus seines Vaters Hand
Den Ring zu haben. — Wie auch wahr! — Nachdem
Er von ihm lange das Versprechen schon
Gehabt, des Ringes Vorrecht einmal zu
Genießen. — Wie nicht minder wahr! — Der Vater,
2000 Beteu'rte jeder, könne gegen ihn
Nicht falsch gewesen sein! und eh' er dieses
Von ihm, von einem solchen lieben Vater,
Argwohnen lass': eh' müss' er seine Brüder,
So gern er sonst von ihnen nur das Beste
2005 Bereit zu glauben sei, des falschen Spiels

Bezeihen, und er wolle die Verräter
Schon auszufinden wissen, sich schon rächen.

Saladin.

Und nun, der Richter? — Mich verlangt zu hören,
Was du den Richter sagen lässest. Sprich!

Nathan.

2010 Der Richter sprach: Wenn ihr mir nun den Vater
Nicht bald zur Stelle schafft, so weis' ich euch
Von meinem Stuhle. Denkt ihr, daß ich Rätsel
Zu lösen da bin? Oder harret ihr,
Bis daß der rechte Ring den Mund eröffne? —
2015 Doch halt! Ich höre ja, der rechte Ring
Besitzt die Wunderkraft, beliebt zu machen,
Vor Gott und Menschen angenehm. Das muß
Entscheiden! Denn die falschen Ringe werden
Doch das nicht können! — Nun, wen lieben zwei
2020 Von euch am meisten? — Macht, sagt an! Ihr schweigt?
Die Ringe wirken nur zurück? und nicht
Nach außen? Jeder liebt sich selber nur
Am meisten? — O, so seid ihr alle drei
Betrogene Betrieger! Eure Ringe
2025 Sind alle drei nicht echt. Der echte Ring
Vermutlich ging verloren. Den Verlust
Zu bergen, zu ersetzen, ließ der Vater
Die drei für einen machen.

Saladin.

Herrlich! herrlich!

Nathan.

Und also, fuhr der Richter fort, wenn ihr
2030 Nicht meinen Rat statt meines Spruches wollt:

Geht nur! — mein Rat ist aber der: ihr nehmt
Die Sache völlig wie sie liegt. Hat von
Euch jeder seinen Ring von seinem Vater,
So glaube jeder sicher seinen Ring
2035 Den echten. — Möglich, daß der Vater nun
Die Tyrannei des einen Rings nicht länger
In seinem Hause dulden wollen! — Und gewiß,
Daß er euch alle drei geliebt und gleich
Geliebt, indem er zwei nicht drücken mögen,
2040 Um einen zu begünstigen. — Wohlan!
Es eifre jeder seiner unbestochnen,
Von Vorurteilen freien Liebe nach!
Es strebe von euch jeder um die Wette,
Die Kraft des Steins in seinem Ring an Tag
2045 Zu legen! komme dieser Kraft mit Sanftmut,
Mit herzlicher Verträglichkeit, mit Wohlthun,
Mit innigster Ergebenheit in Gott
Zu Hilf'! Und wenn sich dann der Steine Kräfte
Bei euern Kindes-Kindeskindern äußern,
2050 So lad' ich über tausend tausend Jahre
Sie wiederum vor diesen Stuhl. Da wird
Ein weis'rer Mann auf diesem Stuhle sitzen
Als ich, und sprechen. Geht! — So sagte der
Bescheidne Richter.

Saladin.

Gott! Gott!

Nathan.

Saladin,
2055 Wenn du dich fühlest, dieser weisere
Versprochne Mann zu sein . . .

Saladin
(der auf ihn zustürzt und seine Hand ergreift, die er bis zu Ende nicht wieder fahren läßt).

Ich Staub? Ich Nichts?
O Gott!

Nathan.

Was ist dir, Sultan?

Saladin.

Nathan, lieber Nathan! —
Die tausend tausend Jahre deines Richters
Sind noch nicht um. — Sein Richterstuhl ist nicht
2060 Der meine. — Geh! — Geh! — Aber sei mein Freund.

Nathan.

Und weiter hätte Saladin mir nichts
Zu sagen?

Saladin.

Nichts.

Nathan.

Nichts?

Saladin.

Gar nichts. — Und warum?

Nathan.

Ich hätte noch Gelegenheit gewünscht,
Dir eine Bitte vorzutragen.

Saladin.

Braucht's
2065 Gelegenheit zu einer Bitte? — Rede!

Nathan.

Ich komm' von einer weiten Reis', auf welcher
Ich Schulden eingetrieben. — Fast hab' ich

Des baren Gelds zuviel. — Die Zeit beginnt
Bedenklich wiederum zu werden, — und
2070 Ich weiß nicht recht, wo sicher damit hin. —
Da dacht' ich, ob nicht du vielleicht, — weil doch
Ein naher Krieg des Geldes immer mehr
Erfordert, — etwas brauchen könntest.

Saladin

(ihm tief in die Augen sehend).

Nathan! —
Ich will nicht fragen, ob Al-Hafi schon
2075 Bei dir gewesen, — will nicht untersuchen,
Ob dich nicht sonst ein Argwohn treibt, mir dieses
Erbieten freierdings zu thun . . .

Nathan.

Ein Argwohn?

Saladin.

Ich bin ihn wert. — Verzeih mir! — Denn was hilft's?
Ich muß dir nur gestehen, daß ich im
2080 Begriffe war —

Nathan.

Doch nicht, das nämliche
An mich zu suchen?

Saladin.

Allerdings.

Nathan.

So wär'
Uns beiden ja geholfen! Daß ich aber
Dir alle meine Barschaft nicht kann schicken,
Das macht der junge Tempelherr. Du kennst
2085 Ihn ja. Ihm hab' ich eine große Post
Vorher noch zu bezahlen.

Saladin.

Tempelherr?
Du wirst doch meine schlimmsten Feinde nicht
Mit deinem Geld auch unterstützen wollen?

Nathan.

Ich spreche von dem einen nur, dem du
2090 Das Leben spartest . . .

Saladin.

Ah! woran erinnerst
Du mich! — Hab' ich doch diesen Jüngling ganz
Vergessen! — Kennst du ihn? — Wo ist er?

Nathan.

Wie?
So weißt du nicht, wie viel von deiner Gnade
Für ihn, durch ihn auf mich geflossen? Er,
2095 Er mit Gefahr des neu erhaltnen Lebens
Hat meine Tochter aus dem Feu'r gerettet.

Saladin.

Er? Hat er das? — Ha! darnach sah er aus.
Das hätte traun mein Bruder auch gethan,
Dem er so ähnelt! — Ist er denn noch hier?
2100 So bring ihn her! — Ich habe meiner Schwester
Von diesem ihren Bruder, den sie nicht
Gekannt, so viel erzählet, daß ich sie
Sein Ebenbild doch auch muß sehen lassen! —
Geh, hol ihn! — Wie aus einer guten That,
2105 Gebar sie auch schon bloße Leidenschaft,
Doch so viel andre gute Thaten fließen!
Geh, hol ihn!

Nathan
(indem er Saladins Hand fahren läßt).

Augenblicks! Und bei dem andern
Bleibt es doch auch? (Ab.)

Saladin.

Ah! daß ich meine Schwester
Nicht horchen lassen! — Zu ihr! zu ihr! — Denn
2110 Wie soll ich alles das ihr nun erzählen?
(Ab von der andern Seite.)

Achter Auftritt.

Die Scene: unter den Palmen, in der Nähe des Klosters, wo der Tempelherr Nathans wartet.

Tempelherr
(geht, mit sich selbst kämpfend, auf und ab, bis er losbricht).

— Hier hält das Opfertier ermüdet still. —
Nun gut! Ich mag nicht, mag nicht näher wissen,
Was in mir vorgeht; mag voraus nicht wittern,
Was vorgehn wird. — Genug, ich bin umsonst
2115 Geflohn, umsonst. — Und weiter konnt' ich doch
Auch nichts als fliehn! — Nun komm', was kommen soll! —
Ihm auszubeugen, war der Streich zu schnell
Gefallen, unter den zu kommen ich
So lang und viel mich weigerte. — Sie sehn,
2120 Die ich zu sehn so wenig lüstern war, —
Sie sehn, und der Entschluß, sie wieder aus
Den Augen nie zu lassen — Was Entschluß?
Entschluß ist Vorsatz, That: und ich, ich litt',

Ich litte bloß. Sie sehn, und das Gefühl,
2125 An sie verstrickt, in sie verwebt zu sein,
War eins. — Bleibt eins. — Von ihr getrennt
Zu leben, ist mir ganz undenkbar, wär'
Mein Tod, — und wo wir immer nach dem Tode
Noch sind, auch da mein Tod. — Ist das nun Liebe:
2130 So — liebt der Tempelritter freilich, — liebt
Der Christ das Judenmädchen freilich. — Hm!
Was thut's? — Ich hab' in dem gelobten Lande —
Und drum auch mir gelobt auf immerdar! —
Der Vorurteile mehr schon abgelegt. —
2135 Was will mein Orden auch? Ich Tempelherr
Bin tot, war von dem Augenblick ihm tot,
Der mich zu Saladins Gefangnen machte.
Der Kopf, den Saladin mir schenkte, wär'
Mein alter? — Ist ein neuer, der von allem
2140 Nichts weiß, was jenem eingeplaudert ward,
Was jenen band. — Und ist ein bess'rer, für
Den väterlichen Himmel mehr gemacht.
Das spür' ich ja. Denn erst mit ihm beginn'
Ich so zu denken, wie mein Vater hier
2145 Gedacht muß haben, wenn man Märchen nicht
Von ihm mir vorgelogen. — Märchen? — doch
Ganz glaubliche, die glaublicher mir nie
Als jetzt geschienen, da ich nur Gefahr
Zu straucheln laufe, wo er fiel. — Er fiel?
2150 Ich will mit Männern lieber fallen, als
Mit Kindern stehn. — Sein Beispiel bürget mir
Für seinen Beifall. Und an wessen Beifall
Liegt mir denn sonst? — An Nathans? — O, an dessen

Ermuntrung mehr als Beifall kann es mir
2155 Noch weniger gebrechen. — Welch ein Jude! —
Und der so ganz nur Jude scheinen will!
Da kömmt er, kömmt mit Hast, glüht heitre Freude.
Wer kam vom Saladin je anders? He!
He, Nathan!

Neunter Auftritt.

Nathan und der Tempelherr.

Nathan.

Wie? seid Ihr's?

Tempelherr.

Ihr habt
2160 Sehr lang' Euch bei dem Sultan aufgehalten.

Nathan.

So lange nun wohl nicht. Ich ward im Hingehn
Zu viel verweilt. — Ah, wahrlich, Curd, der Mann
Steht seinen Ruhm. Sein Ruhm ist bloß sein Schatten.—
Doch laßt vor allen Dingen Euch geschwind
2165 Nur sagen . . .

Tempelherr.

Was?

Nathan.

Er will Euch sprechen, will,
Daß ungesäumt Ihr zu ihm kommt. Begleitet
Mich nur nach Hause, wo ich noch für ihn
Erst etwas andres zu verfügen habe:
Und dann, so gehn wir.

Tempelherr.

Nathan, Euer Haus
2170 Betret' ich wieder eher nicht . . .

Nathan.

So seid
Ihr doch indes schon da gewesen? habt
Indeß sie doch gesprochen? — Nun? — Sagt, wie
Gefällt Euch Recha?

Tempelherr.

Über allen Ausdruck! —
Allein, — sie wiedersehn — das werd' ich nie!
2175 Nie! nie! — Ihr müßtet mir zur Stelle denn
Versprechen, — daß ich sie auf immer, immer —
Soll können sehn.

Nathan.

Wie wollt Ihr, daß ich das
Versteh'?

Tempelherr
(nach einer kurzen Pause ihm plötzlich um den Hals fallend.)

Mein Vater!

Nathan.

— Junger Mann!

Tempelherr
(ihn ebenso plötzlich wieder lassend).

Nicht Sohn? —
Ich bitt' Euch, Nathan! —

Nathan.

Lieber junger Mann!

Tempelherr.

2180 Nicht Sohn? — Ich bitt' Euch, Nathan! — Ich beschwör'
Euch bei den ersten Banden der Natur! —
Zieht ihnen spätre Fesseln doch nicht vor! —
Benügt Euch doch, ein Mensch zu sein! — Stoßt mich
Nicht von Euch!

Nathan.

Lieber, lieber Freund! . . .

Tempelherr.

Und Sohn?
2185 Sohn nicht? — Auch dann nicht, dann nicht einmal, wenn
Erkenntlichkeit zum Herzen Eurer Tochter
Der Liebe schon den Weg gebahnet hätte?
Auch dann nicht einmal, wenn in eins zu schmelzen,
Auf Euern Wink nur beide warteten? —
2190 Ihr schweigt?

Nathan.

Ihr überrascht mich, junger Ritter.

Tempelherr.

Ich überrasch' Euch? — überrasch' Euch, Nathan,
Mit Euern eigenen Gedanken? — Ihr
Verkennt sie doch in meinem Munde nicht? —
Ich überrasch' Euch?

Nathan.

Eh' ich einmal weiß,
2195 Was für ein Stauffen Euer Vater denn
Gewesen ist!

Tempelherr.

Was sagt Ihr, Nathan? was? —
In diesem Augenblicke fühlt Ihr nichts
Als Neubegier?

Nathan.

Denn seht! Ich habe selbst
Wohl einen Stauffen ehedem gekannt,
2200 Der Konrad hieß.

Tempelherr.

Nun, — wenn mein Vater denn
Nun ebenso geheißen hätte?

Nathan.

Wahrlich?

Tempelherr.

Ich heiße selber ja nach meinem Vater: Curd
Ist Konrad.

Nathan.

Nun — so war mein Konrad doch
Nicht Euer Vater. Denn mein Konrad war,
2205 Was Ihr, war Tempelherr, war nie vermählt.

Tempelherr.

O darum!

Nathan.

Wie?

Tempelherr.

O, darum könnt' er doch
Mein Vater wohl gewesen sein.

Nathan.

Ihr scherzt.

Tempelherr.

Und Ihr nehmt's wahrlich zu genau! — Was wär's
Denn nun? So was von Bastard oder Bankert!

2210 Der Schlag ist auch nicht zu verachten. — Doch
Entlaßt mich immer meiner Ahnenprobe.
Ich will Euch Eurer wiederum entlassen.
Nicht zwar, als ob ich den geringsten Zweifel
In Euern Stammbaum setzte. Gott behüte!
2215 Ihr könnt ihn Blatt für Blatt bis Abraham
Hinauf belegen. Und von da so weiter
Weiß ich ihn selbst, will ich ihn selbst beschwören.

Nathan.

Ihr werdet bitter. — Doch verdien' ich's? — Schlug
Ich denn Euch schon was ab? — Ich will Euch ja
2220 Nur bei dem Worte nicht den Augenblick
So fassen. — Weiter nichts.

Tempelherr.

Gewiß? — Nichts weiter?
O, so vergebt! . . .

Nathan.

Nun kommt nur, kommt!

Tempelherr.

Wohin?
Nein! — Mit in Euer Haus? — Das nicht! das nicht! —
Da brennt's! — Ich will Euch hier erwarten. Geht! —
2225 Soll ich sie wiedersehn, so seh' ich sie
Noch oft genug. Wo nicht, so sah ich sie
Schon viel zuviel . . .

Nathan.

Ich will mich möglichst eilen.

Zehnter Auftritt.

Der Tempelherr und bald darauf Daja.

Tempelherr.

Schon mehr als g'nug! — Des Menschen Hirn faßt so
Unendlich viel, und ist doch manchmal auch
2230 So plötzlich voll! — von einer Kleinigkeit
So plötzlich voll! Taugt nichts, taugt nichts, es sei
Auch voll, wovon es will. — Doch nur Geduld!
Die Seele wirkt den aufgedunſ'nen Stoff
Bald in einander, schafft sich Raum, und Licht
2235 Und Ordnung kommen wieder. — Lieb' ich denn
Zum erstenmale? — Oder war, was ich
Als Liebe kenne, Liebe nicht? — Ist Liebe
Nur, was ich jetzt empfinde? . . .

Daja
(die sich von der Seite herbeigeschlichen).

Ritter! Ritter!

Tempelherr.

Wer ruft? — Ha, Daja, Ihr?

Daja.

Ich habe mich
2240 Bei ihm vorbeigeschlichen. Aber noch
Könnt' er uns sehn, wo Ihr da steht. — Drum kommt
Doch näher zu mir, hinter diesen Baum.

Tempelherr.

Was giebt's denn? — So geheimnisvoll? — Was ist's?

Daja.

Ja wohl betrifft es ein Geheimnis, was
2245 Mich zu Euch bringt, und zwar ein doppeltes.

Das eine weiß nur ich; das andre wißt
Nur Ihr. — Wie wär' es, wenn wir tauschten?
Vertraut mir Euers, so vertrau' ich Euch
Das meine.

Tempelherr.

Mit Vergnügen. — Wenn ich nur
2250 Erst weiß, was Ihr für meines achtet. Doch
Das wird aus Euerm wohl erhellen. — Fangt
Nur immer an.

Daja.

Ei, denkt doch! — Nein, Herr Ritter,
Erst Ihr; ich folge. — Denn versichert, mein
Geheimnis kann Euch gar nichts nützen, wenn
2255 Ich nicht zuvor das Eure habe. — Nur
Geschwind! — Denn frag' ich's Euch erst ab, so habt
Ihr nichts vertrauet. Mein Geheimnis dann
Bleibt mein Geheimnis, und das Eure seid
Ihr los. — Doch, armer Ritter! — Daß ihr Männer
2260 Ein solch Geheimnis vor uns Weibern haben
Zu können auch nur glaubt!

Tempelherr.

Das wir zu haben
Oft selbst nicht wissen.

Daja.

Kann wohl sein. Drum muß
Ich freilich erst, Euch selbst damit bekannt
Zu machen, schon die Freundschaft haben. — Sagt:
2265 Was hieß denn das, daß Ihr so Knall und Fall
Euch aus dem Staube machtet? daß Ihr uns
So sitzen ließet? — daß Ihr nun mit Nathan

Nicht wiederkommt? — Hat Recha denn so wenig
Auf Euch gewirkt? wie? oder auch so viel? —
2270 So viel! so viel! — Lehrt Ihr des armen Vogels,
Der an der Rute klebt, Geflattre mich
Doch kennen! — Kurz, gesteht es mir nur gleich,
Daß Ihr sie liebt, liebt bis zum Unsinn, und
Ich sag' Euch was . . .

Tempelherr.

Zum Unsinn? Wahrlich, Ihr
2275 Versteht Euch trefflich drauf.

Daja.

Nun, gebt mir nur
Die Liebe zu; den Unsinn will ich Euch
Erlassen.

Tempelherr.

Weil er sich von selbst versteht? —
Ein Tempelherr ein Judenmädchen lieben! . . .

Daja.

Scheint freilich wenig Sinn zu haben. — Doch
2280 Zuweilen ist des Sinns in einer Sache
Auch mehr, als wir vermuten; und es wäre
So unerhört doch nicht, daß uns der Heiland
Auf Wegen zu sich zöge, die der Kluge
Von selbst nicht leicht betreten würde.

Tempelherr.

Das
2285 So feierlich? — (Und setz' ich statt des Heilands
Die Vorsicht: hat sie denn nicht recht?) Ihr macht
Mich neubegieriger, als ich wohl sonst
Zu sein gewohnt bin.

Daja.

O! das ist das Land
Der Wunder!

Tempelherr.

(Nun! — des Wunderbaren. Kann
2290 Es auch wohl anders sein? Die ganze Welt
Drängt sich ja hier zusammen.) — Liebe Daja,
Nehmt für gestanden an, was Ihr verlangt:
Daß ich sie liebe, daß ich nicht begreife,
Wie ohne sie ich leben werde, daß . . .

Daja.

2295 Gewiß? gewiß? — So schwört mir, Ritter, sie
Zur Eurigen zu machen, sie zu retten,
Sie zeitlich hier, sie ewig dort zu retten.

Tempelherr.

Und wie? — Wie kann ich? — Kann ich schwören, was
In meiner Macht nicht steht?

Daja.

In Eurer Macht
2300 Steht es. Ich bring' es durch ein einzig Wort
In Eure Macht.

Tempelherr.

Daß selbst der Vater nichts
Dawider hätte?

Daja.

Ei, was Vater! Vater!
Der Vater soll schon müssen.

Tempelherr.

Müssen, Daja? —
Noch ist er unter Räuber nicht gefallen. —
2305 Er muß nicht müssen.

Daja.

Nun, so muß er wollen,
Muß gern am Ende wollen.

Tempelherr.

Muß und gern! —
Doch, Daja, wenn ich Euch nun sage, daß
Ich selber diese Sait' ihm anzuschlagen
Bereits versucht?

Daja.

Was? und er fiel nicht ein?

Tempelherr.

2310 Er fiel mit einem Mißlaut ein, der mich —
Beleidigte.

Daja.

Was sagt Ihr? — Wie? Ihr hättet
Den Schatten eines Wunsches nur nach Recha
Ihm blicken lassen, und er wär' vor Freuden
Nicht aufgesprungen? hätte frostig sich
2315 Zurückgezogen? hätte Schwierigkeiten
Gemacht?

Tempelherr.

So ungefähr.

Daja.

So will ich denn
Mich länger keinen Augenblick bedenken —
(Pause.)

Tempelherr.

Und Ihr bedenkt Euch doch?

Daja.

Der Mann ist sonst
So gut! — Ich selber bin so viel ihm schuldig! —

2320 Daß er doch gar nicht hören will! — Gott weiß,
Das Herze blutet mir, ihn so zu zwingen.

Tempelherr.

Ich bitt' Euch, Daja, setzt mich kurz und gut
Aus dieser Ungewißheit. Seid Ihr aber
Noch selber ungewiß, ob, was Ihr vorhabt,
2325 Gut oder böse, schändlich oder löblich
Zu nennen: — schweigt! Ich will vergessen, daß
Ihr etwas zu verschweigen habt.

Daja.

Das spornt,
Anstatt zu halten. Nun, so wißt denn: Recha
Ist keine Jüdin, ist — ist eine Christin.

Tempelherr (kalt).

2330 So? Wünsch' Euch Glück! Hat's schwer gehalten? Laßt
Euch nicht die Wehen schrecken! — Fahret ja
Mit Eifer fort, den Himmel zu bevölkern,
Wenn Ihr die Erde nicht mehr könnt!

Daja.

Wie, Ritter?
Verdienet meine Nachricht diesen Spott?
2335 Daß Recha eine Christin ist, das freuet
Euch, einen Christen, einen Tempelherrn
Der Ihr sie liebt, nicht mehr?

Tempelherr.

Besonders, da
Sie eine Christin ist von Eurer Mache.

Daja.

Ach! so versteht Ihr's? So mag's gelten! — Nein!
2340 Den will ich sehn, der die bekehren soll!

Ihr Glück ist, längst zu sein, was sie zu werden
Verdorben ist.

Tempelherr.

Erklärt Euch, oder — geht!

Daja.

Sie ist ein Christenkind, von Christeneltern
Geboren, ist getauft . . .

Tempelherr (hastig).

Und Nathan?

Daja.

Nicht
2345 Ihr Vater!

Tempelherr.

Nathan nicht ihr Vater? — Wißt
Ihr, was Ihr sagt?

Daja.

Die Wahrheit, die so oft
Mich blut'ge Thränen weinen machen. — Nein,
Er ist ihr Vater nicht . . .

Tempelherr.

Und hätte sie
Als seine Tochter nur erzogen? hätte
2350 Das Christenkind als eine Jüdin sich
Erzogen?

Daja.

Ganz gewiß.

Tempelherr.

Sie wüßte nicht,
Was sie geboren sei? — Sie hätt' es nie
Von ihm erfahren, daß sie eine Christin
Geboren sei, und keine Jüdin?

Daja.

Nie!

Tempelherr.

2355 Er hätt' in diesem Wahne nicht das Kind
Bloß auferzogen? ließ das Mädchen noch
In diesem Wahne?

Daja.

Leider!

Tempelherr.

Nathan — Wie? —
Der weise, gute Nathan hätte sich
Erlaubt, die Stimme der Natur so zu
2360 Verfälschen? — Die Ergießung eines Herzens
So zu verlenken, die, sich selbst gelassen,
Ganz andre Wege nehmen würde? — Daja,
Ihr habt mir allerdings etwas vertraut —
Von Wichtigkeit, — was Folgen haben kann, —
2365 Was mich verwirrt, — worauf ich gleich nicht weiß,
Was mir zu thun. — Drum laßt mir Zeit. — Drum geht!
Er kommt hier wiederum vorbei. Er möcht'
Uns überfallen. Geht!

Daja.

Ich wär' des Todes!

Tempelherr.

Ich bin ihn jetzt zu sprechen ganz und gar
2370 Nicht fähig. Wenn Ihr ihm begegnet, sagt
Ihm nur, daß wir einander bei dem Sultan
Schon finden würden.

Daja.

Aber laßt Euch ja
Nichts merken gegen ihn — Das soll nur so

Den letzten Druck dem Dinge geben, soll
8375 Euch, Rechas wegen, alle Skrupel nur
Benehmen! — Wenn Ihr aber dann sie nach
Europa führt, so laßt Ihr doch mich nicht
Zurück?

Tempelherr.

Das wird sich finden. Geht nur, geht!

Vierter Aufzug.

Erster Auftritt.

Scene: in den Kreuzgängen des Klosters.

Der Klosterbruder und bald darauf der Tempelherr.

Klosterbruder.

Ja, ja! er hat schon recht, der Patriarch!
2380 Es hat mir freilich noch von alledem
Nicht viel gelingen wollen, was er mir
So aufgetragen. — Warum trägt er mir
Auch lauter solche Sachen auf? — Ich mag
Nicht fein sein, mag nicht überreden, mag
2385 Mein Näschen nicht in alles stecken, mag
Mein Händchen nicht in allem haben. — Bin
Ich darum aus der Welt geschieden, ich
Für mich, um mich für andre mit der Welt
Noch erst recht zu verwickeln?

Tempelherr

(mit Hast auf ihn zukommend).

Guter Bruder!
2390 Da seid Ihr ja. Ich hab' Euch lange schon
Gesucht.

Klosterbruder.

Mich, Herr?

Tempelherr.

Ihr kennt mich schon nicht mehr?

Klosterbruder.

Doch, doch! Ich glaubte nur, daß ich den Herrn
In meinem Leben wieder nie zu sehn
Bekommen würde. Denn ich hofft' es zu
2395 Dem lieben Gott. — Der liebe Gott, der weiß,
Wie sauer mir der Antrag ward, den ich
Dem Herrn zu thun verbunden war. Er weiß,
Ob ich gewünscht, ein offnes Ohr bei Euch
Zu finden, weiß, wie sehr ich mich gefreut,
2400 Im Innersten gefreut, daß Ihr so rund
Das alles, ohne viel Bedenken, von
Euch wies't, was einem Ritter nicht geziemt. —
Nun kommt Ihr doch; nun hat's doch nachgewirkt!

Tempelherr.

Ihr wißt es schon, warum ich komme? Kaum
2405 Weiß ich es selbst.

Klosterbruder.

Ihr habt's nun überlegt,
Habt nun gefunden, daß der Patriarch
So unrecht doch nicht hat; daß Ehr' und Geld
Durch seinen Anschlag zu gewinnen; daß
Ein Feind ein Feind ist, wenn er unser Engel
2410 Auch siebenmal gewesen wäre. Das,
Das habt Ihr nun mit Fleisch und Blut erwogen
Und kommt und tragt Euch wieder an. — Ach Gott!

Tempelherr.

Mein frommer, lieber Mann! Gebt Euch zufrieden.
Deswegen komm' ich nicht; deswegen will

2415 Ich nicht den Patriarchen sprechen. Noch,
Noch denk' ich über jenen Punkt, wie ich
Gedacht, und wollt' um alles in der Welt
Die gute Meinung nicht verlieren, deren
Mich ein so grader, frommer, lieber Mann
2420 Einmal gewürdigt. — Ich komme bloß,
Den Patriarchen über eine Sache
Um Rat zu fragen . . .

Klosterbruder.

Ihr den Patriarchen?
Ein Ritter einen — Pfaffen?

(Sich schüchtern umsehend.)

Tempelherr.

Ja; — die Sach'
Ist ziemlich pfäffisch.

Klosterbruder.

Gleichwohl fragt der Pfaffe
2425 Den Ritter nie, die Sache sei auch noch
So ritterlich.

Tempelherr.

Weil er das Vorrecht hat,
Sich zu vergehn, das unsereiner ihm
Nicht sehr beneidet. — Freilich, wenn ich nur
Für mich zu handeln hätte; freilich, wenn
2430 Ich Rechenschaft nur mir zu geben hätte,
Was braucht' ich Euers Patriarchen? Aber
Gewisse Dinge will ich lieber schlecht
Nach andrer Willen machen, als allein
Nach meinem gut. — Zudem, ich seh' nun wohl,
2435 Religion ist auch Partei, und wer
Sich drob auch noch so unparteiisch glaubt,
Hält, ohn' es selbst zu wissen, doch nur seiner

Die Stange. Weil das einmal nun so ist,
Wird's so wohl recht sein.

Klosterbruder.

Dazu schweig' ich lieber.
2440 Denn ich versteh' den Herrn nicht recht.

Tempelherr.

Und doch! —
(Laß sehn, warum mir eigentlich zu thun!
Um Machtspruch oder Rat? — Um lautern oder
Gelehrten Rat?) — Ich dank' Euch, Bruder, dank'
Euch für den guten Wink. — Was Patriarch? —
2445 Seid Ihr mein Patriarch! Ich will ja doch
Den Christen mehr im Patriarchen als
Den Patriarchen in dem Christen fragen. —
Die Sach' ist die ...

Klosterbruder.

Nicht weiter, Herr, nicht weiter!
Wozu? — Der Herr verkennt mich. — Wer viel weiß,
2450 Hat viel zu sorgen, und ich habe ja
Mich Einer Sorge nur gelobt. — O gut!
Hört! seht! Dort kömmt, zu meinem Glück, er selbst.
Bleibt hier nur stehn. Er hat Euch schon erblickt.

Zweiter Auftritt.

Der Patriarch, welcher mit allem geistlichen Pomp den einen Kreuzgang heraufkömmt, und die Vorigen.

Tempelherr.

Ich wich' ihm lieber aus. — Wär' nicht mein Mann! —
2455 Ein dicker, roter, freundlicher Prälat!
Und welcher Prunk!

Klosterbruder.

Ihr solltet ihn erst sehn
Nach Hofe sich erheben. Jetzo kömmt
Er nur von einem Kranken.

Tempelherr.

Wie sich da
Nicht Saladin wird schämen müssen!

Patriarch
(indem er näher kommt, winkt dem Bruder).

Hier! —
2460 Das ist ja wohl der Tempelherr. Was will
Er?

Klosterbruder.

Weiß nicht.

Patriarch
(auf ihn zugehend, indem der Bruder und das Gefolge zurücktreten).

Nun, Herr Ritter! — Sehr erfreut,
Den braven jungen Mann zu sehn! — Ei, noch
So gar jung! — Nun, mit Gottes Hilfe, daraus
Kann etwas werden.

Tempelherr.

Mehr, ehrwürd'ger Herr,
2465 Wohl schwerlich, als schon ist. Und eher noch
Was weniger.

Patriarch.

Ich wünsche wenigstens,
Daß so ein frommer Ritter lange noch
Der lieben Christenheit, der Sache Gottes
Zu Ehr' und Frommen blühn und grünen möge!
2470 Das wird denn auch nicht fehlen, wenn nur fein
Die junge Tapferkeit dem reifen Rate

Des Alters folgen will! — Womit wär' sonst
Dem Herrn zu dienen?

Tempelherr.

Mit dem nämlichen,
Woran es meiner Jugend fehlt: mit Rat.

Patriarch.

2475 Recht gern! — Nur ist der Rat auch anzunehmen.

Tempelherr.

Doch blindlings nicht?

Patriarch.

Wer sagt denn das? — Ei freilich
Muß niemand die Vernunft, die Gott ihm gab,
Zu brauchen unterlassen, — wo sie hin
Gehört. — Gehört sie aber überall
2480 Denn hin? — O nein! — Zum Beispiel: wenn uns Gott
Durch einen seiner Engel, — ist zu sagen,
Durch einen Diener seines Worts, — ein Mittel
Bekannt zu machen würdiget, das Wohl
Der ganzen Christenheit, das Heil der Kirche
2485 Auf irgend eine ganz besondre Weise
Zu fördern, zu befestigen: wer darf
Sich da noch unterstehn, die Willkür des,
Der die Vernunft erschaffen, nach Vernunft
Zu untersuchen? und das ewige
2490 Gesetz der Herrlichkeit des Himmels, nach
Den kleinen Regeln einer eiteln Ehre
Zu prüfen? — Doch hiervon genug. — Was ist
Es denn, worüber unsern Rat für jetzt
Der Herr verlangt?

Tempelherr.

Gesetzt, ehrwürd'ger Vater,
2495 Ein Jude hätt' ein einzig Kind, — es sei
Ein Mädchen, — das er mit der größten Sorgfalt
Zu allem Guten auferzogen, das
Er liebe mehr als seine Seele, das
Ihn wieder mit der frömmsten Liebe liebe.
2500 Und nun würd' unsereinem hinterbracht,
Dies Mädchen sei des Juden Tochter nicht;
Er hab' es in der Kindheit aufgelesen,
Gekauft, gestohlen, — was Ihr wollt; man wisse,
Das Mädchen sei ein Christenkind und sei
2505 Getauft; der Jude hab' es nur als Jüdin
Erzogen, lass' es nur als Jüdin und
Als seine Tochter so verharren: — sagt,
Ehrwürd'ger Vater, was wär' hierbei wohl
Zu thun?

Patriarch.

Mich schaudert! — Doch zu allererst
2510 Erkläre sich der Herr, ob so ein Fall
Ein Faktum oder eine Hypothes'.
Das ist zu sagen: ob der Herr sich das
Nur bloß so dichtet, oder ob's geschehn
Und fortfährt zu geschehn.

Tempelherr.

Ich glaubte, das
2515 Sei eins, um Euer Hochehrwürden Meinung
Bloß zu vernehmen.

Patriarch.

Eins? — da seh' der Herr,
Wie sich die stolze menschliche Vernunft

Im Geistlichen doch irren kann. — Mit nichten!
Denn ist der vorgetragne Fall nur so
2520 Ein Spiel des Witzes, so verlohnt es sich
Der Mühe nicht, im Ernst ihn durchzudenken.
Ich will den Herrn damit auf das Theater
Verwiesen haben, wo dergleichen pro
Et contra sich mit vielem Beifall könnte
2525 Behandeln lassen. — Hat der Herr mich aber
Nicht bloß mit einer theatral'schen Schnurre
Zum besten; ist der Fall ein Faktum; hätt'
Er sich wohl gar in unsrer Diöces',
In unsrer lieben Stadt Jerusalem
2530 Eräugnet: — ja alsdann —

Tempelherr.

Und was alsdann?

Patriarch.

Dann wäre an dem Juden fördersamst
Die Strafe zu vollziehn, die päpstliches
Und kaiserliches Recht so einem Frevel,
So einer Lasterthat bestimmen.

Tempelherr.

So?

Patriarch.

2535 Und zwar bestimmen obbesagte Rechte
Dem Juden, welcher einen Christen zur
Apostasie verführt, — den Scheiterhaufen,
Den Holzstoß —

Tempelherr.

So?

Patriarch.

Und wie vielmehr dem Juden,
Der mit Gewalt ein armes Christenkind
2540 Dem Bunde seiner Tauf' entreißt! Denn ist
Nicht alles, was man Kindern thut, Gewalt? —
Zu sagen: — ausgenommen, was die Kirch'
An Kindern thut.

Tempelherr.

Wenn aber nun das Kind,
Erbarmte seiner sich der Jude nicht,
2545 Vielleicht im Elend umgekommen wäre?

Patriarch.

Thut nichts! der Jude wird verbrannt. — Denn besser,
Es wäre hier im Elend umgekommen,
Als daß zu seinem ewigen Verderben
Es so gerettet ward. — Zu dem, was hat
2550 Der Jude Gott denn vorzugreifen? Gott
Kann, wen er retten will, schon ohn' ihn retten.

Tempelherr.

Auch trotz ihm, sollt' ich meinen, — selig machen.

Patriarch.

Thut nichts! der Jude wird verbrannt.

Tempelherr.

Das geht
Mir nah'! Besonders, da man sagt, er habe
2555 Das Mädchen nicht sowohl in seinem als
Vielmehr in keinem Glauben auferzogen
Und sie von Gott nicht mehr nicht wenige
Gelehrt, als der Vernunft genügt.

Patriarch.

Thut nichts!
Der Jude wird verbrannt . . . Ja, wär' allein
2560 Schon dieserwegen wert, dreimal verbrannt
Zu werden! — Was? ein Kind ohn' allen Glauben
Erwachsen lassen? — Wie? die große Pflicht,
Zu glauben, ganz und gar ein Kind nicht lehren?
Das ist zu arg! — Mich wundert sehr, Herr Ritter,
2565 Euch selbst . . .

Tempelherr.

Ehrwürd'ger Herr, das übrige,
Wenn Gott will, in der Beichte. (Will gehn.)

Patriarch.

Was? mir nur
Nicht einmal Rede stehn? — Den Bösewicht,
Den Juden mir nicht nennen? — mir ihn nicht
Zur Stelle schaffen? — O, da weiß ich Rat!
2570 Ich geh' sogleich zum Sultan. — Saladin,
Vermöge der Kapitulation,
Die er beschworen, muß uns, muß uns schützen,
Bei allen Rechten, allen Lehren schützen,
Die wir zu unsrer allerheiligsten
2575 Religion nur immer rechnen dürfen!
Gottlob! wir haben das Original.
Wir haben seine Hand, sein Siegel. Wir! —
Auch mach' ich ihm gar leicht begreiflich, wie
Gefährlich selber für den Staat es ist,
2580 Nichts glauben! Alle bürgerliche Bande
Sind aufgelöset, sind zerrissen, wenn
Der Mensch nichts glauben darf. — Hinweg! hinweg
Mit solchem Frevel . . .

Tempelherr.

Schade, daß ich nicht
Den trefflichen Sermon mit beſſ'rer Muße
2585 Genießen kann! Ich bin zum Saladin
Gerufen.

Patriarch.

Ja? — Nun ſo — Nun freilich — Dann —

Tempelherr.

Ich will den Sultan vorbereiten, wenn
Es Eurer Hochehrwürden ſo gefällt.

Patriarch.

O, oh! — Ich weiß, der Herr hat Gnade funden
2590 Vor Saladin! — Ich bitte, meiner nur
Im beſten bei ihm eingedenk zu ſein. —
Mich treibt der Eifer Gottes lediglich.
Was ich zuviel thu', thu' ich ihm. — Das wolle
Doch ja der Herr erwägen! — Und nicht wahr,
2595 Herr Ritter? das vorhin Erwähnte von
Dem Juden war nur ein Problema? — iſt
Zu ſagen —

Tempelherr.

Ein Problema.

(Geht ab.)

Patriarch.

(Dem ich tiefer
Doch auf den Grund zu kommen ſuchen muß.
Das wär' ſo wiederum ein Auftrag für
2600 Den Bruder Bonafides.) — Hier, mein Sohn!

(Er ſpricht im Abgehn mit dem Kloſterbruder.)

Dritter Auftritt.

Scene: ein Zimmer im Palaste des Saladin, in welches von Sklaven eine Menge Beutel getragen und auf dem Boden neben einander gestellt werden.

Saladin und bald darauf Sittah.

Saladin (der dazu kommt).

Nun wahrlich! das hat noch kein Ende. — Ist
Des Dings noch viel zurück?

Ein Sklave.

Wohl noch die Hälfte.

Saladin.

So tragt das übrige zu Sittah. — Und
Wo bleibt Al-Hafi? Das hier soll sogleich
2605 Al-Hafi zu sich nehmen. — Oder ob
Ich's nicht vielmehr dem Vater schicke? Hier
Fällt mir es doch nur durch die Finger. — Zwar
Man wird wohl endlich hart, und nun gewiß
Soll's Künste kosten, mir viel abzuzwacken.
2610 Bis wenigstens die Gelder aus Ägypten
Zur Stelle kommen, mag das Armut sehn,
Wie's fertig wird! — Die Spenden bei dem Grabe,
Wenn die nur fortgehn! Wenn die Christenpilger
Mit leeren Händen nur nicht abziehn dürfen!
2615 Wenn nur —

Sittah.

Was soll nun das? Was soll das Geld
Bei mir?

Saladin.

Mach dich davon bezahlt und leg
Auf Vorrat, wenn was übrig bleibt.

Sittah.

Ist Nathan
Noch mit dem Tempelherrn nicht da?

Saladin.

Er sucht
Ihn aller Orten.

Sittah.

Sieh doch, was ich hier,
2620 Indem mir so mein alt Geschmeide durch
Die Hände geht, gefunden.

(Ihm ein klein Gemälde zeigend.)

Saladin.

Ha! mein Bruder!
Das ist er, ist er! — War er! war er! ah! —
Ah, wackrer, lieber Junge, daß ich dich
So früh verlor! Was hätt' ich erst mit dir,
2625 An deiner Seit' erst unternommen! — Sittah,
Laß mir das Bild. Auch kenn' ich's schon; er gab
Es deiner ältern Schwester, seiner Lilla,
Die eines Morgens ihn so ganz und gar
Nicht aus den Armen lassen wollt'. Es war
2630 Der letzte, den er ausritt. — Ah, ich ließ
Ihn reiten, und allein! — Ah, Lilla starb
Vor Gram und hat mir's nie vergeben, daß
Ich so allein ihn reiten lassen. — Er
Blieb weg!

Sittah.

Der arme Bruder!

Saladin.

Laß nur gut
2635 Sein! — Einmal bleiben wir doch alle weg! —
Zudem, — wer weiß? Der Tod ist's nicht allein,
Der einem Jüngling seiner Art das Ziel
Verrückt. Er hat der Feinde mehr, und oft
Erliegt der Stärkste gleich dem Schwächsten. — Nun,
2640 Sei wie ihm sei! — Ich muß das Bild doch mit
Dem jungen Tempelherrn vergleichen, muß
Doch sehn, wie viel mich meine Phantasie
Getäuscht.

Sittah.

Nur darum bring' ich's. Aber gieb
Doch, gieb! Ich will dir das wohl sagen; das
2645 Versteht ein weiblich Aug' am besten.

Saladin
(zu einem Thürsteher, der hereintritt).

Wer
Ist da? — der Tempelherr? — Er komm'!

Sittah.

Euch nicht
Zu stören, ihn mit meiner Neugier nicht
Zu irren —
(Sie setzt sich seitwärts auf einen Sofa und läßt den Schleier fallen.)

Saladin.

Gut so! gut! — (Und nun sein Ton!
Wie der wohl sein wird! — Assads Ton
2650 Schläft auch wohl wo in meiner Seele noch!)

Vierter Auftritt.

Der Tempelherr und Saladin.

Tempelherr.

Ich, dein Gefangner, Sultan . . .

Saladin.

Mein Gefangner?
Wem ich das Leben schenke, werd' ich dem
Nicht auch die Freiheit schenken?

Tempelherr.

Was dir ziemt
Zu thun, ziemt mir, erst zu vernehmen, nicht
2655 Vorauszusetzen. Aber, Sultan, — Dank,
Besondern Dank dir für mein Leben zu
Beteuern, stimmt mit meinem Stand' und meinem
Charakter nicht. — Es steht in allen Fällen
Zu deinen Diensten wieder.

Saladin.

Brauch' es nur
2660 Nicht wider mich! — Zwar ein Paar Hände mehr,
Die gönnt' ich meinem Feinde gern. Allein
Ihm so ein Herz auch mehr zu gönnen, fällt
Mir schwer. — Ich habe mich mit dir in nichts
Betrogen, braver junger Mann! Du bist
2665 Mit Seel' und Leib mein Assad. Sieh! ich könnte
Dich fragen, wo du denn die ganze Zeit
Gesteckt? in welcher Höhle du geschlafen?
In welchem Ginnistan, von welcher guten
Div diese Blume fort und fort so frisch
2670 Erhalten worden? Sieh! ich könnte dich

Erinnern wollen, was wir dort und dort
Zusammen ausgeführt. Ich könnte mit
Dir zanken, daß du Ein Geheimnis doch
Vor mir gehabt! Ein Abenteuer mir
2675 Doch unterschlagen: — Ja, das könnt' ich, wenn
Ich dich nur säh' und nicht auch mich. — Nun, mag's!
Von dieser süßen Träumerei ist immer
Doch so viel wahr, daß mir in meinem Herbst
Ein Assad wieder blühen soll. — Du bist
2680 Es doch zufrieden, Ritter?

Tempelherr.

Alles, was
Von dir mir kömmt, — sei was es will — das lag
Als Wunsch in meiner Seele.

Saladin.

Laß uns das
Sogleich versuchen. — Bliebst du wohl bei mir?
Um mir? — Als Christ, als Muselmann, gleichviel!
2685 Im weißen Mantel oder Jamerlonk;
Im Tulban oder deinem Filze: wie
Du willst! Gleichviel! Ich habe nie verlangt,
Daß allen Bäumen Eine Rinde wachse.

Tempelherr.

Sonst wärst du wohl auch schwerlich, der du bist:
2690 Der Held, der lieber Gottes Gärtner wäre.

Saladin.

Nun dann, wenn du nicht schlechter von mir denkst,
So wären wir ja halb schon richtig?

Tempelherr.

Ganz!

Saladin

(ihm die Hand bietend).

Ein Wort?

Tempelherr (einschlagend).

Ein Mann! — Hiermit empfange mehr,
Als du mir nehmen konntest. Ganz der deine!

Saladin.

2695 Zuviel Gewinn für einen Tag! zuviel! —
Kam er nicht mit?

Tempelherr.

Wer?

Saladin.

Nathan.

Tempelherr (frostig).

Nein. Ich kam
Allein.

Saladin.

Welch eine That von dir! Und welch
Ein weises Glück, das eine solche That
Zum Besten eines solchen Mannes ausschlug.

Tempelherr.

2700 Ja, ja!

Saladin.

So kalt? — Nein, junger Mann! wenn Gott
Was Gutes durch uns thut, muß man so kalt
Nicht sein! — selbst aus Bescheidenheit so kalt
Nicht scheinen wollen!

Tempelherr.

Daß doch in der Welt
Ein jedes Ding so manche Seiten hat! —

2705 Von denen oft sich gar nicht denken läßt,
Wie sie zusammenpassen!

Saladin.

Halte dich
Nur immer an die best' und preise Gott!
Der weiß, wie sie zusammenpassen. — Aber,
Wenn du so schwierig sein willst, junger Mann,
2710 So werd' auch ich ja wohl auf meiner Hut
Mich mit dir halten müssen? Leider bin
Auch ich ein Ding von vielen Seiten, die
Oft nicht so recht zu passen scheinen mögen.

Tempelherr.

Das schmerzt! — Denn Argwohn ist so wenig sonst
2715 Mein Fehler —

Saladin.

Nun, so sage doch, mit wem
Du's hast? — Es schien ja gar, mit Nathan. Wie?
Auf Nathan Argwohn? Du? — Erklär dich! sprich!
Komm, gieb mir deines Zutrauns erste Probe.

Tempelherr.

Ich habe wider Nathan nichts. Ich zürn'
2720 Allein mit mir —

Saladin.

Und über was?

Tempelherr.

Daß mir
Geträumt, ein Jude könn' auch wohl ein Jude
Zu sein verlernen; daß mir wachend so
Geträumt.

Saladin.

Heraus mit diesem wachen Traume!

Tempelherr.

Du weißt von Nathans Tochter, Sultan. Was
2725 Ich für sie that, das that ich, — weil ich's that.
Zu stolz, Dank einzuernten, wo ich ihn
Nicht säete, verschmäht' ich Tag für Tag,
Das Mädchen noch einmal zu sehn. Der Vater
War fern; er kömmt; er hört; er sucht mich auf;
2730 Er dankt; er wünscht, daß seine Tochter mir
Gefallen möge, spricht von Aussicht, spricht
Von heitern Fernen. — Nun, ich lasse mich
Beschwatzen, komme, sehe, finde wirklich
Ein Mädchen . . . Ah, ich muß mich schämen, Sultan! —

Saladin.

2735 Dich schämen? — daß ein Judenmädchen auf
Dich Eindruck machte, doch wohl nimmermehr?

Tempelherr.

Daß diesem Eindruck auf das liebliche
Geschwätz des Vaters hin, mein rasches Herz
So wenig Widerstand entgegensetzte! —
2740 Ich Tropf! ich sprang zum zweitenmal ins Feuer. —
Denn nun warb i ch, und nun ward i ch verschmäht.

Saladin.

Verschmäht?

Tempelherr.

Der weise Vater schlägt nun wohl
Mich platterdings nicht aus. Der weise Vater
Muß aber doch sich erst erkunden, erst
2745 Besinnen. Allerdings! That ich denn das
Nicht auch? Erkundete, besann ich denn
Mich erst nicht auch, als sie im Feuer schrie? —
Fürwahr! bei Gott! Es ist doch gar was Schönes,
So weise, so bedächtig sein!

Saladin.

Nun, nun!
2750 So sieh doch einem Alten etwas nach!
Wie lange können seine Weigerungen
Denn dauern? Wird er denn von dir verlangen,
Daß du erst Jude werden sollst?

Tempelherr.

Wer weiß!

Saladin.

Wer weiß? — der diesen Nathan besser kennt.

Tempelherr.

2755 Der Aberglaub', in dem wir aufgewachsen,
Verliert, auch wenn wir ihn erkennen, darum
Doch seine Macht nicht über uns. — Es sind
Nicht alle frei, die ihrer Ketten spotten.

Saladin.

Sehr reif bemerkt! Doch Nathan wahrlich, Nathan...

Tempelherr.

2760 Der Aberglauben schlimmster ist, den seinen
Für den erträglichern zu halten...

Saladin.

Mag
Wohl sein! Doch Nathan...

Tempelherr.

Dem allein
Die blöde Menschheit zu vertrauen, bis
Sie hellern Wahrheitstag gewöhne; dem
2765 Allein...

Saladin.

Gut! Aber Nathan! — Nathans Los
Ist diese Schwachheit nicht.

Tempelherr.

So dacht' ich auch! ...
Wenn gleichwohl dieser Ausbund aller Menschen
So ein gemeiner Jude wäre, daß
Er Christenkinder zu bekommen suchte,
2770 Um sie als Juden aufzuziehn: — wie dann?

Saladin.

Wer sagt ihm so was nach?

Tempelherr.

Das Mädchen selbst,
Mit welcher er mich körnt, mit deren Hoffnung
Er gern mir zu bezahlen schiene, was
Ich nicht umsonst für sie gethan soll haben: —
2775 Dies Mädchen selbst ist seine Tochter — nicht,
Ist ein verzettelt Christenkind.

Saladin.

Das er
Dem ungeachtet dir nicht geben wollte?

Tempelherr (heftig).

Woll' oder wolle nicht! Er ist entdeckt.
Der tolerante Schwätzer ist entdeckt!
2780 Ich werde hinter diesen jüd'schen Wolf
Im philosoph'schen Schafpelz Hunde schon
Zu bringen wissen, die ihn zausen sollen!

Saladin (ernst).

Sei ruhig, Christ!

Tempelherr.

Was? ruhig, Christ? — Wenn Jud'
Und Muselmann auf Jud', auf Muselmann
2785 Bestehen, soll allein der Christ den Christen
Nicht machen dürfen?

Saladin (noch ernster).

Ruhig, Christ!

Tempelherr (gelassen).

Ich fühle
Des Vorwurfs ganze Last, — die Saladin
In diese Silbe preßt! Ah, wenn ich wüßte,
Wie Assad, — Assad sich an meiner Stelle
2790 Hierbei genommen hätte!

Saladin.

Nicht viel besser! —
Vermutlich, ganz so brausend! — Doch, wer hat
Denn dich auch schon gelehrt, mich so wie er
Mit Einem Worte zu bestechen? Freilich,
Wenn alles sich verhält, wie du mir sagest,
2795 Kann ich mich selber kaum in Nathan finden. —
Indeß, er ist mein Freund, und meiner Freunde
Muß keiner mit dem andern hadern. — Laß
Dich weisen! Geh behutsam! Gieb ihn nicht
Sofort den Schwärmern deines Pöbels preis!
2800 Verschweig, was deine Geistlichkeit an ihm
Zu rächen mir so nahe legen würde!
Sei keinem Juden, keinem Muselmanne
Zum Trotz ein Christ!

Tempelherr.

Bald wär's damit zu spät!
Doch Dank der Blutbegier des Patriarchen,
2805 Des Werkzeug mir zu werden graute!

Saladin.

Wie?
Du kamst zum Patriarchen eher als
Zu mir?

Tempelherr.

Im Sturm der Leidenschaft, im Wirbel
Der Unentschlossenheit! — Verzeih! — Du wirst
Von deinem Assad, fürcht' ich, ferner nun
2810 Nichts mehr in mir erkennen wollen.

Saladin.

Wär'
Es diese Furcht nicht selbst! Mich dünkt, ich weiß,
Aus welchen Fehlern unsre Tugend keimt.
Pfleg diese ferner nur, und jene sollen
Bei mir dir wenig schaden. — Aber geh!
2815 Such du nun Nathan, wie er dich gesucht,
Und bring ihn her. Ich muß euch doch zusammen
Verständigen. — Wär' um das Mädchen dir
Im Ernst zu thun: sei ruhig. Sie ist dein!
Auch soll es Nathan schon empfinden, daß
2820 Er ohne Schweinefleisch ein Christenkind
Erziehen dürfen! — Geh!

(Der Tempelherr geht ab, und Sittah verläßt den Sofa.)

Fünfter Auftritt.

Saladin und Sittah.

Sittah.

Ganz sonderbar!

Saladin.

Gelt, Sittah? Muß mein Assad nicht ein braver,
Ein schöner junger Mann gewesen sein?

Sittah.

Wenn er so war, und nicht zu diesem Bilde
2825 Der Tempelherr vielmehr gesessen! — Aber
Wie hast du doch vergessen können, dich
Nach seinen Eltern zu erkundigen?

Saladin.

Und insbesondre wohl nach seiner Mutter?
Ob seine Mutter hier zu Lande nie
2830 Gewesen sei? — Nicht wahr?

Sittah.

Das machst du gut!

Saladin.

O, möglicher wär' nichts! Denn Assad war
Bei hübschen Christendamen so willkommen,
Auf hübsche Christendamen so erpicht,
Daß einmal gar die Rede ging — Nun, nun,
2835 Man spricht nicht gern davon. — Genug, ich hab'
Ihn wieder! — will mit allen seinen Fehlern,
Mit allen Launen seines weichen Herzens
Ihn wieder haben! — Oh! das Mädchen muß
Ihm Nathan geben. Meinst du nicht?

Sittah.

Ihm geben?

2840 Ihm lassen!

Saladin.

Allerdings! Was hätte Nathan,
Sobald er nicht ihr Vater ist, für Recht
Auf sie? Wer ihr das Leben so erhielt,
Tritt einzig in die Rechte des, der ihr
Es gab.

Sittah.

Wie also, Saladin? wenn du
2845 Nur gleich das Mädchen zu dir nähmst? Sie nur
Dem unrechtmäßigen Besitzer gleich
Entzögest?

Saladin.

Thäte das wohl not?

Sittah.

Not nun
Wohl eben nicht! — Die liebe Neubegier
Treibt mich allein, dir diesen Rat zu geben.
2850 Denn von gewissen Männern mag ich gar
Zu gern so bald wie möglich wissen, was
Sie für ein Mädchen lieben können.

Saladin.

Nun,
So schick und laß sie holen.

Sittah.

Darf ich, Bruder?

Saladin.

Nur schone Nathans! Nathan muß durchaus
2855 Nicht glauben, daß man mit Gewalt ihn von
Ihr trennen wolle.

Sittah.

Sorge nicht.

Saladin.

Und ich,
Ich muß schon selbst sehn, wo Al-Hafi bleibt.

Sechster Auftritt.

Scene: die offne Flur in Nathans Hause, gegen die Palmen zu, wie im ersten Auftritte des ersten Aufzuges. Ein Teil der Waren und Kostbarkeiten liegt ausgekramt, deren ebendaselbst gedacht wird.

Nathan und Daja.

Daja.

O, alles herrlich! Alles auserlesen!
O, alles — wie nur Ihr es geben könnt.
2860 Wo wird der Silberstoff mit goldnen Ranken
Gemacht? Was kostet er? — Das nenn' ich noch
Ein Brautkleid! Keine Königin verlangt
Es besser.

Nathan.

Brautkleid? Warum Brautkleid eben?

Daja.

Je nun! Ihr dachtet daran freilich nicht,
2865 Als Ihr ihn kauftet. — Aber wahrlich, Nathan,
Der und kein andrer muß es sein! Er ist
Zum Brautkleid wie bestellt. Der weiße Grund
Ein Bild der Unschuld, und die goldnen Ströme,
Die aller Orten diesen Grund durchschlängeln,
2870 Ein Bild des Reichtums. Seht Ihr? Allerliebst!

Nathan.

Was witzelst du mir da? Von wessen Brautkleid
Sinnbilderst du mir so gelehrt? — Bist du
Denn Braut?

Daja.

Ich?

Nathan.

Nun wer denn?

Daja.

Ich? — lieber Gott!

Nathan.

Wer denn? Von wessen Brautkleid sprichst du denn? —
2875 Das alles ist ja dein und keiner andern.

Daja.

Ist mein? Soll mein sein? — Ist für Recha nicht?

Nathan.

Was ich für Recha mitgebracht, das liegt
In einem andern Ballen. Mach! nimm weg!
Trag deine Siebensachen fort!

Daja.

Versucher!
2880 Nein, wären es die Kostbarkeiten auch
Der ganzen Welt! Nicht rühr an! wenn Ihr mir
Vorher nicht schwört, von dieser einzigen
Gelegenheit, dergleichen Euch der Himmel
Nicht zweimal schicken wird, Gebrauch zu machen.

Nathan.

2885 Gebrauch? von was? — Gelegenheit? wozu?

Daja.

O stellt Euch nicht so fremd! — Mit kurzen Worten:
Der Tempelherr liebt Recha; gebt sie ihm!

So hat doch einmal Eure Sünde, die
Ich länger nicht verschweigen kann, ein Ende.
2890 So kömmt das Mädchen wieder unter Christen,
Wird wieder, was sie ist, ist wieder, was
Sie ward: und Ihr, Ihr habt mit all dem Guten,
Das wir Euch nicht genug verdanken können,
Nicht Feuerkohlen bloß auf Euer Haupt
2895 Gesammelt.

Nathan.

Doch die alte Leier wieder? —
Mit einer neuen Saite nur bezogen,
Die, fürcht' ich, weder stimmt noch hält.

Daja.

Wie so?

Nathan.

Mir wär' der Tempelherr schon recht. Ihm gönnt'
Ich Recha mehr als einem in der Welt.
2900 Allein ... Nun, habe nur Geduld.

Daja.

Geduld?
Geduld ist Eure alte Leier nun
Wohl nicht?

Nathan.

Nur wenig Tage noch Geduld!
Sieh doch! — Wer kommt denn dort? Ein Klosterbruder?
Geh, frag ihn, was er will.

Daja.

Was wird er wollen?

(Sie geht auf ihn zu und fragt.)

Nathan.

2905 So gieb! — und eh' er bittet. — (Wüßt' ich nur
Dem Tempelherrn erst beizukommen, ohne

Die Ursach meiner Neugier ihm zu sagen!
Denn wenn ich sie ihm sag', und der Verdacht
Ist ohne Grund, so hab' ich ganz umsonst
2910 Den Vater auf das Spiel gesetzt.) — Was ist's?

Daja.

Er will Euch sprechen.

Nathan.

Nun, so laß ihn kommen,
Und geh indeß.

Siebenter Auftritt.

Nathan und der Klosterbruder.

Nathan.

(Ich bliebe Rechas Vater
Doch gar zu gern! — Zwar kann ich's denn nicht bleiben,
Auch wenn ich aufhör', es zu heißen? — Ihr,
2915 Ihr selbst werd' ich's doch immer auch noch heißen,
Wenn sie erkennt, wie gern ich's wäre.) — Geh! —
Was ist zu Euern Diensten, frommer Bruder?

Klosterbruder.

Nicht eben viel. — Ich freue mich, Herr Nathan,
Euch annoch wohl zu sehn.

Nathan.

So kennt Ihr mich?

Klosterbruder.

2920 Je nu, wer kennt Euch nicht? Ihr habt so manchem
Ja Euern Namen in die Hand gedrückt.
Er steht in meiner auch seit vielen Jahren.

Nathan

(nach seinem Beutel langend).

Kommt, Bruder, kommt; ich frisch' ihn auf.

Klosterbruder.

Habt Dank!

Ich würd' es Ärmern stehlen, nehme nichts. —
2925 Wenn Ihr mir nur erlauben wollt, ein wenig
Euch meinen Namen aufzufrischen. Denn
Ich kann mich rühmen, auch in Eure Hand
Etwas gelegt zu haben, was nicht zu
Verachten war.

Nathan.

Verzeiht! — Ich schäme mich —
2930 Sagt, was? — und nehmt zur Buße siebenfach
Den Wert desselben von mir an.

Klosterbruder.

Hört doch
Vor allen Dingen, wie ich selber nur
Erst heut' an dies mein Euch vertrautes Pfand
Erinnert worden.

Nathan.

Mir vertrautes Pfand?

Klosterbruder.

2935 Vor kurzem saß ich noch als Eremit
Auf Quarantana, unweit Jericho.
Da kam arabisch Raubgesindel, brach
Mein Gotteshäuschen ab und meine Zelle
Und schleppte mich mit fort. Zum Glück entkam
2940 Ich noch und floh hierher zum Patriarchen,
Um mir ein ander Plätzchen auszubitten,

Allwo ich meinem Gott in Einsamkeit
Bis an mein selig Ende dienen könne.

Nathan.

Ich steh' auf Kohlen, guter Bruder. Macht
2945 Es kurz. Das Pfand! das mir vertraute Pfand!

Klosterbruder.

Sogleich, Herr Nathan. — Nun, der Patriarch
Versprach mir eine Siedelei auf Thabor,
Sobald als eine leer, und hieß inzwischen
Im Kloster mich als Laienbruder bleiben.
2950 Da bin ich jetzt, Herr Nathan, und verlange
Des Tags wohl hundertmal auf Thabor. Denn
Der Patriarch braucht mich zu allerlei,
Wovor ich großen Ekel habe. Zum
Exempel:

Nathan.

Macht, ich bitt' Euch!

Klosterbruder.

Nun, es kömmt!
2955 Da hat ihm jemand heut' ins Ohr gesetzt,
Es lebe hier herum ein Jude, der
Ein Christenkind als seine Tochter sich
Erzöge.

Nathan.

Wie? (Betroffen.)

Klosterbruder.

Hört mich nur aus! — Indem
Er mir nun aufträgt, diesem Juden stracks,
2960 Wo möglich, auf die Spur zu kommen, und
Gewaltig sich ob eines solchen Frevels

Erzürnt, der ihm die wahre Sünde wider
Den heil'gen Geist bedünkt; — das ist, die Sünde,
Die aller Sünden größte Sünd' uns gilt,
2965 Nur daß wir, Gott sei Dank, so recht nicht wissen,
Worin sie eigentlich besteht: — da wacht
Mit einmal mein Gewissen auf, und mir
Fällt bei, ich könnte selber wohl vor Zeiten
Zu dieser unverzeihlich großen Sünde
2970 Gelegenheit gegeben haben. — Sagt:
Hat Euch ein Reitknecht nicht vor achtzehn Jahren
Ein Töchterchen gebracht von wenig Wochen?

Nathan.

Wie das? — Nun freilich — allerdings —

Klosterbruder.

Ei, seht
Mich doch recht an! — Der Reitknecht, der bin ich.

Nathan.

2975 Seid Ihr?

Klosterbruder.

Der Herr, von welchem ich's Euch brachte,
War — ist mir recht — ein Herr von Filnek. — Wolf
Von Filnek!

Nathan.

Richtig!

Klosterbruder.

Weil die Mutter kurz
Vorher gestorben war, und sich der Vater
Nach — mein' ich — Gazza plötzlich werfen mußte,
2980 Wohin das Würmchen ihm nicht folgen konnte,
So sandt' er's Euch. Und traf ich Euch damit
Nicht in Darun?

Nathan.

Ganz recht!

Klosterbruder.

Es wär' kein Wunder,
Wenn mein Gedächtnis mich betrög'. Ich habe
Der braven Herrn so viel gehabt, und diesem
2985 Hab' ich nur gar zu kurze Zeit gedient.
Er blieb bald drauf bei Askalon und war
Wohl sonst ein lieber Herr.

Nathan.

Ja wohl! ja wohl!
Dem ich so viel, so viel zu danken habe!
Der mehr als einmal mich dem Schwert entrissen!

Klosterbruder.

2990 O schön! So werd't Ihr seines Töchterchens
Euch um so lieber angenommen haben.

Nathan.

Das könnt Ihr denken.

Klosterbruder.

Nun, wo ist es denn?
Es ist doch wohl nicht etwa gar gestorben? —
Laßt's lieber nicht gestorben sein! — Wenn sonst
2995 Nur niemand um die Sache weiß, so hat
Es gute Wege.

Nathan.

Hat es?

Klosterbruder.

Traut mir, Nathan!
Denn seht, ich denke so! Wenn an das Gute,
Das ich zu thun vermeine, gar zu nah

Was gar zu Schlimmes grenzt, so thu' ich lieber
3000 Das Gute nicht; weil wir das Schlimme zwar
So ziemlich zuverlässig kennen, aber
Bei weiten nicht das Gute. — War ja wohl
Natürlich, wenn das Christentöchterchen
Recht gut von Euch erzogen werden sollte,
3005 Daß Ihr's als Euer eigen Töchterchen
Erzögt. — Das hättet Ihr mit aller Lieb'
Und Treue nun gethan, und müßtet so
Belohnet werden? Das will mir nicht ein.
Ei freilich, klüger hättet Ihr gethan,
3010 Wenn Ihr die Christin durch die zweite Hand
Als Christin auferziehen lassen; aber
So hättet Ihr das Kindchen Eures Freunds
Auch nicht geliebt. Und Kinder brauchen Liebe,
Wär's eines wilden Tieres Lieb' auch nur,
3015 In solchen Jahren mehr als Christentum.
Zum Christentume hat's noch immer Zeit.
Wenn nur das Mädchen sonst gesund und fromm
Vor Euern Augen aufgewachsen ist,
So blieb's vor Gottes Augen, was es war.
3020 Und ist denn nicht das ganze Christentum
Aufs Judentum gebaut? Es hat mich oft
Geärgert, hat mir Thränen g'nug gekostet,
Wenn Christen gar so sehr vergessen konnten,
Daß unser Herr ja selbst ein Jude war.

Nathan.

3025 Ihr, guter Bruder, müßt mein Fürsprach sein,
Wenn Haß und Gleißnerei sich gegen mich
Erheben sollten — wegen einer That —
Ah, wegen einer That! — Nur Ihr, Ihr sollt

Sie wissen! — Nehmt sie aber mit ins Grab!
3030 Noch hat mich nie die Eitelkeit versucht,
Sie jemand andern zu erzählen. Euch
Allein erzähl' ich sie. Der frommen Einfalt
Allein erzähl' ich sie. Weil die allein
Versteht, was sich der gottergebne Mensch
3035 Für Thaten abgewinnen kann.

Klosterbruder.

Ihr seid
Gerührt, und Euer Auge steht voll Wasser?

Nathan.

Ihr traft mich mit dem Kinde zu Darun.
Ihr wißt wohl aber nicht, daß wenig Tage
Zuvor in Gath die Christen alle Juden
3040 Mit Weib und Kind ermordet hatten, wißt
Wohl nicht, daß unter diesen meine Frau
Mit sieben hoffnungsvollen Söhnen sich
Befunden, die in meines Bruders Hause,
Zu dem ich sie geflüchtet, insgesamt
3045 Verbrennen müssen.

Klosterbruder.

Allgerechter!

Nathan.

Als
Ihr kamt, hatt' ich drei Tag' und Nächt' in Asch'
Und Staub vor Gott gelegen und geweint. —
Geweint? Beiher mit Gott auch wohl gerechtet,
Gezürnt, getobt, mich und die Welt verwünscht,
3050 Der Christenheit den unversöhnlichsten
Haß zugeschworen —

Klosterbruder.

Ach! Ich glaub's Euch wohl!

Nathan.

Doch nun kam die Vernunft allmählich wieder.
Sie sprach mit sanfter Stimm': „Und doch ist Gott!
Doch war auch Gottes Ratschluß das! Wohlan!
3055 Komm! übe, was du längst begriffen hast,
Was sicherlich zu üben schwerer nicht
Als zu begreifen ist, wenn du nur willst.
Steh auf!" — Ich stand! und rief zu Gott: Ich will!
Willst du nur, daß ich will! — Indem stiegt Ihr
3060 Vom Pferd' und überreichtet mir das Kind,
In Euern Mantel eingehüllt. — Was Ihr
Mir damals sagtet, was ich Euch, hab' ich
Vergessen. So viel weiß ich nur: ich nahm
Das Kind, trug's auf mein Lager, küßt' es, warf
3065 Mich auf die Knie und schluchzte: Gott! auf sieben
Doch nun schon eines wieder!

Klosterbruder.

Nathan! Nathan!
Ihr seid ein Christ! — Bei Gott, Ihr seid ein Christ!
Ein bess'rer Christ war nie!

Nathan.

Wohl uns! Denn was
Mich Euch zum Christen macht, das macht Euch mir
3070 Zum Juden! — Aber laßt uns länger nicht
Einander nur erweichen. Hier braucht's That!
Und ob mich siebenfache Liebe schon
Bald an dies einz'ge fremde Mädchen band,
Ob der Gedanke mich schon tötet, daß
3075 Ich meine sieben Söhn' in ihr aufs neue

Verlieren soll: — wenn sie von meinen Händen
Die Vorsicht wieder fordert, — ich gehorche!

Klosterbruder.

Nun vollends! — Eben das bedacht' ich mich
So viel, Euch anzuraten! Und so hat's
3080 Euch Euer guter Geist schon angeraten!

Nathan.

Nur muß der erste beste mir sie nicht
Entreißen wollen!

Klosterbruder.

Nein, gewiß nicht!

Nathan.

Wer
Auf sie nicht größ're Rechte hat als ich,
Muß frühere zum minsten haben —

Klosterbruder.

Freilich!

Nathan.

3085 Die ihm Natur und Blut erteilen.

Klosterbruder.

So
Mein' ich es auch!

Nathan.

Drum nennt mir nur geschwind
Den Mann, der ihr als Bruder oder Ohm,
Als Vetter oder sonst als Sipp verwandt:
Ihm will ich sie nicht vorenthalten — sie,
3090 Die jedes Hauses, jedes Glaubens Zierde
Zu sein erschaffen und erzogen ward. —
Ich hoff', Ihr wißt von diesem Euern Herrn
Und dem Geschlechte dessen mehr als ich.

Klosterbruder.

Das, guter Nathan, wohl nun schwerlich! — Denn
3095 Ihr habt ja schon gehört, daß ich nur gar
Zu kurze Zeit bei ihm gewesen.

Nathan.

Wißt
Ihr denn nicht wenigstens, was für Geschlechts
Die Mutter war? — War sie nicht eine Stauffin?

Klosterbruder.

Wohl möglich! — Ja, mich dünkt.

Nathan.

Hieß nicht ihr Bruder
3100 Konrad von Stauffen? — und war Tempelherr?

Klosterbruder.

Wenn mich's nicht triegt. Doch halt! Da fällt mir ein,
Daß ich vom sel'gen Herrn ein Büchelchen
Noch hab'. Ich zog's ihm aus dem Busen, als
Wir ihn bei Askalon verscharrten.

Nathan.

Nun?

Klosterbruder.

3105 Es sind Gebete drin. Wir nennen's ein
Brevier. — Das, dacht' ich, kann ein Christenmensch
Ja wohl noch brauchen. — Ich nun freilich nicht —
Ich kann nicht lesen —

Nathan.

Thut nichts! — Nur zur Sache

Klosterbruder.

In diesem Büchelchen stehn vorn und hinten,
3110 Wie ich mir sagen lassen, mit des Herrn

Selbeigner Hand, die Angehörigen
Von ihm und ihr geschrieben.

Nathan.

O erwünscht!
Geht! lauft! holt mir das Büchelchen. Geschwind!
Ich bin bereit, mit Gold es aufzuwiegen,
3115 Und tausend Dank dazu! Eilt! lauft!

Klosterbruder.

Recht gern!
Es ist arabisch aber, was der Herr
Hineingeschrieben. (Ab.)

Nathan.

Einerlei! Nur her! —
Gott! wenn ich doch das Mädchen noch behalten
Und einen solchen Eidam mir damit
3120 Erkaufen könnte! — Schwerlich wohl! — Nun, fall'
Es aus, wie's will! — Wer mag es aber denn
Gewesen sein, der bei dem Patriarchen
So etwas angebracht? Das muß ich doch
Zu fragen nicht vergessen. — Wenn es gar
3125 Von Daja käme?

Achter Auftritt.

Daja und Nathan.

Daja
(eilig und verlegen).

Denkt doch, Nathan!

Nathan.

Nun?

Daja.

Das arme Kind erschrak wohl recht darüber!
Da schickt . . .

Nathan.

Der Patriarch?

Daja.

Des Sultans Schwester,
Prinzessin Sittah . . .

Nathan.

Nicht der Patriarch?

Daja.

Nein, Sittah! — Hört Ihr nicht? — Prinzessin Sittah
3130 Schickt her und läßt sie zu sich holen.

Nathan.

Wen?
Läßt Recha holen? — Sittah läßt sie holen. —
Nun, wenn sie Sittah holen läßt, und nicht
Der Patriarch . . .

Daja.

Wie kommt Ihr denn auf den?

Nathan.

So hast du kürzlich nichts von ihm gehört?
3135 Gewiß nicht? Auch ihm nichts gesteckt?

Daja.

Ich? ihm?

Nathan.

Wo sind die Boten?

Daja.

Vorn.

Nathan.

Ich will sie doch
Aus Vorsicht selber sprechen. Komm! — Wenn nur
Vom Patriarchen nichts dahinter steckt. (Ab.)

Daja.

Und ich — ich fürchte ganz was andres noch.
3140 Was gilt's? die einzige vermeinte Tochter
So eines reichen Juden wär' auch wohl
Für einen Muselmann nicht übel? — Hui,
Der Tempelherr ist drum. Ist drum, wenn ich
Den zweiten Schritt nicht auch noch wage, nicht
3145 Auch ihr noch selbst entdecke, wer sie ist! —
Getrost! Laß mich den ersten Augenblick,
Den ich allein sie habe, dazu brauchen!
Und der wird sein — vielleicht nun eben, wenn
Ich sie begleite. So ein erster Wink
3150 Kann unterwegens wenigstens nicht schaden.
Ja, ja! Nur zu! Jetzt oder nie! Nur zu! (Ihm nach.)

Fünfter Aufzug.

Erster Auftritt.

Scene: das Zimmer in Saladins Palaste, in welches die Beutel mit Geld getragen worden, die noch zu sehen.

Saladin und bald darauf verschiedene Mamelucken.

Saladin (im Hereintreten).

Da steht das Geld nun noch! Und niemand weiß
Den Derwisch aufzufinden, der vermutlich
Ans Schachbrett irgendwo geraten ist,
3155 Das ihn wohl seiner selbst vergessen macht; —
Warum nicht meiner? — Nun, Geduld! Was giebt's?

Ein Mameluck.

Erwünschte Nachricht, Sultan! Freude, Sultan!
Die Karawane von Kahira kömmt,
Ist glücklich da! mit siebenjährigem
3160 Tribut des reichen Nils.

Saladin.

Brav, Ibrahim!
Du bist mir wahrlich ein willkommner Bote! —
Ha! endlich einmal! endlich! — Habe Dank
Der guten Zeitung.

Der Mameluck (wartend).

(Nun? nur her damit!)

Saladin.

Was wart'st du? — Geh nur wieder.

Der Mameluck.

Dem Willkommnen

3165 Sonst nichts?

Saladin.

Was denn noch sonst?

Der Mameluck.

Dem guten Boten

Kein Botenbrot? — So wär' ich ja der erste,

Den Saladin mit Worten abzulohnen

Doch endlich lernte? — Auch ein Ruhm! — **der** erste,

Mit dem er knickerte.

Saladin.

So nimm dir nur

3170 Dort einen Beutel.

Der Mameluck.

Nein, nun nicht! Du kannst

Mir sie nun alle schenken wollen.

Saladin.

Trotz! —

Komm her! Da hast du zwei. — Im Ernst? er geht?

Thut mir's an Edelmut zuvor? — Denn sicher

Muß ihm es saurer werden, auszuschlagen,

3175 Als mir zu geben. — Ibrahim! — Was kommt

Mir denn auch ein, so kurz vor meinem Abtritt

Auf einmal ganz ein andrer sein zu wollen? —

Will Saladin als Saladin nicht sterben? —

So mußt' er auch als Saladin nicht leben.

Ein zweiter Mameluck.

3180 Nun, Sultan! . . .

Saladin.

Wenn du mir zu melden kömmst ...

Zweiter Mameluck.

Daß aus Ägypten der Transport nun da!

Saladin.

Ich weiß schon.

Zweiter Mameluck.

Kam ich doch zu spät!

Saladin.

Warum
Zu spät? — Dä nimm für deinen guten Willen
Der Beutel einen oder zwei.

Zweiter Mameluck.

Macht drei!

Saladin.

3185 Ja, wenn du rechnen kannst! — So nimm sie nur

Zweiter Mameluck.

Es wird wohl noch ein dritter kommen, — wenn
Er anders kommen kann.

Saladin.

Wie das?

Zweiter Mameluck.

Je nu,
Er hat auch wohl den Hals gebrochen! Denn
Sobald wir drei der Ankunft des Transports
3190 Versichert waren, sprengte jeder frisch
Davon. Der vorderste, der stürzt; und so

Komm' ich nun vor und bleib' auch vor bis in
Die Stadt, wo aber Ibrahim, der Lecker,
Die Gassen besser kennt.

Saladin.

O, der Gestürzte!
3195 Freund, der Gestürzte! — Reit ihm doch entgegen.

Zweiter Mameluck.

Das werd' ich ja wohl thun! — Und wenn er lebt,
So ist die Hälfte dieser Beutel sein.

(Geht ab.)

Saladin.

Sieh, welch ein guter, edler Kerl auch das! —
Wer kann sich solcher Mamelucken rühmen?
3200 Und wär' mir denn zu denken nicht erlaubt,
Daß sie mein Beispiel bilden helfen? — Fort
Mit dem Gedanken, sie zu guter Letzt
Noch an ein andres zu gewöhnen! ...

Ein dritter Mameluck.

Sultan, ...

Saladin.

Bist du's, der stürzte?

Dritter Mameluck.

Nein. Ich melde nur, —
3205 Daß Emir Mansor, der die Karawane
Geführt, vom Pferde steigt ...

Saladin.

Bring ihn! geschwind! —
Da ist er ja! —

Zweiter Auftritt.

Emil Mansor und Saladin.

Saladin.

Willkommen, Emir! Nun,
Wie ist's gegangen? — Mansor, Mansor, hast
Uns lange warten lassen!

Mansor.

Dieser Brief
3210 Berichtet, was dein Abulkassem erst
Für Unruh' in Thebais dämpfen müssen,
Eh' wir es wagen durften, abzugehen.
Den Zug darauf hab' ich beschleuniget
So viel, wie möglich war.

Saladin.

Ich glaube dir! —
3215 Und nimm nur, guter Mansor, nimm sogleich . . .
Du thust es aber doch auch gern? . . . nimm frische
Bedeckung nur sogleich. Du mußt sogleich
Noch weiter, mußt der Gelder größern Teil
Auf Libanon zum Vater bringen.

Mansor.

Gern!
3220 Sehr gern!

Saladin.

Und nimm dir die Bedeckung ja
Nur nicht zu schwach. Es ist um Libanon
Nicht alles mehr zu sicher. Hast du nicht
Gehört? Die Tempelherren sind wieder rege.
Sei wohl auf deiner Hut! — Komm nur! Wo hält
3225 Der Zug? Ich will ihn sehn und alles selbst
Betreiben. — Ihr! ich bin sodann bei Sittah.

Dritter Auftritt.

Scene: die Palmen vor Nathans Hause, wo der Tempelherr auf und nieder geht.

Tempelherr.

Ins Haus nun will ich einmal nicht. — Er wird
Sich endlich doch wohl sehen lassen! — Man
Bemerkte mich ja sonst so bald, so gern! —
3230 Will's noch erleben, daß er sich's verbittet,
Vor seinem Hause mich so fleißig finden
Zu lassen. — Hm! — ich bin doch aber auch
Sehr ärgerlich. — Was hat mich denn nun so
Erbittert gegen ihn? — Er sagte ja:
3235 Noch schlüg' er mir nichts ab. Und Saladin
Hat's über sich genommen, ihn zu stimmen. —
Wie? sollte wirklich wohl in mir der Christ
Noch tiefer nisten als in ihm der Jude? —
Wer kennt sich recht? Wie könnt ich ihm denn sonst
3240 Den kleinen Raub nicht gönnen wollen, den
Er sich's zu solcher Angelegenheit
Gemacht, den Christen abzujagen? — Freilich,
Kein kleiner Raub, ein solch Geschöpf! — Geschöpf?
Und wessen? — doch des Sklaven nicht, der auf
3245 Des Lebens öden Strand den Block geflößt
Und sich davon gemacht? Des Künstlers doch
Wohl mehr, der in dem hingeworfnen Blocke
Die göttliche Gestalt sich dachte, die
Er dargestellt? — Ach! Rechas wahrer Vater
3250 Bleibt, trotz dem Christen, der sie zeugte, — bleibt
In Ewigkeit der Jude. — Wenn ich mir
Sie lediglich als Christendirne denke,
Sie sonder alles das mir denke, was
Allein ihr so ein Jude geben konnte: —

3255 Sprich, Herz, — was wär' an ihr, das dir gefiel?
Nichts! Wenig! Selbst ihr Lächeln, wär' es nichts
Als sanfte, schöne Zuckung ihrer Muskeln,
Wär', was sie lächeln macht, des Reizes unwert,
In den es sich auf ihrem Munde kleidet: —
3260 Nein, selbst ihr Lächeln nicht! Ich hab' es ja
Wohl schöner noch an Aberwitz, an Tand,
An Höhnerei, an Schmeichler und an Buhler
Verschwenden sehn! — Hat's da mich auch bezaubert?
Hat's da mir auch den Wunsch entlockt, mein Leben
3265 In seinem Sonnenscheine zu verflattern? —
Ich wüßte nicht. Und bin auf den doch launisch,
Der diesen höhern Wert allein ihr gab?
Wie das? warum? — Wenn ich den Spott verdiente,
Mit dem mich Saladin entließ! Schon schlimm
3270 Genug, daß Saladin es glauben konnte!
Wie klein ich ihm da scheinen mußte! wie
Verächtlich! — Und das alles um ein Mädchen? —
Curd! Curd! das geht so nicht. Lenk ein! Wenn vollends
Mir Daja nur was vorgeplaudert hätte,
3275 Was schwerlich zu erweisen stünde? — Sieh,
Da tritt er endlich, in Gespräch vertieft,
Aus seinem Hause! — Ha! mit wem! — Mit ihm?
Mit meinem Klosterbruder? — Ha! so weiß
Er sicherlich schon alles! ist wohl gar
3280 Dem Patriarchen schon verraten! — Ha!
Was hab' ich Querkopf nun gestiftet! — Daß
Ein einz'ger Funken dieser Leidenschaft
Doch unsers Hirns so viel verbrennen kann! —
Geschwind entschließ dich, was nunmehr zu thun!
3285 Ich will hier seitwärts ihrer warten, — ob
Vielleicht der Klosterbruder ihn verläßt.

Vierter Auftritt.

Nathan und der Klosterbruder.

Nathan (im Näherkommen).

Habt nochmals, guter Bruder, vielen Dank!

Klosterbruder.

Und Ihr desgleichen!

Nathan.

Ich? von Euch? wofür?
Für meinen Eigensinn, Euch aufzudringen,
3290 Was Ihr nicht braucht? — Ja, wenn ihm Eurer nur
Auch nachgegeben hätt', Ihr mit Gewalt
Nicht wolltet reicher sein als ich.

Klosterbruder.

Das Buch
Gehört ja ohnedem nicht mir, gehört
Ja ohnedem der Tochter, ist ja so
3295 Der Tochter ganzes väterliches Erbe. —
Je nun, sie hat ja Euch. — Gott gebe nur,
Daß Ihr es nie bereuen dürft, so viel
Für sie gethan zu haben!

Nathan.

Kann ich das?
Das kann ich nie. Seid unbesorgt!

Klosterbruder.

Nu, nu!
3300 Die Patriarchen und die Tempelherren . . .

Nathan.

Vermögen mir des Bösen nie so viel
Zu thun, daß irgend was mich reuen könnte,
Geschweige, das! — Und seid Ihr denn so ganz

Versichert, daß ein Tempelherr es ist,
3305 Der Euern Patriarchen hetzt?

Klosterbruder.

Es kann
Beinah kein andrer sein. Ein Tempelherr
Sprach kurz vorher mit ihm, und was ich hörte,
Das klang darnach.

Nathan.

Es ist doch aber nur
Ein einziger jetzt in Jerusalem,
3310 Und diesen kenn' ich. Dieser ist mein Freund,
Ein junger, edler, offner Mann!

Klosterbruder.

Ganz recht,
Der nämliche! — Doch was man ist, und was
Man sein muß in der Welt, das paßt ja wohl
Nicht immer.

Nathan.

Leider nicht. — So thue, wer's
3315 Auch immer ist, sein Schlimmstes oder Bestes!
Mit Euerm Buche, Bruder, trotz' ich allen
Und gehe graden Wegs damit zum Sultan.

Klosterbruder.

Viel Glücks! Ich will Euch denn nur hier verlassen.

Nathan.

Und habt sie nicht einmal gesehn! — Kommt ja
3320 Doch bald, doch fleißig wieder. — Wenn nur heut'
Der Patriarch noch nichts erfährt! — Doch was?
Sagt ihm auch heute, was Ihr wollt.

Klosterbruder.

Ich nicht.
Lebt wohl!

(Geht ab.)

Nathan.

Vergeßt uns ja nicht, Bruder! — Gott!
Daß ich nicht gleich hier unter freiem Himmel
3325 Auf meine Kniee sinken kann! Wie sich
Der Knoten, der so oft mir bange machte,
Nun von sich selber löset! — Gott! wie leicht
Mir wird, daß ich nun weiter auf der Welt
Nichts zu verbergen habe! daß ich vor
3330 Den Menschen nun so frei kann wandeln als
Vor dir, der du allein den Menschen nicht
Nach seinen Thaten brauchst zu richten, die
So selten seine Thaten sind, o Gott! —

Fünfter Auftritt.

Nathan und der Tempelherr, der von der Seite auf ihn zukömmt.

Tempelherr.

He! wartet, Nathan, nehmt mich mit!

Nathan.

Wer ruft? —
3335 Seid Ihr es, Ritter? Wo gewesen, daß
Ihr bei dem Sultan Euch nicht treffen lassen?

Tempelherr.

Wir sind einander fehlgegangen. Nehmt's
Nicht übel!

Nathan.

Ich nicht, aber Saladin . .

Tempelherr.

Ihr wart nur eben fort . . .

Nathan.

Und spracht ihn doch?

3340 Nun, so ist's gut.

Tempelherr.

Er will uns aber beide
Zusammen sprechen.

Nathan.

Desto besser. Kommt
Nur mit. Mein Gang stand ohnehin zu ihm. —

Tempelherr.

Ich darf ja doch wohl fragen, Nathan, wer
Euch da verließ?

Nathan.

Ihr kennt ihn doch wohl nicht?

Tempelherr.

3345 War's nicht die gute Haut, der Laienbruder,
Des sich der Patriarch so gern zum Stöber
Bedient?

Nathan.

Kann sein! Beim Patriarchen ist
Er allerdings.

Tempelherr.

Der Pfiff ist gar nicht übel,
Die Einfalt vor der Schurkerei voraus
3350 Zu schicken.

Nathan.

Ja, die dumme, — nicht die fromme.

Tempelherr.

An fromme glaubt kein Patriarch.

Nathan.

Für den
Nun steh' ich. Der wird seinem Patriarchen
Nichts Ungebührliches vollziehen helfen.

Tempelherr.

So stellt er wenigstens sich an. — Doch hat
3355 Er Euch von mir denn nichts gesagt?

Nathan.

Von Euch?
Von Euch nun namentlich wohl nichts. — Er weiß
Ja wohl auch schwerlich Euern Namen?

Tempelherr.

Schwerlich.

Nathan.

Von einem Tempelherren freilich hat
Er mir gesagt . . .

Tempelherr.

Und was?

Nathan.

Womit er Euch
3360 Doch ein- für allemal nicht meinen kann!

Tempelherr.

Wer weiß? Laßt doch nur hören.

Nathan.

Daß mich einer
Bei seinem Patriarchen angeklagt . . .

Tempelherr.

Euch angeklagt? — Das ist, mit seiner Gunst —
Erlogen. — Hört mich, Nathan! — Ich bin nicht
3365 Der Mensch, der irgend etwas abzuleugnen

Imstande wäre. Was ich that, das that ich!
Doch bin ich auch nicht der, der alles, was
Er that, als wohlgethan verteid'gen möchte.
Was sollt' ich eines Fehls mich schämen? Hab'
3370 Ich nicht den festen Vorsatz, ihn zu bessern?
Und weiß ich etwa nicht, wie weit mit dem
Es Menschen bringen können? — Hört mich, Nathan! —
Ich bin des Laienbruders Tempelherr,
Der Euch verklagt soll haben, allerdings. —
3375 Ihr wißt ja, was mich wurmisch machte! was
Mein Blut in allen Adern sieden machte!
Ich Gauch! — ich kam, so ganz mit Leib' und Seel'
Euch in die Arme mich zu werfen. Wie
Ihr mich empfingt — wie kalt — wie lau — denn lau
3380 Ist schlimmer noch als kalt; wie abgemessen
Mir auszubeugen Ihr beflissen wart;
Mit welchen aus der Luft gegriffnen Fragen
Ihr Antwort mir zu geben scheinen wolltet:
Das darf ich kaum mir jetzt noch denken, wenn
3385 Ich soll gelassen bleiben. — Hört mich, Nathan! —
In dieser Gährung schlich mir Daja nach
Und warf mir ihr Geheimnis an den Kopf,
Das mir den Aufschluß Euers rätselhaften
Betragens zu enthalten schien.

Nathan.

Wie das?

Tempelherr.

3390 Hört mich nur aus! — Ich bildete mir ein,
Ihr wolltet, was Ihr einmal nun den Christen
So abgejagt, an einen Christen wieder
Nicht gern verlieren. Und so fiel mir ein,

Euch kurz und gut das Messer an die Kehle
3395 Zu setzen.

Nathan.

Kurz und gut? und gut? — Wo steckt
Das Gute?

Tempelherr.

Hört mich, Nathan! — Allerdings,
Ich that nicht recht! — Ihr seid wohl gar nicht schuldig. —
Die Närrin Daja weiß nicht, was sie spricht, —
Ist Euch gehässig, — sucht Euch nur damit
3400 In einen bösen Handel zu verwickeln; —
Kann sein! kann sein! — Ich bin ein junger Laffe,
Der immer nur an beiden Enden schwärmt,
Bald viel zu viel, bald viel zu wenig thut; —
Auch das kann sein! Verzeiht mir, Nathan.

Nathan.

Wenn
3405 Ihr so mich freilich fasset —

Tempelherr.

Kurz, ich ging
Zum Patriarchen! — hab' Euch aber nicht
Genannt. Das ist erlogen, wie gesagt!
Ich hab' ihm bloß den Fall ganz allgemein
Erzählt, um seine Meinung zu vernehmen. —
3410 Auch das hätt' unterbleiben können; ja doch! —
Denn kannt' ich nicht den Patriarchen schon
Als einen Schurken? Konnt' ich Euch nicht selber
Nur gleich zur Rede stellen? — Mußt' ich der
Gefahr, so einen Vater zu verlieren,
3415 Das arme Mädchen opfern? — Nun, was thut's?
Die Schurkerei des Patriarchen, die

So ähnlich immer sich erhält, hat mich
Des nächsten Weges wieder zu mir selbst
Gebracht. — Denn hört mich, Nathan, hört mich aus! —
3420 Gesetzt, er wüßt' auch Euern Namen, was
Nun mehr, was mehr? — Er kann Euch ja das Mädchen
Nur nehmen, wenn sie niemands ist als Euer.
Er kann sie doch aus Euerm Hause nur
Ins Kloster schleppen. — Also — gebt sie mir!
3425 Gebt sie nur mir und laßt ihn kommen. Ha!
Er soll's wohl bleiben lassen, mir mein Weib
Zu nehmen. — Gebt sie mir, geschwind! — Sie sei
Nun Eure Tochter, oder sei es nicht!
Sei Christin oder Jüdin oder keines!
3430 Gleichviel! gleichviel! Ich werd' Euch weder jetzt
Noch jemals sonst in meinem ganzen Leben
Darum befragen. Sei, wie's sei!

Nathan.

Ihr wähnt
Wohl gar, daß mir die Wahrheit zu verbergen
Sehr nötig?

Tempelherr.

Sei, wie's sei!

Nathan.

Ich hab' es ja
3435 Euch — oder wem es sonst zu wissen ziemt —
Noch nicht geleugnet, daß sie eine Christin
Und nichts als meine Pflegetochter ist. —
Warum ich's aber ihr noch nicht entdeckt? —
Darüber brauch' ich nur bei ihr mich zu
3440 Entschuldigen.

Tempelherr.

Das sollt Ihr auch bei ihr
Nicht brauchen. — Gönnt's ihr doch, daß sie Euch nie

Mit andern Augen darf betrachten! Spart
Ihr die Entdeckung doch! — Noch habt Ihr ja,
Ihr ganz allein, mit ihr zu schalten. Gebt
3445 Sie mir! Ich bitt' Euch, Nathan, gebt sie mir!
Ich bin's allein, der sie zum zweitenmale
Euch retten kann — und will.

Nathan.

Ja — konnte! konnte!
Nun auch nicht mehr. Es ist damit zu spät.

Tempelherr.

Wie so? zu spät?

Nathan.

Dank sei dem Patriarchen . . .

Tempelherr.

3450 Dem Patriarchen? Dank? ihm Dank? wofür?
Dank hätte der bei uns verdienen wollen?
Wofür? wofür?

Nathan.

Daß wir nun wissen, wem
Sie anverwandt, nun wissen, wessen Händen
Sie sicher ausgeliefert werden kann.

Tempelherr.

3455 Das dank' ihm — wer für mehr ihm danken wird!

Nathan.

Aus diesen müßt Ihr sie nun auch erhalten
Und nicht aus meinen.

Tempelherr.

Arme Recha! Was
Dir alles zustößt, arme Recha! Was
Ein Glück für andre Waisen wäre, wird

3460 Dein Unglück! — Nathan! — Und wo sind sie, diese
Verwandte?

Nathan.

Wo sie sind?

Tempelherr.

Und wer sie sind?

Nathan.

Besonders hat ein Bruder sich gefunden,
Bei dem Ihr um sie werben müßt.

Tempelherr.

Ein Bruder?
Was ist er, dieser Bruder? Ein Soldat?
3465 Ein Geistlicher? — Laßt hören, was ich mir
Versprechen darf.

Nathan.

Ich glaube, daß er keines
Von beiden — oder beides ist. Ich kenn'
Ihn noch nicht recht.

Tempelherr.

Und sonst?

Nathan.

Ein braver Mann!
Bei dem sich Recha gar nicht übel wird
3470 Befinden.

Tempelherr.

Doch ein Christ! — Ich weiß zu Zeiten
Auch gar nicht, was ich von Euch denken soll; —
Nehmt mir's nicht ungut, Nathan. — Wird sie nicht
Die Christin spielen müssen unter Christen?
Und wird sie, was sie lange g'nug gespielt,

3475 Nicht endlich werden? Wird den lautern Weizen,
Den Ihr gesä't, das Unkraut endlich nicht
Ersticken? — Und das kümmert Euch so wenig?
Dem ungeachtet könnt Ihr sagen — Ihr? —
Daß sie bei ihrem Bruder sich nicht übel
3480 Befinden werde?

Nathan.

Denk' ich! hoff ich! — Wenn
Ihr ja bei ihm was mangeln sollte, hat
Sie Euch und mich denn nicht noch immer? —

Tempelherr.

Oh!
Was wird bei ihm ihr mangeln können! Wird
Das Brüderchen mit Essen und mit Kleidung,
3485 Mit Naschwerk und mit Putz das Schwesterchen
Nicht reichlich g'nug versorgen? Und was braucht
Ein Schwesterchen denn mehr? — Ei freilich: auch
Noch einen Mann! Nun, nun, — auch den, auch den
Wird ihr das Brüderchen zu seiner Zeit
3490 Schon schaffen, wie er immer nur zu finden!
Der christlichste der beste! — Nathan, Nathan!
Welch einen Engel hattet Ihr gebildet,
Den Euch nun andre so verhunzen werden!

Nathan.

Hat keine Not! Er wird sich unsrer Liebe
3495 Noch immer wert genug behaupten.

Tempelherr.

Sagt
Das nicht! Von meiner Liebe sagt das nicht!
Denn die läßt nichts sich unterschlagen, nichts,
Es sei auch noch so klein! auch keinen Namen! —

Doch halt! — Argwohnt sie wohl bereits, was mit
3500 Ihr vorgeht?

Nathan.

Möglich; ob ich schon nicht wüßte,
Woher?

Tempelherr.

Auch eben viel; sie soll — sie muß
In beiden Fällen, was ihr Schicksal droht,
Von mir zuerst erfahren. Mein Gedanke,
Sie eher wieder nicht zu sehn, zu sprechen,
3505 Als bis ich sie die meine nennen dürfe,
Fällt weg. Ich eile ...

Nathan.

Bleibt! wohin?

Tempelherr.

Zu ihr!
Zu sehn, ob diese Mädchenseele Manns genug
Wohl ist, den einzigen Entschluß zu fassen,
Der ihrer würdig wäre!

Nathan.

Welchen?

Tempelherr.

Den:
3510 Nach Euch und ihrem Bruder weiter nicht
Zu fragen —

Nathan.

Und?

Tempelherr.

Und mir zu folgen, — wenn
Sie drüber eines Muselmannes Frau
Auch werden müßte.

Nathan.

Bleibt! Ihr trefft sie nicht;
Sie ist bei Sittah, bei des Sultans Schwester.

Tempelherr.

3515 Seit wenn? warum?

Nathan.

Und wollt Ihr da bei ihnen
Zugleich den Bruder finden, kommt nur mit.

Tempelherr.

Den Bruder? welchen? Sittahs oder Rechas?

Nathan.

Leicht beide. Kommt nur mit! Ich bitt' Euch, kommt!

(Er führt ihn fort.)

Sechster Auftritt.

Scene: in Sittahs Harem.

Sittah und Recha in Unterhaltung begriffen.

Sittah.

Was freu' ich mich nicht deiner, süßes Mädchen! —
3520 Sei so beklemmt nur nicht! so angst! so schüchtern! —
Sei munter! sei gesprächiger! vertrauter!

Recha.

Prinzessin, . . .

Sittah.

Nicht doch! nicht Prinzessin! Nenn
Mich Sittah, — deine Freundin, — deine Schwester.
Nenn mich dein Mütterchen! — Ich könnte das

3525 Ja schier auch sein. — So jung! so klug! so fromm!
Was du nicht alles weißt! nicht alles mußt
Gelesen haben

Recha.

Ich gelesen? — Sittah,
Du spottest deiner kleinen albern Schwester.
Ich kann kaum lesen.

Sittah.

Kannst kaum, Lügnerin!

Recha.

3530 Ein wenig meines Vaters Hand! — Ich meinte,
Du sprächst von Büchern.

Sittah.

Allerdings! von Büchern.

Recha.

Nun, Bücher wird mir wahrlich schwer zu lesen! —

Sittah.

Im Ernst?

Recha.

In ganzem Ernst. Mein Vater liebt
Die kalte Buchgelehrsamkeit, die sich
3535 Mit toten Zeichen ins Gehirn nur drückt,
Zu wenig.

Sittah.

Ei, was sagst du! — Hat indeß
Wohl nicht sehr unrecht! — Und so manches, was
Du weißt . . .?

Recha.

Weiß ich allein aus seinem Munde
Und könnte bei dem meisten dir noch sagen,
3540 Wie? wo? warum? er mich's gelehrt.

Sittah.

So hängt
Sich freilich alles besser an. So lernt
Mit eins die ganze Seele.

Recha.

Sicher hat
Auch Sittah wenig oder nichts gelesen!

Sittah.

Wie so? — Ich bin nicht stolz aufs Gegenteil. —
3545 Allein wie so? Dein Grund! Sprich dreist. Dein Grund?

Recha.

Sie ist so schlecht und recht, und unverkünstelt,
So ganz sich selbst nur ähnlich . . .

Sittah.

Nun?

Recha.

Das sollen
Die Bücher uns nur selten lassen, sagt
Mein Vater.

Sittah.

O, was ist dein Vater für
3550 Ein Mann!

Recha.

Nicht wahr?

Sittah.

Wie nah er immer doch
Zum Ziele trifft!

Recha.

Nicht wahr? — Und diesen Vater —

Sittah.

Was ist dir, Liebe?

Recha.

Diesen Vater —

Sittah.

Gott!

Du weinst?

Recha.

Und diesen Vater — Ah! es muß
Heraus! Mein Herz will Luft, will Luft ...

(Wirft sich, von Thränen überwältigt, zu ihren Füßen.)

Sittah.

Kind, was
3555 Geschieht dir? Recha?

Recha.

Diesen Vater soll —
Soll ich verlieren!

Sittah.

Du? verlieren? ihn?
Wie das? — Sei ruhig! — nimmermehr! — Steh auf!

Recha.

Du sollst vergebens dich zu meiner Freundin,
Zu meiner Schwester nicht erboten haben!

Sittah.

3560 Ich bin's ja! bin's! — Steh doch nur auf! Ich muß
Sonst Hilfe rufen.

Recha

(die sich ermannt und aufsteht).

Ah! verzeih! vergieb! —
Mein Schmerz hat mich vergessen machen, wer
Du bist. Vor Sittah gilt kein Winseln, kein
Verzweifeln. Kalte, ruhige Vernunft

3565 Will alles über sie allein vermögen.
Wes Sache diese bei ihr führt, der siegt!

Sittah.

Nun dann?

Recha.

Nein, meine Freundin, meine Schwester
Giebt das nicht zu! Giebt nimmer zu, daß mir
Ein andrer Vater aufgedrungen werde!

Sittah.

3570 Ein andrer Vater? aufgedrungen? Dir?
Wer kann das? kann das auch nur wollen, Liebe?

Recha.

Wer? Meine gute böse Daja kann
Das wollen, — will das können. — Ja, du kennst
Wohl diese gute böse Daja nicht?
3575 Nun, Gott vergeb' es ihr! — belohn' es ihr!
Sie hat mir so viel Gutes, — so viel Böses
Erwiesen!

Sittah.

Böses dir? — So muß sie Gutes
Doch wahrlich wenig haben.

Recha.

Doch! recht viel,
Recht viel!

Sittah.

Wer ist sie?

Recha.

Eine Christin, die
3580 In meiner Kindheit mich gepflegt, mich so
Gepflegt! — Du glaubst nicht! — die mir eine Mutter
So wenig missen lassen! — Gott vergelt'

Es ihr! — die aber mich auch so geängstet!
Mich so gequält!

Sittah.

Und über was? warum?

3585 Wie?

Recha.

Ach! die arme Frau — ich sag' dir's ja —
Ist eine Christin, — muß aus Liebe quälen, —
Ist eine von den Schwärmerinnen, die
Den allgemeinen, einzig wahren Weg
Nach Gott zu wissen wähnen!

Sittah.

Nun versteh' ich!

Recha.

3590 Und sich gedrungen fühlen, einen jeden,
Der dieses Wegs verfehlt, darauf zu lenken. —
Kaum können sie auch anders. Denn ist's wahr,
Daß dieser Weg allein nur richtig führt:
Wie sollen sie gelassen ihre Freunde
3595 Auf einem andern wandeln sehn, — der ins
Verderben stürzt, ins ewige Verderben?
Es müßte möglich sein, denselben Menschen
Zur selben Zeit zu lieben und zu hassen. —
Auch ist's das nicht, was endlich laute Klagen
3600 Mich über sie zu führen zwingt. Ihr Seufzen,
Ihr Warnen, ihr Gebet, ihr Drohen hätt'
Ich gern noch länger ausgehalten, gern!
Es brachte mich doch immer auf Gedanken,
Die gut und nützlich. Und wem schmeichelt's doch
3605 Im Grunde nicht, sich gar so wert und teuer,
Von wem's auch sei, gehalten fühlen, daß

Er den Gedanken nicht ertragen kann,
Er müss' einmal auf ewig uns entbehren!

Sittah.

Sehr wahr!

Recha.

Allein — allein — das geht zu weit!
3610 Dem kann ich nichts entgegensetzen, nicht
Geduld, nicht Überlegung, nichts!

Sittah.

Was? wem?

Recha.

Was sie mir eben jetzt entdeckt will haben.

Sittah.

Entdeckt? und eben jetzt?

Recha.

Nur eben jetzt!
Wir nahten auf dem Weg' hierher uns einem
3615 Verfallnen Christentempel. Plötzlich stand
Sie still, schien mit sich selbst zu kämpfen, blickte
Mit nassen Augen bald gen Himmel, bald
Auf mich. Komm, sprach sie endlich, laß uns hier
Durch diesen Tempel in die Richte gehn!
3620 Sie geht; ich folg' ihr, und mein Auge schweift
Mit Graus die wankenden Ruinen durch.
Nun steht sie wieder, und ich sehe mich
An den versunknen Stufen eines morschen
Altars mit ihr. Wie ward mir? als sie da
3625 Mit heißen Thränen, mit gerungnen Händen.
Zu meinen Füßen stürzte . . .

Sittah.

Gutes Kind!

Recha.

Und bei der Göttlichen, die da wohl sonst
So manch Gebet erhört, so manches Wunder
Verrichtet habe, mich beschwor, — mit Blicken
3630 Des wahren Mitleids mich beschwor, mich meiner
Doch zu erbarmen! — wenigstens ihr zu
Vergeben, wenn sie mir entdecken müsse,
Was ihre Kirch' auf mich für Anspruch habe.

Sittah.

(Unglückliche! — Es ahnte mir!)

Recha.

Ich sei
3635 Aus christlichem Geblüte, sei getauft,
Sei Nathans Tochter nicht, er nicht mein Vater! —
Gott! Gott! Er nicht mein Vater! — Sittah! Sittah!
Sieh mich aufs neu' zu deinen Füßen . . .

Sittah.

Recha!
Nicht doch! steh auf! — Mein Bruder kömmt! steh auf!

Siebenter Auftritt.

Saladin und die Vorigen.

Saladin.

3640 Was giebt's hier, Sittah?

Sittah.

Sie ist von sich! Gott!

Saladin.

Wer ist's?

Sittah.

Du weißt ja . . .

Saladin.

Unsers Nathans Tochter?

Was fehlt ihr?

Sittah.

Komm doch zu dir, Kind! — Der Sultan . . .

Recha

(die sich auf den Knieen zu Saladins Füßen schleppt, den Kopf zur Erden gesenkt).

Ich steh' nicht auf! nicht eher auf! — mag eher
Des Sultans Antlitz nicht erblicken! — eher
3645 Den Abglanz ewiger Gerechtigkeit
Und Güte nicht in seinen Augen, nicht
Auf seiner Stirn bewundern . . .

Saladin.

Steh . . . steh auf!

Recha.

Eh' er mir nicht verspricht . . .

Saladin.

Komm! ich verspreche . . .

Sei was es will!

Recha.

Nicht mehr, nicht weniger,
3650 Als meinen Vater mir zu lassen und
Mich ihm! — Noch weiß ich nicht, wer sonst mein Vater
Zu sein verlangt, — verlangen kann. Will's auch
Nicht wissen. Aber macht denn nur das Blut
Den Vater? nur das Blut?

Saladin (der sie aufhebt).

Ich merke wohl! —
3655 Wer war so grausam denn, dir selbst — dir selbst
Dergleichen in den Kopf zu setzen? Ist
Es denn schon völlig ausgemacht? erwiesen?

Recha.

Muß wohl! Denn Daja will von meiner Amm'
Es haben.

Saladin.

Deiner Amme!

Recha.

Die es sterbend
3660 Ihr zu vertrauen sich verbunden fühlte.

Saladin.

Gar sterbend! — Nicht auch faselnd schon? — Und wär's
Auch wahr! — Ja wohl: das Blut, das Blut allein
Macht lange noch den Vater nicht! macht kaum
Den Vater eines Tieres! giebt zum höchsten
3665 Das erste Recht, sich diesen Namen zu
Erwerben! Laß dir doch nicht bange sein! —
Und weißt du was? Sobald der Väter zwei
Sich um dich streiten, — laß sie beide, nimm
Den dritten! — Nimm dann mich zu deinem Vater!

Sittah.

3670 O thu's! o thu's!

Saladin.

Ich will ein guter Vater,
Recht guter Vater sein! — Doch halt! mir fällt
Noch viel was Beff'res bei. — Was brauchst du denn
Der Väter überhaupt? Wenn sie nun sterben?

Bei Zeiten sich nach einem umgesehn,
3675 Der mit uns um die Wette leben will!
Kennst du noch keinen? . . .

Sittah.

Mach sie nicht erröten!

Saladin.

Das hab' ich allerdings mir vorgesetzt.
Erröten macht die Häßlichen so schön,
Und sollte Schöne nicht noch schöner machen? —
3680 Ich habe deinen Vater Nathan und
Noch einen — einen noch hierher bestellt.
Errätst du ihn? — Hierher! Du wirst mir doch
Erlauben, Sittah?

Sittah.

Bruder!

Saladin.

Daß du ja
Vor ihm recht sehr erröteſt, liebes Mädchen!

Recha.

3685 Vor wem? erröten? . . .

Saladin.

Kleine Heuchlerin!
Nun, so erblasse lieber! — Wie du willst
Und kannst! —

(Eine Sklavin tritt herein und nahet sich Sittah.)

Sie sind doch etwa nicht schon da?

Sittah.

Gut! laß sie nur herein. — Sie sind es, Bruder!

Letzter Auftritt.

Nathan und der Tempelherr zu den Vorigen.

Saladin.

Ah, meine guten, lieben Freunde! — Dich,
3690 Dich, Nathan, muß ich nur vor allen Dingen
Bedeuten, daß du nun, sobald du willst,
Dein Geld kannst wieder holen lassen! . . .

Nathan.

Sultan! . . .

Saladin.

Nun steh' ich auch zu deinen Diensten . . .

Nathan.

Sultan! . . .

Saladin.

Die Karawan' ist da. Ich bin so reich
3695 Nun wieder, als ich lange nicht gewesen. —
Komm, sag mir, was du brauchst, so recht was Großes
Zu unternehmen! Denn auch ihr, auch ihr,
Ihr Handelsleute, könnt des baren Geldes
Zuviel nie haben!

Nathan.

Und warum zuerst
3700 Von dieser Kleinigkeit? — Ich sehe dort
Ein Aug' in Thränen, das zu trocknen mir
Weit angelegner ist. (Geht auf Recha zu.) Du hast geweint?
Was fehlt dir? — bist doch meine Tochter noch?

Recha.

Mein Vater! . . .

Nathan.

Wir verstehen uns. Genug! —
3705 Sei heiter! Sei gefaßt! Wenn sonst dein Herz
Nur dein noch ist! Wenn deinem Herzen sonst
Nur kein Verlust nicht droht! — Dein Vater ist
Dir unverloren!

Recha.

Keiner, keiner sonst!

Tempelherr.

Sonst keiner? — Nun! so hab ich mich betrogen.
3710 Was man nicht zu verlieren fürchtet, hat
Man zu besitzen nie geglaubt und nie
Gewünscht. — Recht wohl! recht wohl! — Das ändert,
Das ändert alles! — Saladin, wir kamen [Nathan,
Auf dein Geheiß. Allein, ich hatte dich
3715 Verleitet; jetzt bemüh dich nur nicht weiter!

Saladin.

Wie gach nun wieder, junger Mann! — Soll alles
Dir denn entgegen kommen? Alles dich
Erraten?

Tempelherr.

Nun, du hörst ja! siehst ja, Sultan!

Saladin.

Ei wahrlich! — Schlimm genug, daß deiner Sache
3720 Du nicht gewisser warst!

Tempelherr.

So bin ich's nun.

Saladin.

Wer so auf irgend eine Wohlthat trotzt,
Nimmt sie zurück. Was du gerettet, ist

Deswegen nicht dein Eigentum. Sonst wär'
Der Räuber, den sein Geiz ins Feuer jagt,
3725 So gut ein Held wie du!
(Auf Recha zugehend, um sie dem Tempelherrn zuzuführen.)
Komm, liebes Mädchen,
Komm! Nimm's mit ihm nicht so genau. Denn wär'
Er anders, wär' er minder warm und stolz,
Er hätt' es bleiben lassen, dich zu retten.
Du mußt ihm eins fürs andre rechnen. — Komm!
3730 Beschäm ihn! thu was ihm zu thun geziemte!
Bekenn ihm deine Liebe! trage dich ihm an!
Und wenn er dich verschmäht, dir's je vergißt,
Wie ungleich mehr in diesem Schritte du
Für ihn gethan, als er für dich ... Was hat
3735 Er denn für dich gethan? Ein wenig sich
Beräuchern lassen! — ist was Recht's! — so hat
Er meines Bruders, meines Assad, nichts!
So trägt er seine Larve, nicht sein Herz.
Komm, Liebe ...

Sittah.

Geh! geh, Liebe, geh! Es ist
3740 Für deine Dankbarkeit noch immer wenig,
Noch immer nichts.

Nathan.

Halt, Saladin! halt, Sittah!

Saladin.

Auch du?

Nathan.

Hier hat noch einer mit zu sprechen ...

Saladin.

Wer leugnet das? — Unstreitig, Nathan, kömmt
So einem Pflegevater eine Stimme

3745 Mit zu! Die erste, wenn du willst. — Du hörst,
Ich weiß der Sache ganze Lage.

Nathan.

Nicht so ganz! —
Ich rede nicht von mir. Es ist ein andrer,
Weit, weit ein andrer, den ich, Saladin,
Doch auch vorher zu hören bitte.

Saladin.

Wer?

Nathan.

3750 Ihr Bruder!

Saladin.

Rechas Bruder?

Nathan.

Ja!

Recha.

Mein Bruder?
So hab' ich einen Bruder?

Tempelherr
(aus seiner wilden, stummen Zerstreuung auffahrend).

Wo? wo ist
Er, dieser Bruder? Noch nicht hier? Ich sollt'
Ihn hier ja treffen.

Nathan.

Nur Geduld!

Tempelherr (äußerst bitter).

Er hat
Ihr einen Vater aufgebunden: — wird
3755 Er keinen Bruder für sie finden?

Saladin.

Das
Hat noch gefehlt! Christ! ein so niedriger

Verdacht wär' über Assads Lippen nicht
Gekommen. — Gut! fahr nur so fort!

Nathan.

Verzeih

Ihm! — Ich verzeih' ihm gern. — Wer weiß, was wir
3760 An seiner Stell', in seinem Alter dächten!

(Freundschaftlich auf ihn zugehend.)

Natürlich, Ritter! — Argwohn folgt auf Mißtrau'n! —
Wenn Ihr mich Eures wahren Namens gleich
Gewürdigt hättet . . .

Tempelherr.

Wie?

Nathan.

Ihr seid kein Stauffen!

Tempelherr.

Wer bin ich denn?

Nathan.

Heißt Curd von Stauffen nicht!

Tempelherr.

3765 Wie heiß ich denn?

Nathan.

Heißt Leu von Filnek.

Tempelherr.

Wie?

Nathan.

Ihr stutzt?

Tempelherr.

Mit Recht! Wer sagt das?

Nathan.

Ich, der mehr,

Noch mehr Euch sagen kann. Ich straf' indeß
Euch keiner Lüge.

Tempelherr.

Nicht?

Nathan.

Kann doch wohl sein,
Daß jener Nam' Euch ebenfalls gebührt.

Tempelherr.

3770 Das sollt' ich meinen! — (Das hieß Gott ihn sprechen!)

Nathan.

Denn Eure Mutter — die war eine Stauffin.
Ihr Bruder, Euer Ohm, der Euch erzogen,
Dem Eure Eltern Euch in Deutschland ließen,
Als, von dem rauhen Himmel dort vertrieben,
3775 Sie wieder hier zu Lande kamen: — der
Hieß Curd von Stauffen, mag an Kindesstatt
Vielleicht Euch angenommen haben! — Seid
Ihr lange schon mit ihm nun auch herüber
Gekommen? Und er lebt doch noch?

Tempelherr.

Was soll
3780 Ich sagen? — Nathan! — Allerdings! So ist's!
Er selbst ist tot. Ich kam erst mit der letzten
Verstärkung unsers Ordens. — Aber, aber —
Was hat mit diesem allem Rechas Bruder
Zu schaffen?

Nathan.

Euer Vater . . .

Tempelherr.

Wie? auch den
3785 Habt Ihr gekannt? Auch den?

Nathan.

Er war mein Freund.

Tempelherr.

War Euer Freund? Ist's möglich, Nathan! . . .

Nathan.

Nannte

Sich Wolf von Filnek, aber war kein Deutscher . . .

Tempelherr.

Ihr wißt auch das?

Nathan.

War einer Deutschen nur

Vermählt, war Eurer Mutter nur nach Deutschland

3790 Auf kurze Zeit gefolgt . . .

Tempelherr.

Nicht mehr! Ich bitt'

Euch! — Aber Rechas Bruder? Rechas Bruder . . .

Nathan.

Seid Ihr!

Tempelherr.

Ich? ich ihr Bruder?

Recha.

Er mein Bruder?

Sittah.

Geschwister!

Saladin.

Sie Geschwister!

Recha (will auf ihn zu).

Ah! mein Bruder

Tempelherr (tritt zurück).

Ihr Bruder!

Recha

(hält an und wendet sich zu Nathan).

Kann nicht sein! nicht sein! Sein Herz
3795 Weiß nichts davon! — Wir sind Betrieger! Gott!

Saladin (zum Tempelherrn).

Betrieger? — wie? Das denkst du? kannst du denken?
Betrieger selbst! Denn alles ist erlogen
An dir: Gesicht und Stimm' und Gang! Nichts dein!
So eine Schwester nicht erkennen wollen! Geh!

Tempelherr

(sich demütig ihm nahend).

3800 Mißdeut auch du nicht mein Erstaunen, Sultan!
Verkenn in einem Augenblick', in dem
Du schwerlich deinen Assad je gesehen,
Nicht ihn und mich!

(Auf Nathan zueilend.)

Ihr nehmt und gebt mir, Nathan!
Mit vollen Händen beides! — Nein! Ihr gebt
3805 Mir mehr, als Ihr mir nehmt! unendlich mehr!

(Recha um den Hals fallend.)

Ah meine Schwester! meine Schwester!

Nathan.

Blanda
Von Filnek!

Tempelherr.

Blanda? Blanda? — Recha nicht?
Nicht Eure Recha mehr? — Gott! Ihr verstoßt
Sie, gebt ihr ihren Christennamen wieder!
3810 Verstoßt sie meinetwegen! — Nathan! Nathan!
Warum es sie entgelten lassen? sie!

Nathan.

Und was? — O meine Kinder! meine Kinder! —
Denn meiner Tochter Bruder wär' mein Kind
Nicht auch, — sobald er will?

(Indem er sich ihren Umarmungen überläßt, tritt Saladin mit unruhigem Erstaunen zu seiner Schwester

Saladin.

Was sagst du, Schwester?

Sittah.

3815 Ich bin gerührt . . .

Saladin.

Und ich, — ich schaudere
Vor einer größern Rührung fast zurück!
Bereite dich nur drauf, so gut du kannst.

Sittah.

Wie?

Saladin.

Nathan, auf ein Wort! ein Wort!

(Indem Nathan zu ihm tritt, tritt Sittah zu dem Geschwister, ihm ihre Teilnahme zu bezeigen, und Nathan und Saladin sprechen leiser.)

Hör! hör doch, Nathan! Sagtest du vorhin
3820 Nicht —?

Nathan.

Was?

Saladin.

Aus Deutschland sei ihr Vater nicht
Gewesen, ein geborner Deutscher nicht.
Was war er denn? Wo war er sonst denn her?

Nathan.

Das hat er selbst mir nie vertrauen wollen.
Aus seinem Munde weiß ich nichts davon.

Saladin.

3825 Und war auch sonst kein Frank'? kein Abendländer?

Nathan.

O! daß er der nicht sei, gestand er wohl. —
Er sprach am liebsten persisch . . .

Saladin.

Persisch? Persisch?
Was will ich mehr? — Er ist's! Er war es!

Nathan.

Wer?

Saladin.

Mein Bruder! ganz gewiß! Mein Assad! ganz
3830 Gewiß!

Nathan.

Nun, wenn du selbst darauf verfällst: —
Nimm die Versichrung hier in diesem Buche!

(Ihm das Brevier überreichend.)

Saladin

(es begierig aufschlagend).

Ah! seine Hand! Auch die erkenn' ich wieder!

Nathan.

Noch wissen sie von nichts! Noch steht's bei dir
Allein, was sie davon erfahren sollen!

Saladin

(indeß er darin geblättert).

3835 Ich meines Bruders Kinder nicht erkennen?
Ich meine Neffen — meine Kinder nicht?

Sie nicht erkennen? ich? Sie dir wohl lassen?

(Wieder laut.)

Sie sind's! sie sind es, Sittah, sind! Sie sind's!
Sind beide meines . . . deines Bruders Kinder!

(Er rennt in ihre Umarmungen.)

Sittah (ihm folgend).

3840 Was hör' ich! — Konnt's auch anders, anders sein! —

Saladin (zum Tempelherrn).

Nun mußt du doch wohl, Trotzkopf, mußt mich lieben!

(Zu Recha.)

Nun bin ich doch, wozu ich mich erbot?
Magst wollen oder nicht!

Sittah.

Ich auch! ich auch!

Saladin

(zum Tempelherrn zurück).

Mein Sohn! mein Assad! meines Assads Sohn!

Tempelherr.

3845 Ich deines Bluts! — So waren jene Träume,
Womit man meine Kindheit wiegte, doch —
Doch mehr als Träume!

(Ihm zu Füßen fallend.)

Saladin (ihn aufhebend).

Seht den Bösewicht!
Er wußte was davon und konnte mich
Zu seinem Mörder machen wollen! Wart!

(Unter stummer Wiederholung allseitiger Umarmungen fällt der Vorhang.)

NOTES.

ACT FIRST.

TITLE.—**Nathan.** In Boccaccio the Jew's name is Melchisedec, reminding of that priest of Jehovah called the prototype of Christ (Heb. v. 6; Ps. cx. 4), though we see no special reason for the selection. Possibly the prophet Nathan (2 Sam. xii. 1–14), who made David see his wrong by a simple parable, had an influence upon Lessing's choice; possibly the Nathan in Boccaccio's story (10, 3; see Introduction, p. xxvi) suggested the name. However, it is a common Jewish name, is euphonious and suited the verse better than Melchisedec.

MOTTO.—**Introite, nam et heic Dii sunt** (Apud Gellium): *Enter, for here, too, are gods.* These words were put by Aristotle into the mouth of Heraclitus, the Ionian philosopher of Ephesus, when visited by some friends who were reluctant to enter into a stable where he was warming himself. They were interpolated, in this Latin form, by Phil. Beroaldus into the preface of Aulus Gellius to his *Noctes Atticae* and transmitted to recent times as a saying of Gellius. Lessing preferred the Latin form, probably as the best known.

ACT I. SCENE 1.

* **Scene: Flur in Nathans Hause. Flur** is *entrance-hall,*—frequently paved—from which one enters either directly into the rooms of a house, or into a corridor.

* **Daja.** In the first sketch this name is Dina, but Lessing's friend Ramler having suggested that *Daja* in Persian and Arabic meant nurse,

* Shows that the note is on a word occurring in the stage directions.

or foster-mother, he changed it to Daja. He also found the name Daja in an Arabic history of Saladin.

2. **Daß ihr doch endlich einmal wiederkommt,** *that at last you really return once more.* The accumulation of particles (doch endlich einmal) well express Daja's anxiety and intense desire for Nathan's return. —**Ihr.** The use of the vocative throughout the play conforms in general to the usage of the Mid. H. G. period. Ihr is very respectful, and, through English and French influence, is very popular on the stage, while Sie (pl.) is scarcely admitted in serious and elevated poetry (except in the drama and the novel). Ihr is used in addressing superiors (as Daja and Al-Hafi to Nathan, Daja to the Templar, etc.). It is also used by children to parents as a mark of respect (as Recha to Nathan); and in polite address.

5. **Babylon.** After the destruction of its defenses by Darius Hystaspes, and later, by Xerxes, Babylon never rose again and had at this epoch no special significance.

7. **Seitab.** Here this word evidently means Seitenwege, Abwege machen, vom graden Wege abgehen, and the preposition ab does not have its usual force, as in bergab, stromab, etc., but denotes direction towards the side and from the main road. For Nathan is not travelling on a side-way, by-way, but is obliged to make constant deviations from the direct course, either on account of the unsettled times (third Crusade, 1192–3), or for business purposes, as lines 9–10 would indicate.

8. **Gut zwei hundert Meilen.** The German mile equals about four and three-fourths English miles. The distance from Babylon to Jerusalem is about 140 German or 700 English miles.

10. **Födert** for fördert. Possibly a mistake, for this form does not again occur in the play, though the true form does (l. 2486); or else Lessing is not consistent. It is a dialectic form preferred in the 18th century by many because they considered it more euphonious.

11. **Von der Hand schlagen** = rasch abmachen, *to do quickly, to cause no trouble.* Cf. von der Hand gehen, and Lessing in a letter to Ramler, von der Hand wegschlagen.

12–13. These words of Daja explain her former „Gott sei Dank," etc. For the fire had made Nathan's absence doubly painful. The form indeß is now generally written indes.

Das brannte, that (the house), and nothing else, burned; **das** is emphatic; for it indicates that Nathan had heard of the burning of his house, but was not aware that anybody's life had been endangered by the fire.

18. **Schon wahr!** *Quite true, but* (das ist schon wahr, aber). The schon is here concessive as in wenn schon, obschon.

27. **Würdet Ihr von mir es hören?** Daja implies that she would either have burned with Recha or never have awaited his return.

42. Babylon was noted for its silks and woollens and Damascus for its jewelry.

53. **Und schweig.** The more natural interpretation of these words seems to be that Nathan wishes Daja to take his gifts as he gives them, without many words, though she understands them in another sense. This interpretation would be more in accordance with Nathan's generous nature. However, we feel that his real danger lies in Daja's pricking conscience, and there may be the ulterior meaning of bribery to this conscience.

54–55. **Wer zweifelt, Nathan, das ihr nicht,** etc. The negation here violates the grammar, and is in imitation of the Latin *quis dubitat, quin,* and the Romance Languages, especially the French. But such Gallicisms are found in the best writers.

61. **Komm' über Euch!** cf. Matt. xxvii, 25: Sein Blut komme über uns und unsre Kinder. Daja knows her Bible well and likes to quote it. Or is it Lessing that knows his Bible so well and likes to put it in Daja's mouth? For at the time of the Crusades the Bible was laid on the shelf and no one knew anything about it, not even the priests. Only a select few may have had some knowledge of it.

63. **Wenn du mich hintergehst!** Recha's non-appearance causes Nathan to doubt whether he has heard the whole truth or not.

65–67. In her feverish excitement her mind continually dwells on fire. **sie** (was sie malet) refers to Phantasie. She passes from the sleeping to the waking state indifferently, and not at stated intervals as with one in the normal condition of life; while awake her mind is feverish, turbid, visionary, and while asleep she dreams.

68–69. **Bald weniger als Tier, bald mehr als Engel.** Recha still has a vague dread that she may be burned alive, and in consequence of her excitement her sleep is only broken, so that in the day she feels weary. Having no knowledge of psychological truths, Daja describes her visionary condition at night as superhuman, nay, superior to that of an angel, and her exhaustion by day as weaker than that of an animal, which, at least, has the full use of its senses. It is well-known that the words of those in such a state can be very apt and even betray what seems to be superhuman knowledge.

70. Cf. Ps. viii. 4 and Job vii. 17. Nathan is reminded of the weakness of the flesh.

71 ff. Here we have one of those wonderful mental visions so often observed in such cases. Buchheim calls it "Expectant Attention" and credits Lessing with "having given the first *psychological* explanation — in 1779, at a time when mesmerism was in vogue — of the manifestations of animal magnetism." This particular phase of these phenomena is usually called clairvoyance (or second sight), and the *expectant state* is a necessary part of the explanation.

74. **Indem** = indessen, während dessen.

75. **Brach sich ihr Auge wieder,** *Her eye grew dim again.*

76. **Dem seines Armes Stütze sich entzog.** Sein refers to Haupt, for the arm is considered the natural support of the head, and not to the Templar as some would interpret it. For in that case Recha would have to be talking in her dreams and supposing that her head rested on the Templar's arm; but she believed the Templar an angel and not a human being (see Düntzer on this passage).

77. **Stürzt'** = fiel, sank. In her vivid description Daja uses strong expressions.

79. **Was Wunder.** In Mid. H. G. the genitive after wer and was was the usual construction, but this construction has now passed into simple apposition, though it still remains in phrases like was des Teufels, was Henkers, was ist Weißes dort am grünen Walde, etc.

90. **Seinen unvermuteten Gewinst** = sein unvermutet ihm geschenktes Leben. The figure is taken from gambling where the winner is ever ready to risk the stakes he has unexpectedly won.

91. **Frisch,** *boldly.* **War** = wäre . . . gewesen. When a negative reality is to be represented, then the preterite indicative is (often) used instead of the subjunctive, as „Jene hat gelebt (that is, lebt nicht mehr), wenn ich dies Blatt aus meinen Händen gebe."

94. **vors erste** = fürs erste. Formerly vor and für were interchangeable.

98. **Des Hauses.** The insertion of the genitive between the governing noun and its modifying adjective is a very bold imitation of the classic construction, but found in the German of the 15th century in translations from the Latin.

Kundschaft = Kunde, Kenntnis, Bekanntschaft. This is an earlier meaning of the word, now obsolete. The more general construction would be with von rather than with the genitive.

100. **Mit vorgespreiztem Mantel** = mit nach vorn ausgebreitetem Mantel. The cloak was held out before him and drawn together so as to shield him from the fire.

104. **Mit eins** (eines, old acc.; cf. auf eins, in eins, both from Lessing) = mit einmal or einem Male = plötzlich.

105. **Empor sie tragend** = emporhaltend, trug er sie.

110. **Untern** = unter den. This contraction of the article and preposition is very rare.

111. **Des Auferstandenen Grab.** Even at that period there was a church of the Holy Sepulchre which was said to contain a monument enclosing the grave of the Lord. The real grave in this church was a sarcophagus of bluish white marble, they say. The very site of the church is unknown.

113. **Entbot.** The real meaning of entbieten is durch einen Boten sagen lassen. But Daja is the messenger, not the one sending the message, hence Lessing must have transferred its meaning from the sender to the messenger. Erhob in the same line seems also to be used in a peculiar sense, for it means 'to raise,' 'to exalt,' 'to praise.' We may translate, *I thanked, implored (praised), urged, conjured.*

120. **Jemand antreten** = nahe Jemand treten = mit einer Bitte oder überhaupt mit einer Forderung nahe zu Jemand treten. Antreten is more forcible here than angehen would be. Cf. l. 517.

125. **Unsers Auferstandenen.** In the first sketch Lessing wrote seines, etc. Cf. l. 1550. Daja intentionally includes herself in the blessing of a risen Lord and also gently hints to Nathan that Recha belongs to the same faith.

133. **Sich zanken,** a more forcible, but a less elegant expression than sich streiten. The high esteem we have comes from the judgment (Kopf), our inclination (angezogen werden) from the heart. Nothing hurts more than contempt for our judgment, hence we easily hate the

one despising our high esteem and possibly transfer this to all mankind. But Recha's feelings are stronger than her reason, and this cool, indifferent treatment would naturally depress her and lead to melancholy (Schwermut). Notice the figure of chiasmus, as Menschenhaß refers to Kopf and Schwermut to Herz. For the better definition of **Schwärmer** (visionary, enthusiast, dreamer) see "Education of the Human Race," § 90, in Lessing's Complete Works (Lachmann's ed.), X, 325, and XI (2), 67 ff. In the normal condition reason and feeling are in accord; in the visionary state they exchange places; the head feels, the heart reflects. The distorted fancies of the brain become inspirations of the feelings and the excitement of the feelings reflections of reason. Hence Nathan says: Das letztere ist Rechas Fall: sie schwärmt. She had lost the equilibrium between reason and feelings.

141. **Geschwärmt.** The special idiomatic use of the past participle after heißen, sein, nennen is well-known. Cf. Das heißt schlecht geworfen, unter ehrlichen Leuten nennt man das gelogen, Frisch gewagt ist halb gewonnen, and our example: Ist doch auch geschwärmt (*is indeed also visionary dreaming*).

142. **Eine — Grille.** The dash indicates that Daja suddenly realizes that Nathan will only mock her superstitions and substitutes Grille (whim, caprice) for Glauben (belief, faith). Therefore she cleverly conceals from him (cf. 1577) that she had made Recha believe that an angel had saved her, thus condemning her own work in the one word Grille.

144 **Keines irdischen** (Vaters Sohn) is pleonastic, though quite oriental and not foreign to Greek and Latin. It is the Saxon genitive.

148. After verhüllt supply gewesen sei, and after geschwebt in the next line habe. Such omissions are common in German.

For mit eins cf. l. 104.

152. The belief of the active interference of angels in bodily form in the affairs of men was common to Christians, Jews and Mussulmans at that period.

156–177. **Den Wilden** = den ungesitteten, for he had rudely refused thanks. **Launigen** = launischen, *splenetic, moody.*

158. The fine irony of the passage as seen in the words hiernieden and wallen is exquisite. Wallen is used of those on a pilgrimage and Waller means a pilgrim. The thrust is directed against the too common sanctimoniousness of the age.

159. **Ungesittet Ritterschaft zu treiben.** Ritterschaft = **ritterliches Thun.** His deed was chivalrous, but his conduct since the deed has been rude.

163–4. Compare Lessing also in Minna von Barnhelm, Act Fifth, Scene Ninth: „Minna wäre sonst ein Engel, den ich mit Schaudern verehren müßte, den ich nicht lieben könnte." Lessing also wrote the following epigram in the album of one who believed that he had a friend without a blemish and that his beloved was an angel: —

„Trau keinem Freunde sonder Mängel,
Und lieb ein Mädchen, keinen Engel."

167. **Schlimm** = schlau, *bad* or *wicked*, in a playful sense. Nathan ridicules the idea of an angel having come to rescue Recha.

ACT I. SCENE 2.

169–70. In lines 72–4, Recha in her visionary state hears her father's voice, but his long delay in coming to her makes her believe that his voice had only preceded him, hence her joyous surprise on seeing him bodily before her eyes.

177. **Garstig,** in the sense of abscheulich. It refers to the implied Abscheu or Schauder which Recha feels at the thought of such a death. The tremor of fright caused by the thought is indicated by the "O." According to the stage direction in the first sketch she rushes into her fathers' arms at the words „mein Kind, mein liebes Kind."

189. **Die ungetreuen Ström'.** Cf. Schiller's auf ungetreuen Wellen in the ring of Polycrates. The Romans frequently called the sea *perfidus*, *treacherous* (*perfida freta*), and the idea is as old as poetry and the knowledge of the sea.

193. **Vorgespreizter Mantel.** Cf. line 100 and the note. The Templars wore white (weiße) linen mantles.

195. **Durchs Feuer trüg', von seinem Fittiche verweht.** A rather bold construction in German, as verweht must modify Feuer ([the fire] *blown* away by his wing) the object of a preposition, rather than Recha (mich), to which some refer it.

198–9. The fond father is speaking here when he makes his daughter equal to an angel. Perhaps there is just a touch of self-adulation in these words, which imply that the father of such a daughter must also have angelic qualities. Recha hints as much in her reply.

200. **Wem schmeichelt ihr?** etc. This reading was suggested by Ramler, though no one knows just what the original reading was. Düntzer suggests „mir, mein Vater?" instead of „wem? dem Engel?" Some have interpreted the words as indicating that Recha considered herself the image of her father, but this does not seem a logical deduction. For, however much a personal resemblance might flatter his vanity, it would not make him prouder of her or more inclined to compare her with an angel. The passage is difficult to understand exactly, but seems to mean: "Are you complimenting the angel on his remarkable insight, or yourself for being the father of such a daughter?" Of course the words are playful.

203. **Gewähren** = hervorbringen, *produce;* or perhaps its usual meaning of *offer*, *present*, suffices for a fair rendering of the thought, though it could not 'offer' without 'producing.'

212. **Von aller Ewigkeit.** This Biblical phrase adds force and beauty to the idea expressed.

220. **Ohn' dieses** is a violent apocope.

225. **Hirn** = Gehirn. According to Lessing, Hirn is more sonorous and forceful and perhaps for that reason better adapted to poetry, though Gehirn is possibly not less frequent in poetry. Here it may be a mere question of meter. The brain is likened to a stringed instrument whose strings snap when over-strained.

226. **Subtilitäten.** Rather learned for Daja, but probably she had heard Nathan himself use it in some of his philosophical talks.

227. **Zersprengen** = zersprengen machen; for it is used in a causative sense.

228. **Wunders nicht genug.** In the earlier history of the language the use of the partitive genitive was more frequent than now. But it is still used with genug and in expressions like **Wer und was Anders**, Jemand, Niemand Anders, viel, wenig, mehr Gutes, etc.

232. **Eines Tempelherrn verschont.** The genitive is the older construction with schonen and its compound verschonen and is often used now. Historical facts do not confirm this statement (cf. also line 88), as Saladin frequently spared Templars and other warriors.

232–236. The true Templars preferred death at the hands of

Saladin, the greatest enemy of Christianity, to pardon, and therefore never asked to be spared. The statement in lines 235–6 rests upon a historical fact related in Marin, Histoire de Saladin, I, 249 f. In a battle Odo de St. Amaud had been taken prisoner; the Sultan offered him his liberty in exchange for one of his Emirs who was a prisoner of the Templars. His reply was that a Templar ought either to conquer or die, and could only give his sword and belt as ransom.

235. Ledern = ledernen. When the adjective already ends in **n** Lessing frequently omits the ending -en. Cf. lines 294, **silbern** = silbernen; 897, 3528, albern = albernen.

237. Das schließt für mich = das spricht für mich, beweist für mich. The commentators claim that schließen has this meaning only here and in one or two other places. Cf. Sanders, Wörterb. 3, 958, 2 col. Then Recha considers Nathan's remark an argument in her favor; but by giving the expression a slightly different shade of meaning it would refer to Recha's inner conviction that she had seen an angel face to face and needs no further argument to convince her. However, it may only mean "that argues for me."

251. Viele zwanzig Jahre her. In Silesia and Lusatia viel joined with zwanzig denotes an indefinite number: Viel zwanzig kommen den Tag zum Herrn und wollen ihn sprechen. Cf. also einige zwanzig where und after einige is omitted. As Lessing was from Lusatia this idiom was familiar to him.

252. In line 2649 we learn that the name was Assad.

253. Line 2986 informs us that he fell at Ascalon.

258. Unglaublichers. That is, the angel theory. For the syncopated form cf. lines 458, abgeschmackters; 783, bessers; 1664, Wichtigers, and in Goethe, liebers, abgeschmackters, gräulichers. Lessing also has geringres, schönres, where the first e is syncopated.

260. Sein Geschwister. Das Geschwister is here used in the collective sense, and therefore properly stands in the singular. Marin (l. c. I, 111, 112) tells us that Saladin was very fond of his family.

266. Seit wenn? Modern usage requires seit wann. Originally wann and wenn, dann and denn were not different and even now are interchangeable in colloquial language. About the middle of the 18th century the two terms were differentiated in the written language. In Mid. H. G. and in the older Mod. H. G. wenn was preferred.

268–9. Nathan had urged a natural miracle for Recha's rescue; that is, the pardon of the Templar who rescued her, all in the natural order of things; Daja required an unnatural miracle; that is, an angel. Either case required equally strong belief; hence Nathan's pleasant raillery.

272–5. Certainly an elevated Christian idea that the counsels and plots of kings serve God's purposes. He makes them his sport and scorn by destroying them. Cf. Ps. ii. 2–5. **Sein Spiel** will be best considered as the accusative in apposition with **Entschlüsse** and **Entwürfe** and the clause wenn nicht sein Spott = wenn (sie) nicht sein Spott (sind), (indem er sie vernichtet).

275–6. The repetition of **mein Vater** is emphatic; for Lessing would hardly be guilty of repetition to fill out the verse as some critics pretend. Any good actor would manage the phrases without difficulty.

283. **Bug** = Biegung.

284. **Wilden,** *barbarous.* "Jews and Mussulmans were then the only learned men," says Lessing in one of his fragments, and the East was then in a higher state of civilization than the West. And yet the adjective may refer especially to the Templar, who was rude and impetuous in his nature.

286. **Wündersücht'ges Volk.** A colloquial expression used in good-natured irony (*wonder-loving people*).

293 ff. This parable sounds oriental, but Düntzer is probably right in ascribing its invention to Lessing.

299–300. The meaning is not quite clear. If we believe we can be nearer God by merely "feeling ourselves so much nearer," then we abase the true conception of God, and detract from his majesty by our boasting; otherwise, as Nathan says, Daja's words are "nonsense."

310. Since the fifth century angel-worship has been quite common in the Church, and many angels have special days set apart for their worship, as the archangels Gabriel and Michael, and the patron angels. These remarks are intended more especially for Daja the Catholic than for Recha, as the Jews did not have any days set apart for angel-worship.

311–312. **Mich Deucht.** The older conjugation of dünken was: dünken, däuchte (rarely dauchte), gedäucht (rarely gedaucht). Now the verb is regular (dünken, dünkte, gedünkt). From däuchte were then formed the presents däuchten and däuchen. Deucht is only another spelling. The earlier language preferred the accusative with this verb, and it is now the best accredited, though the dative is more common.

320. Cf. line 94 ff., where Nathan expresses the same thought.

323. **Vergnügsam,** now generally genügsam, denotes that state or condition of inner contentment which is satisfied with little. Daja of course means that the Templar has no physical wants.

325. **Untern Palmen.** Cf. line 119.

329. **Schad't,** unusual and harsh contraction; cf. hätt'st, line 354 below, and läd't for ladet. Goethe also uses find't, bild't, etc.

334. **Franke.** Even now Orientals generally call those from the western nations Franks because the first crusaders were mostly Franks, that is, Frenchmen.

335–6. The rules of St. Benedict and of Bernard of Clairvaux were very strict, requiring hard labor and privations; those of the Templars were modelled after them. Hunger and watching belong to the duties of a soldier.

339. **Ah.** Strictly speaking this should be ach, which is generally, though not always, used to express pain, while ah expresses joyful surprise and wonder. But Lessing frequently exchanged them and they are now often exchanged.

340. **Zusprach',** now Zuspruch.

343. "Even Goeze, Lessing's opponent, said in a sermon on love towards those of other religions that we must also love enemies and unbelievers and help them where we can: ‚Genug, es ist ein Mensch, und daher unser Nächster.' " The Templar only needed to know that a human life was at stake to rush to its rescue.

346. **Ihm** refers back to „was," which is here regarded as a person. Cf. „Was sich neckt, das liebt sich"; „Was sich noch jüngst in blut'gem Haß getrennt, das theilt entzückt die allgemeine Lust."

355. He had only wished to cure the Engelschwärmerin, and now comforts her about the Templar.

358. Comforting words to Recha, but not containing an absolute truth; for God does not always reward the good done here in this life. The comfort to Recha lies in the words: **Gewiß, nicht tot!**

360–1. Because Schwärmerei is merely a quiescent state of fancy and feeling, while action requires an effort of the will. One is indolent self-indulgence and the other is true manhood active in good works. **Andächtig Schwärmen,** *indulging in devout contemplation,* as the Quietists.

364. **Dürfen** is here used in its obsolescent signification of nötig haben, brauchen; *in order that he may not need to act well.*

372. **Al-Hafi,** *the barefooted.* See Introduction, p. xxxvi. In this character we may observe Lessing's skillful use of humor, though elevated above the merely comical; for Al-Hafi represents the humorous element in human nature.

374. **Kömmt.** According to Kehrein kömmt is Netherlandish, while kommt is high German. Lessing is very fond of kömmt.

375. **Hinein mit euch** appears a rather brusk expression in the mouth of Nathan. But he has already asked them twice (lines 359 and 367) to withdraw, and this cannot appear harsh, as it was said to hurry them away before the stranger arrived and saw them, a thing not permitted in the East (cf. Düntzer, p. 84, and Niemeyer, p. 99). Some think Nathan had kept Recha secluded, so that no one should find out his secret. Of course Nathan did not easily recognize the Dervish in his fine dress as treasurer.

ACT I. SCENE 3.

376. **Reißt nur die Augen auf,** colloquialism among the lower classes. The cynical Al-Hafi constantly uses such expressions while Nathan speaks in pleasant raillery with him.

381. **So der rechte Derwisch.** So is here used to qualify and restrict the words it introduces and means „ich meine"; „das heißt," *that is, the genuine Dervish.*

385. **Kein Mensch muß müssen.** This celebrated saying evidently means that no one should allow outward force to make him do anything against his inner convictions of what is right and wrong. Nathan refers to this outer force, while the Dervish refers to the inner conviction.

Und ein Derwisch müßte? The battle-cry of the Dervishes was freedom, hence Nathan's surprise that a Dervish must needs do anything.

386–7. **Warum . . . erkennt.** The warum of the first clause implies the omitted was (was er für gut erkennt) of the second and the das of the following clause is the antecedent of both. warum here = um was and is used for the more correct worum.

388. **Bei unserm Gott!** According to the general trend of the drama this can mean nothing else than that Nathan considers God common to all mankind in spite of the differences of their religious beliefs, thus denying a separate God for Jew and Mussulman.

389. **Mensch** is here used in its pregnant sense of a truly noble person. Cf. 1491–2.

390. **Und (ihr) fragt,** etc. The omission of the pronoun in German is rare, but the poet often takes that liberty either to imitate colloquial speech, as here, or in elevated lyric style. Cf. Goethe: Habe nun, ach Philosophie, etc., studirt, etc.; Füllest wieder Busch und Thal Still mit Nebelglanz. Cf. also Grimm IV, 214.

392. **Kerl** denotes one of great physical and even mental strength, but unpolished. As Dervish Al-Hafi was one of nature's sons and as free as the air he breathed, but cynical; this expression belongs to the cynical part of his character.

Des, now dessen, incorrectly often written deß; it is the older form found in Mid. and O. H. G.

396. **Will sein;** will is here used in the sense of *claims; which also claims respect.*

398. **Koch.** Said half seriously and half in earnest. For Nathan has but little faith in the practical ability of the Dervish, and therefore mentions that office as a proper one for his friend, which he might be able to fill with honor and to the satisfaction of his master. But the Dervish thinks he might add steward (line 400) also, as that with Nathan would not be too much.

402. **Worden.** In the Mid. H. G. the participle ge– was not so rigorously required in the formation of the past participle as at present. Luther, Herder, Goethe, Schiller and others, omit it with worden.

403–4. **Des kleinern Schatzes — des größern.** It is said that when Saladin first acquired the office of vizier of Egypt he wished to abdicate in favor of his father Ayoub, so great was his tenderness for him, but the latter refused this dignity and took charge of the finances. The greater treasury was the state treasury, which, according to Lessing's drama, was in charge of Saladin's father; but this is an anachronism, for his father was dead at this time. The lesser treasury was that of Saladin's own household, now in the hands of the Dervish.

406. **Ist von seinem Hause** = gehört zu seinem Hause. The construction is French, *est de sa maison*, and not German.

408. **Mit Strumpf und Stiel vertilgen,** now mit Stumpf und Stiel vertilgen. Notice the alliteration and compare über Stock und Stein, mit Haut und Haar, mit Mann und Maus, Kind und Kegel.

411. **Trotz einem,** *as well as;* er Läuft trotz einem Pferde, *he runs as fast as any horse.*

415–417. Experience teaches that poverty cannot be removed by the greatest generosity, nor should we refuse on that account to listen to the calls of distress. The metaphor begun by the Dervish and finished by Nathan is extremely felicitous.

418–421. Lessing remarks in the first sketch of his drama that the Arabs ascribe this maxim to Aristotle. It would not do for princes to rob their subjects, for the greed of princes would impoverish their people and either drive them to vices of all kinds or to a revolution. That would be bad enough, but it would be ten times worse if the people should plunder the treasury of the princes, for then they (the princes) would have to plunder the rich to satisfy the poor. Nathan cannot assent to this last alternative, as his compassion for the poor is too great.

422. **Ihr habt gut reden** = man mag immerhin reden, es ist umsonst zu reden, in imitation of the French *avoir beau dire, it is in vain to talk.* The Dervish thinks that Nathan would talk differently if he had his experience.

Kommt an. In the Imperative: komm an! employed as a challenge to the waiting opponent to come on; moreover as challenge in general = wohlan, *well, good, done.* Sanders' Wörterb. I, 975. Here it is used in the sense of Acht gegeben. There is a controversy between them about the maxim, and the Dervish calls Nathan's attention to the proof of the justice of his remark.

425. **Wuchern,** here = Zinsen einbringen, and does not have its usual meaning of usury.

432. **Scheidebrief** = 'bill of divorce,' but here in the sense of *farewell* (to our friendship).

435. Al-Hafi could not conduct the finances of Saladin honorably with an empty treasury.

437. **Ihr schüttelt.** Supply den Kopf, an unusual omission.

439–40. Viehoff paraphrases thus: „Al-Hafi Derwisch ist willkommen, an Allem Theil zu nehmen, was ich in meinem Vermögen habe."

441. **Defterdar,** here *treasurer.* It really means Minister of Finance.

444–5. Al-Hafi already contemplated leaving a position so distasteful to him because it brought him too much in contact with the world. Son of Nature as he is he loves the hot sands of the Ganges whence he came; or, perhaps, of the desert, as we may judge from line 497.

450. **Leicht,** that is, freed from his duties as treasurer.

Barfuß. Walking barefooted in the hot sands was a mortification for sins.

451. **Mit meinen Lehrern.** Nodnagel says: "The teachers of Hafi on the Ganges are Brachmins, from the farthest antiquity in possession of the treasures of wisdom, much of which has passed to occidental lore and poetry; they live in voluntary poverty, now as teachers, now as hermits." He belongs to the Parsees or Ghebres, who believe in the Zoroastrian-Brachminical idea of the purification of the soul by means of physical mortifications of the body. They of course despised worldly possessions.

456. **Im Hui,** *in a trice.* Colloquially hui is used as a substantive.

Den reichsten Bettler in einen armen Reichen. This is one of Lessing's favorite antitheses. The contented poor man is richer than the discontented, avaricious, greedy rich man. Düntzer reminds us that Lessing found this thought in a Latin collection of riddles by Hollonius and Setzer (1615).

471. **Unmild mild,** *illiberally liberal.* This figure of speech (oxymoron), the joining of two contradictory ideas, produces a very pleasant epigrammatical effect. Cf. concordia discors, insapiens sapientia, etc. Mild is probably used here in the Mid. H. G. sense of *liberal, generous.*

473 ff. Lessing's fertility in metaphors and similes in this whole scene is remarkable. Already we have had the changing ebb and flood tide, the engulfing canals, the open sluices, and now appears the

stopped pipes sending forth unclean (unrein) and spurting (sprudelnd) the waters they have received clear and calm. The unrein and sprudelnd are perhaps best explained by the unhold and ungestüm above.

477–8. This of course refers to birdsnaring, where the fowlers imitate the calls which decoy the birds into the snare. The Gimpel (bullfinch, redfinch, here blockhead) is so easily snared that the word has become proverbial for simpleton.

478. **Geck,** etc., *self-complaisant fool that I am*, for he says above that he had felt flattered.

481. **Bei hundert tausenden** = in Abtheilungen von hunderttausenden; cf. the English, *by hundreds.* It is not the equivalent here of bei in such expressions as bei fünfzig Tausend = gegen fünfzig Tausend, *about 50,000*, but rather *by hundred thousands.* This is not a true picture of the great ruler — who was celebrated for his clemency, justice, moderation and liberality, and never was known to exact unjust tribute. He often restored what was lawfully his own and gave the rest to his officers, leaving so little property that his funeral expenses had to be raised by contribution among his friends. Therefore Düntzer's interpretation of bei Hunderttausenden = da es hundert tausende gibt, may be right. The idea would then be that, seeing that hundreds of thousands are oppressing, etc., it is folly to wish to appear a philanthropist to individuals. But perhaps the state of passion to which the Dervish had wrought himself will account for his exaggerated statements.

483. **An einzeln.** Either a dative plural from the older form einzel (Mid. H. G. and later), or to be explained as line 235 above. Cf. Matt. v, 45, for the following lines, and remember the fact that Saladin gave to friend and foe, to the needy of all creeds, with unstinted generosity.

496. **Mache.** *Pray, do hasten off into*, etc. Machen here has its colloquial meaning. For the next sentence compare E. von Kleist's saying: Ein wahrer Mensch muß fern von Menschem sein. This is the true character of the Dervish, and the world would only rob him of his real humanity by its disagreeable frictions which he does not understand how to turn to his best interests.

ACT I. SCENE 4.

519. **Weiter ab sich schlägt** = den Weg verläßt. Cf. den Weg einschlagen, *turns aside.*

524. **Absein = Abwesenheit.** Formerly Absein was more frequently employed than now, found in Opitz, Flemming and Hagedorn. Cf. the form Dasein. Notice the noble motive that Nathan gives for the Templar's action and the unpleasant contrast with the real reason given in line 528: er kömmt zu keinem Juden. Nathan is broad and the Templar is narrow and rude.

528. **Euch.** The ethical dative used in an indeterminate way to express the interest of the speaker or hearer.

ACT I. SCENE 5.

Scene: Tempelherr. The order of the Knights Templars was founded about 1118 by some French knights, who "bound themselves by a vow to the Patriarch of Jerusalem to guard the public roads, to live as regular canons, and to fight for the King of Heaven in chastity, obedience, and self-denial." "The Templars almost from their foundation had their quarters in the palace of the Latin kings, which had been the mosque of Mount Moriah. This place was also known as Solomon's Temple," hence the name Templars. It was "a military order from its very origin, inasmuch as its earliest members banded themselves together for the express purpose of giving armed protection to the numerous pilgrims, who, after the first crusade, flocked to Jerusalem and the other sacred sites in the Holy Land."

The palms were near the cloister (cf. Act 3, scene 18, line 2111) from which the Templar has just come, and the friar follows him at a distance.

Adolf Stahr thinks that Lessing saw originals for his friar during his journey in Italy with prince Leopold of Brunswick.

532. **Vor langer Weile** = aus Langweile. He is not following me merely to kill time, merely because he has nothing better to do.

533. **Guter Bruder,** that is, lay brother of a mendicant order; one who has received ordination is called father. Hence the Templar's question: Ich kann euch wohl Vater nennen, nicht? Similarly Götz

von Berlichingen in Goethe's drama (1, 2) greets brother Martin as *worthy father*. And the answers are also similar. The lay brother had to take oath to obedience, celibacy and submission to the cloister; his duties were usually outside the cloister. They often showed true humility and were ready for the most menial services.

536. **Wer . . . was hätte** = Wenn jemand nur selbst was hätte. In O. H. G. wer and was were used as indefinite pronouns, but at present this use is retained only in colloquial language. They are then equivalent to jemand and etwas.

544. **Ein kleines Pilgermahl**, etc. It was considered a part of the duty of the cloisters to keep open house, and many were celebrated for their hospitality.

546. **Herr.** In the 17th century Herr and Frau began to be used in the case of address; Herr is still thus employed. Chamisso is very fond of it and Lessing uses it in this play.

550–551. In Baumgarten's Universal History, IV, 81, we learn that there was danger of blood-heating and ulceration, if foreigners partook of dates, but this statement lacks confirmation.

552. Compare line 1633: Und wart mit Euerm Kummer geiziger Als Euerm Leben? The cause of his melancholy lay chiefly in his lack of everything as captive, though apparently free, in his enforced inactivity, and the latent love for the Jewish maiden (provided that had already made itself felt) whom he had saved from the fire.

555. **Erkunden**, now erkundigen. Cf. also line 2746, erkundete.

Einem auf den Zahn fühlen, "to sound one, to feel one's pulse"; a colloquial expression taken from the dentist who examines the teeth to find the defective ones.

561. That is, true obedience is blind. It wills what another wills, while the seeker for fine distinctions (der klügelt) first tests the right and wrong and then acts upon his own judgment, which, according to the friar, is not true obedience, but independent action. This shows the different principle governing the two characters: the Templar makes nice distinctions (klügelt), the friar obeys without examination of causes, but in such a way that no harm ever comes from it.

The conjunction daß sometimes introduces sentences expressing a wish, a threat, etc., leaving the wish, threat, etc., to be supplied from the verb of the subordinate clause: **Daß du mir nur Wort hältst (Ich** rathe dir, daß, etc.); Daß doch die Einfalt immer recht behält! (Wie wahr ist es, daß doch, etc.). Simplicity is instinctively true where too much philosophizing goes astray. Cf. Schiller's **Worte des Glaubens:**

> Und was kein Verstand der Verständigen sieht,
> Das übet in Einfalt ein kindlich Gemüth.

570. **Das rote Kreuz.** The Templars (Knights Templars) were probably the most renowned of the three great military orders founded in the 12th century, the Hospitallers (Knights of St. John of Jerusalem later Knights of Malta), the Teutonic Knights and the Knights Templars. "The three orders were distinguished from each other by their garb. The Hospitallers wore black mantles with white crosses, the Templars white mantles with red crosses, the Teutonic Knights, white mantles with a black cross. The white color of the Templars signified their own innocence and their mildness for Christians, while the red denoted the bloody martyr-death and the enmity to unbelievers."

573. **Tebnin,** a strong fortress north of Ptolemaïs, near Tyre, on the road to Sidon. It is situated in the mountains between Paneas and Sarepta or Sarphenda. During Saladin's campaign against the Christians in 1187, Ptolemaïs and many other places along the coast were captured by his Emirs, Tebnin among the number. Sidon surrendered to Saladin himself. Tyre was not captured until after a siege of three years. There is no historical account of the breaking of a truce by an attack of the Templars on Tebnin, but they did it elsewhere. Lusignan, king of Jerusalem, broke his oath not to fight against Saladin about this time and had quite a number of skirmishes around Tebnin, but it all seems to have been legitimate warfare.

576. Sidon lies on the Mediterranean Sea; in earlier times it was one of the capitals of Phœnicia and was one of the many Christian cities taken in Saladin's celebrated campaign (cf. above). Now it is a wretched town of no account.

577. **Selbstzwanzigster** = ich mit neunzehn andern Tempelherren, so daß ich selbst der zwanzigste war. To denote the number of persons in one's company, instead of using the full cardinal number, the pronoun selbst is placed before the ordinal. Hence the now nearly obsolete compounds selbander (er selbst der andere [der zweite]), selbdritte (er selbst der dritte), etc. Cf. also the Greek. The cardinal is not common in

this construction, but Lessing has selb fünziger (Emilia Galotti, III, 1).

578. **Vom Saladin.** But compare line 585, where the article is omitted. It may be used or omitted before a well-known proper name.

583. **Er ganz allein.** The friar is humble throughout and uses Der Herr or the polite ihr (see note to line 2). Here er takes the place of Der Herr in the line above and is not to be confounded with the Er often used in address.

585–6. Notice the change of tense from the past to the historical present in order to denote surprise and express the action more vividly.

593. **Aufbehalten** = aufbewahrt. This verb is now nearly obsolete and is seldom used of persons.

593–4. The bitter sarcasm in these words shows that the Templar considered it the "Irony of Fate" that he was spared to rescue a Jewess from burning and escort inquisitive pilgrims to Mt. Sinai. He is not ashamed of saving the Jewess, as some interpret this passage, any more than he would be ashamed of saving a dog, but he considers it unworthy a valorous and heroic young man desirous of winning fame and honor.

595–6. Sinai, that is, in Arabia Petraea, the real Horeb, between the Gulf of Suez and Akabah. Sinai is the name of the desert in which the mountain lies. This is then what caused his absence from the city, and as it is far distant from Jerusalem it must have taken a long time. Contrary to present usage, Lessing, like Herder, omits the article with the names of mountains.

607–8. **Er hätte durch den Herrn Ein Briefchen gern bestellt.** These words express the wish of the Patriarch, *He would have liked to send*, etc. The friar does not wish to emphasize the reality of his statement, but modestly expresses his opinion. We should expect future time, but he is *sounding* the Templar, and we can supply: er sagte, er hätte gern einen Brief durch Sie bestellt, wenn Sie dazu bereit wären.

611–12. **Sagt der Patriarch.** The fidelity of the friar is seen in this refrain; for he delivers his message literally as his superior had enjoined upon him, but at the same time wishes his bearer to understand that he is not responsible for the moral right or wrong of the opinions advanced. They are not his. Cf. Minna von Barnhelm 3, 2, where Just waives all responsibility in the same way.

615–6. Cf. 1 Cor. ix, 25; 2 Tim. iv, 8; 1 Pet. v, 4; Jas. i, 12; Rev. ii, 10, for the special crown offered to the faithful.

618. **Mein Herr** seems to be an imitation of the French polite *monsieur* used in addressing strangers.

619. On account of the following auch, Düntzer suggests changing Denn diese Krone zu verdienen into Und diese, etc.

622. **Sich besehen** = sich umsehen, sehend sich umthun. Cf. also: Daß ich mich in Wien besehen wollte, and In dieser Hitze in Italien herum reisen, um sich zu besehen, all from Lessing.

625. Historically true. Saladin worked zealously on the fortifications of Jerusalem after he had captured it.

628. **Den Streitern Gottes** = den Kreuzfahrern. The expression accords with the mediæval idea that every crusade was a Holy War and the crusaders the warriors of God himself.

632. **König Philipp.** That is, Philip Augustus II, of France, who undertook in 1191 a crusade with Richard the Lionhearted of England. But he had already started home in August of 1191 on account of dissensions with Richard. After his departure Richard concluded a truce of a little more than three years with Saladin. Why Lessing mentions Philip here and not Richard is puzzling; for the friendship existing between Richard and Saladin hardly seems a justifiable reason for this anachronism. However, see note to line 677f.

641. **Es völlig wieder losgeht,** colloquial expression for im Fall der Krieg völlig wieder ausbricht. For the attack of the Templars on Tebnin was only an isolated case and not a general, well-organized outbreak of hostilities.

647. The Templars' attack on Tebnin was a breach of the truce.

654–5. This contradicts the Patriarch's assertion (lines 621–2) that the Templar was free. He considers himself simply a prisoner on parole.

659. **Verübeln** = für übel aufnehmen, *to take amiss.* The friar has an unpleasant duty to perform, and is fearful that the Templar will fall in with the Patriarch's evil propositions. Hence his apparent relief when he finds him honorable.

661. **Ausgattern,** *spy out.* This is a colloquialism, as well also as Den Garaus machen and Das Stück wagen below.

663. **Stecken** = verborgen sein. For Die ungeheuren Summen cf.

lines 403–4, the *greater treasury* in the care of his father, whom history calls an excellent manager. The fortress on Lebanon is Lessing's invention.

671. **Den Garaus ihm zu machen,** d. h., ihn zu töten. Garaus is a substantive formed from the adverbs gar and aus (generally masc., sometimes neut.) and has two principal meanings: (1) the sunrise and sunset bell, hence the end of night and day, then of anything; (2) the emptying of the cup when drinking one's health; cf. Eng. 'carouse' which comes from Garaus.

673. **Maroniten.** This is one of the many Christian sects of the Orient. They probably received their name from the abbot John Maro (?) who lived in the 8th century (?); they dwelt on Lebanon not far from Byblos. But this is all conjecture, as nothing certain is known. They partook of the Lord's Supper in both forms, allowed the inferior priests to marry, were monothelites till they united with the Roman Catholic Church in the 12th century; but they did not conform entirely to its regulations. As they lived on Lebanon, they would therefore know the way. Saladin had founded a cloister there and allowed the Maronites bells.

677–9. As above stated, Philip Augustus was on his way to France and Richard the Lionhearted was still in Palestine. It has been suggested that the poet's reason for exchanging these two kings was on account of the natures of the two men. Philip was not only cunning and secret, but of a shrewd and ignoble mind; nay, he did not even shrink from great crimes, if for his advantage, while Richard was frank and open-hearted. It may be objected that Richard often did wrong, but yet he did not descend to low cunning like Philip.

678. Ptolemaïs was a strong fortress on the boundary of Palestine, also called St. Jean d'Acre and Accho (?).

684. **Gott und der Orden . . .** The priests frequently suffocated every human impulse and moral obligation for the honor of "God and the Order" as they claimed, when anything was to be gained by it. See lines 686–7 for a proof of their sense of moral obligation. In striking contrast to this is the simple, straightforward nature of the friar.

691–2. Specious sophistry, as the Templar's answer shows. The malicious casuistry of lines 695–7 still further brings out the repugnant side of the Patriarch's character and is only too true a copy of the corruption that had crept into the Church.

697. **Unsertwillen.** In the casuistry of the Patriarch the pardoning was done for the sake of Saladin's brother and not for the sake of the Templar.

698. **Und da verlauten wolle,** *and since they pretend* (in the stories in circulation about your pardon).

700–701. This appears to be the first intimation to the Templar of the real reason of his pardon. Cf. line 583ff.

704–710. External resemblance, according to the Templar, should imply an internal one; that is, like features like character. This does not follow, but yet he hopes it may in his case. Nature is true in all its works, for perfect harmony reigns in everything.

ACT I. SCENE 6.

716–17. **Doch muß ich mein Paket nur wagen** = Fr. hasarder, risquer le paquet = es auf gut Glück wagen. Cf. Lessing's French translation of his Laokoon: risquons donc le paquet, *to risk anything, to engage in a doubtful cause.*

718–19. The proverb quoted is unknown to the German, though there are many similar ones; for monks and women were the butt of popular jokes. Weiber sind des Teufels Kloben, darin er fängt, was aufsitzt. Ein altes Weib heißt sprichwörtlich ein Bote des Teufels. The Devil is represented with claws, which he uses to get men in his power. In the first sketch Lessing calls woman the Devil's left claw, so the monk would be the right, referring to the Patriarch's proposals. Prejudice against the Jews is expressed throughout the scene.

736. **Sina** = Arabic form for China. Cf. Apfelsine, 'China apple' or 'orange.'

748–9. **Wie schnell ein Augenblick vorüber ist?** The moment of generous feeling in Nathan would soon be over; for the Templar cannot believe that any Jew could be liberal.

753. **Auch mir ward's vor** (now **an**) **der Wiege nicht gesungen,** etc. This refers to the custom of singing cradle songs predicting their future fate to children. Cf. lines 3845–3847.

756. **Um da ein Judenmädchen zu erziehen.** Cf. also the answer of

the Templar. It is hard to reconcile the statement here with Act IV, Scene 7. The emperor Frederick Barbarossa lost his life on June 10, 1190, so that Daja could have been only two years with Nathan when our piece opens in 1192. We know that Recha was then eighteen years old, and could not have been brought up by Daja. Cf. Introduction, p. XXXIV. A similar scene occurs in Minna von Barnhelm, Act I, Scene 12, where Just proposes to tell Werner's tale.

757. **Knecht** = Kriegsknecht or Reiterknecht, *cavalryman.*

761. **Ersaufen,** coarse expression, to be ascribed to the vexation of the Templar. Ertrinken is the usual word.

769. **Zum Rätsel von mir selbst mir wird.** His (to himself) enigmatical conduct puzzles him when he thinks that he, a Christian, should rescue a Jewess. *Becomes an enigma of myself to myself.*

776-7. **Auch laßt den Vater mir vom Halse.** Cf. also einem damit vom Halse bleiben. *Don't bother me with the father.*

778. **Ein plumper Schwab.** Proverbially the Swabians are called dumm und ehrlich, the Hessians blind and the Pommeranians plump. But here the epithet „plump" is applied to the Swabians. Daja calls him a German bear (l. 786). He half confesses that the maiden's image was and still is in his soul. It could not, however, have been anything but a passing impression, for it was not until his visit that his passion was aroused. Daja appears about to confess Recha's origin when he abruptly leaves.

786. **Du deutscher Bär** denotes the bluntness of the German character which did not yield so early and readily to the refining influence of the Roman and Romanizing civilization as the other nations.

ACT II. SCENE 1.

788. **Wo bist du?** Cares of state will account for Saladin's distraction. The outbreak of the war and his financial distress draw his attention from the game, so that Sittah has to remind him of his mistakes.

789. **Für mich und kaum.** *For me and scarcely that.* He is playing scarcely well enough for Sittah, who modestly assumes that she is a poor player.

791. **Unbedeckt = ungedeckt. So zieh' ich in die Gabel.** They

generally say now die Gabel geben. It means *to fork*, that is, to threaten two pieces at once with one piece, so that one of the threatened pieces must be lost.

793. **Ich setze vor,** *I cover*, or *I interpose.*

800. **Das warst du nicht vermuten?** A rare construction, for the infinitive seldom depends on sein. Gothic and O. H. German furnish no examples and Grimm finds but one case in Mid. H. German. In Greg. we find: *sî wæren vischen*, 774. In the transition period we find many examples and the inifinitive seems to have developed out of a present participle. It is like our progressive form (*you were not expecting that, were you?*)

804–5. **Meine tausend Dinar'.** The possessive pronoun shows that that was the usual stake. A dinar is an Arabian coin worth about four dollars; the naserin is a silver coin worth about one half cent, first coined by the Calif Naser or Nasr.

812. **Den Satz,** *the stake.*

821. **Abschach,** *discover check.* It is a move which leaves the adversary's king exposed to check from some other piece and at the same time attacks a piece with the moving piece, here the queen. They now usually say Abzugsschach. The mention of a queen is here an anachronism, as she was not introduced into the play till 1525.

826. **Bloß mit dem Steine?** would seem to imply that Saladin was not fortunate with his wives, but history tells us nothing of this.

828–30. This may refer to the fact that Saladin had frequently spared Sittah's queen, but probably refers to his treatment of princesses. When the sister of the defeated Saleh, son of Nureddin, appeared before Saladin (1175), he returned her her fortress and loaded her with gifts. The mother of the defeated Sultan Massud was treated with the greatest distinction, though her son's domains were not restored to him. Sybilla, wife of Guy de Lusignan, king of Jerusalem, and Maria, wife of Prince Balian II, were royally treated by Saladin.

839. **Die Glatten Steine.** A passage of the Alcoran (Sure 5) which forbade wine, gaming and images (figures of men and animals) was interpreted as referring to chessmen. A sect of Muhammedans, the Sonnites, therefore only played with smooth pieces (glatte Steine). Lessing found this in the Preliminary Discourse to the Koran by George Sale (1734). Cf. the footnote to Boxberger's Edition, l. 841.

Others, especially Persians, did not follow this rule and used carved pieces. Lessing assumes that all priests use the smooth pieces and supposes that Saladin was usually pleased to play with smooth pieces whenever he played with a priest, in which case he did not have the carved pieces to make him more attentive. However, some believe that Saladin distrusted the Imam of using the smooth pieces in order to get the advantage over him. But Buchheim well observes that Saladin was a strict Mussulman and would never have played with carved pieces. It is the enlightened Saladin of the drama who complains of the smooth pieces suitable to an Imam.

841. **Iman.** Most editions change this form to Imam, which is the prevalent and more correct spelling, but Boxberger (ibid.) shows that the form Iman was more common among Occidental scholars in Lessing's time.

842. **Verlust will Vorwand** is a German proverb: *Loss seeks an excuse.*

849. **Zerstreuung.** She here returns to the cause of Saladin's distraction and care, which naturally makes the sister anxious. Zerstreuung (Zerstreut) could hardly be used in the sense of diversion, amusement, for Sittah would not be likely to be diverted when her brother is anxious and troubled. Her brother's anxiety is enough to make her anxious.

851. **Gieriger** = eifriger, *more zealously.*

852. **Losgeht,** cf. l. 641.

854. **Stillestand** = Waffenstillstand. Lessing used the shorter form in several instances. Stillestand instead of Stillstand is required by the meter. Cf. l. 573 about the breaking of the truce.

857. **Richards Bruder.** History knows nothing of this; it does tell us of a proposed marriage of Saladin's brother Melek el Adel with Richard's sister Joan, widow of king William of Sicily, whom she had accompanied to the East. Lessing enlarged this and proposed a double marriage.

858–9. History often mentions this mutual admiration of these two great men.

870. **Aberglauben.** Sittah does not make any distinction between Aberglauben (superstition) and Glauben (belief, creed).

Wirzt = würzt, as it is derived from Wurz (Eng. wort), *spice.*

875 ff. Virtue is again elevated above belief (creed), morality above religious confession. Christ's name, not his virtues, is to be propagated until it swallows all other names, in that it makes the whole world Christian in name only. The Christians do not wish any longer to hear of *good men*, but only of *good Christians*. Sittah forgets how the Muhammedans propagated their faith with fire and sword.

882. The Christians generally required the conversion of the heathen before intermarriage.

885–6. Sittah asserts that love was not brought into the world by Christians and was not peculiar to them. God created man and woman (Gen. ii, 23 ff.) and implanted this feeling (of conjugal love) in their breast.

891. Saladin's remarks about the Templars are strictly true. From the smallest beginnings they rose to the greatest power and played an important part in the history of the world. But the warlike and secular spirit grew much more rapidly than the religious, and the monkish part of their character was only seen when they wished to cloak their actions.

892. **Acca** = Ptolemaïs, lying on the Syrian coast; it played an important part during the Crusades. Saladin's brother was to receive Palestine and other territories and Joan Acca as dowry.

897. **Albern,** cf. l. 235 note.

903. **Irrte** is used in the sense of **irre machen, stören, verwirren.**

906. Cf. lines 666 ff. As already mentioned Saladin's father was long ago dead; but Lessing was never a martyr to chronology.

910. Lessing's own experiences are speaking here. For no one cared less for money than he and no one had more need of it at times.

ACT II. SCENE 2.

915. Al-Hafi is under the impression that the tribute from Egypt has arrived and that he has been summoned to receive it.

917. **Fein viel** = höchst viel.

921. **Das ist für was (etwas) noch weniger als nichts.** *That is for something still less than nothing;* that is, instead of receiving I am to pay out.

926 **Gönnt's euch nur selber erst!** Sittah had not only not taken the "winnings," but had even been paying the household expenses of Saladin, as we shall soon see. Hence she had begrudged herself the money.

927. **Euer.** The uninflected predicate forms mein, dein, unser, euer, are older than the inflected meiner, meine, meines, etc., and assert ownership pure and simple.

929–30. Sittah is trying to prevent her brother from finding out her secret that the money is out and that she has been paying all expenses for some time. So she wants Al-Hafi to say that he will pay her the stakes. His nun ja is his reply, but he adds something that may betray all.

941–2. Cf. the proverb „wie gewonnen, so zerronnen." Sittah had not really won the game, as Saladin was not yet check-mated, nor was the game actually lost, for Saladin still had chances of winning; she was not to get the stakes as there was no money to pay them, so the proverb "easy come, easy go" applied very well.

947. **Ich hätte ihr Hirn wohl lieber selbst** = Ich wäre lieber selbst so klug wie sie.

953. **Die Mummerei,** that is, the further concealment of financial straits. For him the farce (Mummerei) was over.

958. **Bescheiden** = Einsehen haben, einsichtsvoll, *be prudent and disclose nothing*.

962. **Verbitten,** in the sense of begging one not to do anything.

965. **Dir nicht näher treten** = dir nicht mehr zu Herzen gehen.

970–1. **So sind die Posten stehen geblieben,** *the items (of the account) remain* (unpaid); that is, I shall claim all arrears when the treasury is full.

976. **Ausgeworfen,** that is, the appanage of princes and princesses. Marin, II, 326, relates the following scene at Saladin's death: "He had alms distributed to all poor people, even to Christians. As he had given during his whole life and never saved anything for himself, they were obliged to sell his jewels and furniture. One of his sisters (Sittalscham or Sillah-Abscham, our Sittah), charged with this charity, added her own effects to make the alms more abundant." This probably gave Lessing the idea of the present scene.

989–991. Among Lessing's material to the Nathan is found the following notice: "Saladin never had more than one garment, never more than one horse in his stable. In the midst of riches and superabundance he enjoyed complete poverty. After his death they found in Saladin's treasury no more than a ducat and forty Naserins." Marin says that Saladin on his death-bed ordered his standard bearer to place the garment in which he was to be buried upon a lance and bear it before the people and say that that was all that the conqueror of the East had gained by his conquests. He left neither house, nor garden, nor estate, nor other property. His saying in Lessing's drama: Ein Kleid, ein Schwert, ein Pferd — und einen Gott remains to this day in the Thuringian proverb: ein Rock und ein Gott.

1002. **Abbrechen,** *to pinch one's self, to curtail expenses.* **Einziehen** = einschränken, *retrench.*

1005. **Doch was kann das machen?** As Saladin had always lived in the plainest, simplest manner possible, curtailment, retrenchment, sparing would not amount to much.

1007. **Abzudingen** = abzuhandeln, secure some abatement in his duty to his God. But already his God had been satisfied with his heart, and he could give him no less.

1012. **Spießen.** Death by impaling is still a common punishment in the Orient and is considered both more cruel and more ignominious than strangling.

1013. **drosseln** = erdrosseln. This punishment was that of persons of rank. **Auf Überschuß . . . wär' ergriffen worden,** *If I were caught with a surplus by you.* Saladin's punishment for having a surplus was greater, according to Al-Hafi's view, than for embezzlement.

1014. **Unterschleif,** *embezzlement.* When Saladin's treasurers defrauded him they lost their places, but received no other punishment. For greed of money seemed to the sultan to be as universal as it is sordid. Thus Al-Hafi would have risked nothing by embezzlement.

1017. **Bei niemand andern** = bei niemand anderm, or bei niemand anders, for bei keinem andern.

1020–21. **Auf dem Trocknen sein.** *Stranded, aground* are the corresponding English nautical expressions. *To be dead broke, to be strapped* (slang) renders the German idea. For the German is slangy and sounds strange in the mouth of Sittah. But we must remember that Lessing used the expressive language of his day and ennobled it by his approval.

1023. **Nimm auf** = nimm Geld auf, *borrow money on security.* **Wie du kannst . . . versprich.** When necessary he must promise the highest interest.

1024. **Borgen** = Darlehn nehmen; leihen = Darlehn geben, that is, *borrow money, loan money.* But the Germans are not so careful as we in the use of these words. Lessing uses them correctly here, but in l. 1056 borgen stands for leihen.

1032. Al-Hafi's astonishment is quite natural, because he knows that Sittah refers to Nathan and he does not wish to have him robbed. His awkward efforts to save his friend are amusing.

1035. **Mich denkt** = ich erinnere mich. Lessing found this impersonal construction in Logau and stamped it with his approval. Generally the dative is employed with denken in the sense of sich erinnern.

1037. **Sein Gott** = der Gott der Juden, der Gott seiner Väter, unless the pronoun is used for the sake of the meter. For Sittah knew of Nathan's enlightened character. Cf. line 1123 and Buchheim's note to this passage.

1040–41. To the Dervish living in voluntary poverty riches was the smallest and wisdom the greatest possession, and we do not question his wisdom; for riches have wings and wisdom remains forever with its possessor.

1048. Notice the past tenses. Once it was true, now it is not.

1050. **Die ganze Stadt erschallt** (davon), Was, etc. The particle davon is necessary to make a rounded sentence, but the exigencies of the verse excluded it here.

1055. Al-Hafi had already sounded Nathan and knows that it would be useless to try. Now he is only anxious to save his friend from a forced loan.

1062–3. **Er weiß zu leben** = il sait vivre, *is well-bred, has good manners.*

1067. **Trotz Saladin.** Cf. note to line 411.

1068. **Wenn schon nicht ganz so viel.** Nathan was more circumspect in his giving and did not scatter his money broadcast like Saladin.

1069. Sonder Ansehen = ohne Rücksicht auf das religiöse Bekenntniß. Nathan had risen above the narrow bounds of his own creed and called every human being a brother.

1071. Parsees or Ghebres are the members of a religious sect of Zoroaster. As they worship fire they are peculiarly repugnant to the Mussulmans as heretics. Cf. lines 451 and 1489.

1077. Cf. Boccaccio, Giorn. X, Nov. III, where Mitridones desires to kill his rival for surpassing him in giving (also called Nathan in the novel). See Introduction, p. xxvi.

1078. Lohn von Gott. Every recompense from God, either as thanks from the receiver of the gift, or direct blessings from God for well-doing.

1082. Gesetz, Mosaic law.

1086–7. Übern Fuß mit ihm gespannt; *on bad terms with him.* Cf. über der Hand, über der Achsel sein. Now they generally say simply **mit einem gespannt sein.** The expression comes from wrestling.

ACT II. SCENE 3.

1103 ff. Fancy has ever delighted in finding hidden treasures, especially in the Orient. Josephus (Jewish Antiquities) relates that Solomon buried immense treasures with his father David. At one time Hircanus the High Priest, at another king Herod, opened the grave and took out large sums of money. The royal coffin was, however, so ingeniously concealed that it was never found. Solomon's grave was also said to contain immense treasures, but both only yielded up their hidden wealth at the magic word which was supposed to bring the treasure to light.

1104. Deren Siegel. In ancient times royal graves were frequently sealed for safety, and this must refer to that custom, unless it refers to the ingeniously hidden graves.

1115. Denn er handelt. Commerce is a far more fruitful source of wealth than mines or hidden treasures, though Saladin was hardly of that opinion and he may have said it in contempt.

1116. Saumtier = here Lasttier and the camel is probably meant. as it is the beast of burden in the East.

1118. **Eh** = früher.

1125. **Eingestimmt mit jeder Schönheit** = für jede Schönheit **empfänglich**. Nathan was a man of culture and refinement.

1131–2. **Seinem Volke entfliehen** = den Charakter seines Volkes **verleugnen.** For avarice is the great sin of the Jews, according to Sittah.

1137–8. Boccaccio also states that Saladin would not resort to force.

1142. **Haram** = Harem, though Haram is considered the more correct, if less common, form.

ACT II. SCENE 4.

1162. **Ganz etwas andres,** etc. That is, he thinks love may move her breast instead of gratitude.

1171–2. **Das ein** = für allemal ist abgethan = **Das** ist ein = für allemal abgethan. The unusual order of words is caused by the verse.

1181. **So macht nur, daß er Euch hier nicht gewahr wird;** *Please do hasten away, so that he may not see you here.* Cf. line 496 for the colloquial use of machen.

ACT II. SCENE 5.

1191. **Fast scheu' ich mich des Sonderlings.** Sich scheuen is usually followed by the preposition vor and the dative, or by the simple dative, only rarely by the genitive as here.

1192. **Rauhe Tugend** is a favorite expression with Lessing. Cf. Emilia Galotti, Act II, Scene 5, where the term is applied to Odoardo, whose character is very similar to the Templar's.

The three words scheuen (shrink from), stutzen (startle, puzzle), and verlegen (confuse, perplex) form a descending climax, so to speak. Nathan's approach was not servile, but somewhat uncertain on account of the rugged virtue of the Templar.

1196. **Den drallen Gang,** *the manly gait.* drall means *firm, sturdy, vigorous.*

1198 **Wo sah ich doch dergleichen?** The appearance of the Templar recalls a faint recollection in Nathan's mind of having seen a similar person, which becomes more definite in Scene Seventh, and finally leads to the peaceful solution of the dramatic plot. The following dialogue shows the Jewish traits in Nathan's character: submissive patience, humility and perseverance.

1202. **Verzieht** (verziehen, not verzeihen) is used in the sense of *stay*, that is, *hasten not away till you hear my thanks.*

1207. **Großmut,** say the critics, is not exactly the right word here, but Edelmut. Großmut is a Christian, loving self-abnegation, while Edelmut is merely a generous self-mastery. The Templar in saving Recha did not overcome his Christian pride, for it was repugnant to him to think that he had rescued a Jewess. But he showed Edelmut in the philanthropic exposure of his life to save a fellow-being.

1210 ff. The Templar is applying the Patriarch's casuistry that we owe no one thanks who does not perform the service for our sake. Cf. lines 695–7. He refuses to receive thanks of the father because he did not do the deed for the father's sake. He debases it to a mere deed of a Templar's duty, and legal duty at that, when it was philanthropic. He descends still further when he pleads indifference to life as the leading motive of his action; that is mere egoism.

1218–9. **In die Schanze schlagen** = aufs Spiel setzen. Schanze = *la chance*, which denotes the fortunate throw in dice, then uncertainty, *chance.* Lessing found the word in Logau.

1219–20. The Templar is not telling the truth; he did not know that it was a Jewess. Cf. Act I, Scene 6 and Act IV, Scene 4.

1221. **Groß und abscheulich.** It was grand to rush to the rescue of a human being, but abominable to ascribe it to disgust of life and contempt for Jews. But the generous Nathan excuses it as modesty in order to escape notoriety and admiration.

1232–3. In the first sketch Lessing wrote, — so brauche wenigstens was das beßre an ihm ist — seinen Reichtum, which explains this passage.

1235. **Verreden** = versichern, daß etwas nicht sei, oder sein werde; verschwören, *solemnly renounce.*

1238. **Fetze,** now der Fetzen (rag), though less correct.

1240. **Mit eins.** Cf. line 104.

1245. **Und das bekam er,** etc. It seems strange that the Templar, at the sight of this spot, should now unnecessarily mention a deed which he had hitherto almost ignored, and it is thought that this spot recalled to him the picture of one who had become dear to him, but too many passages contradict that. It was rather a scornful allusion to his burnt cloak for which some day he might claim indemnification. Nathan understood how to make good use of this incident.

1249. **Ihm** refers to **Fleck,** and is repeated in the next line in **den Flecken.**

1252. **Der Tropfen mehr.** The cloak had been exposed to all kinds of weather. Notice the partitive genitive.

1256–8. Nathan's skill in winning the Templar is well shown in these lines. He had noticed that the Templar was weakening and presses his point in a masterly manner. The Templar's reply shows that he had gained his point.

1262–3. **Stellt und verstellt Euch,** *simulate and dissimulate.* "I'll find the kernel out of the bitter shell, however brusk and rude you may be." Nathan repeats a suggestion already made to Daja, lines 523–4.

1268. **Floht ihre Prüfung.** Knowing the feeling of gratitude in the one saved from death and the readiness of servants to enter into love affairs, also remembering the absence of the father you would not put her to the test in order not to win an easy victory. **Ihre Prüfung;** ihre is objective, *test of her.*

1274. **Tragen** = erzeugen, *produce.*

1278. **Mit diesem Unterschied ist's nicht weit her,** *this difference is unimportant.* Nathan's idea is that the equality of man makes the differences non-essential.

1284. **Nur muß der Knorr den Knubben hübsch vertragen.** Now usually Knorren (masc.) and Knubbe (fem.); the meaning is the same for both words (gnarl, excrescence on trees). People must bear and forbear and then all will be well.

1285 ff. *The hillock must not presumptuously pretend that it did not spring from the earth.* Nathan is zealous against any aristocracy in religion.

1286. **Entschossen** = entsprossen.

1293. **Sich entbrechen** = sich mit Gewalt von etwas zurückhalten, *restrain one's self.*

1293–5. Elsewhere Lessing remarks that the Jews are the only people who made a business of spreading their religion. On account of this religious zeal Christ had reproved them and Horace had laughed at them. The Christians had merely taken this zeal from Judaism and carried out the idea in their teachings. The Mussulmans, too, had spread their faith with fire and sword.

1300. **In ihrer schwärzesten Gestalt.** In his Dramaturgy Lessing says that "the crusades themselves, which were at bottom a political move of the popes, became in their execution the most inhuman persecutions of which Christian superstition was ever guilty; true religion had the most and bloodiest Ismenors; and does punishing individual persons who had robbed a mosque compare at all with the fatal rage which depopulated believing Europe in order to devastate unbelieving Asia?"

1301. **Als hier, als jetzt?** = als im Orient, als während der Kreuzzüge? That is, in Palestine, which became the scene of the bloodiest and almost endless religious wars during the crusades. The consensus of opinion seems to be that Lessing is right. They were uncalled for, were cruel, were the hotbed of political ambition, malice and treachery from a human point of view.

1321. **Ferne** = Zukunft.

1325. **Unsrer Recha.** As friend of Nathan in whom he has found a congenial spirit he takes an interest in all that interests his friend. No longer governed by his prejudice against the Jews, his impetuous nature now yields to the favorable impression that Recha had made upon him and his interest grows apace.

Observe the skillful dramatist in Lessing. This inclination is to be intensified by delay. Nathan is here called away to prevent the conversation from dragging out too long, to give an opportunity for the meeting of Recha and the Templar, of Saladin and Nathan, which develops the real plot of the drama. After this slight interruption the second part of the conversation between the Templar and Nathan seems all the fresher and more interesting; for the startling news brought by Daja lends it a new zest.

ACT II. SCENE 6.

The fright of Daja is quite natural; for when the Sultan sent for a rich Jew it boded no good. Her anxiety also served as a foil to set off Nathan's composure, as nothing should disconcert the truly wise man.

1337. **Gestrenger Ritter.** Gestreng was formerly an epithet of the nobility. Cf. English *Dread sovereign;* we now say *worshipful.*

1338. **So bekümmert** (darum), **was,** etc. Verse often requires the omission of particles absolutely necessary in prose.

ACT II. SCENE 7.

1343. No oriental prince has ever had a better reputation than Saladin according to the testimony of all parties. Nathan preferred the pure picture of report for fear that personal knowledge might tarnish the image he had conceived.

1345. **Wenn anders dem so ist,** *if that is really so.*

1346. **Sparung** = Schonung, which is the Mid. H. G. meaning of the word.

1348–9. For he had saved Recha and become his friend, so that Nathan lived a second life in Recha and a third one in the Templar. **Doppelt, dreifach** intensify the expression, but here there was not only a broader life, but also a threefold life for Nathan.

1351. At first Nathan would not lend to Saladin. The cord (Seil) now thrown around him changes the whole situation.

1373. **Euer Name?** The old presentiment that he had seen a person like the Templar rises once more in Nathan's mind, and the Templar's answer only strengthens it. Distrust causes the Templar to conceal his real name (Leu von Filneck) and give the name of his adoption (Curd von Stauffen). Nathan suspects that there is a mystery behind this and he realizes that it must be unraveled before matters go too far.

1378. **Faulen.** His uncle and mother were buried there. Faulen (rot) is a very coarse expression, but suits the Templar's blunt Swabian nature.

1386. **Kundschaft** = Bekanntschaft.

1391. **Wolf (von Filneck)** who was Nathan's friend. See lines 3784–3785. **Wolfs Gang;** it was ein „draller" Gang. Cf. line 1196.

1395. **Das Feuer seines Blicks.** The Templar had einen trotzigen Blick (1196). Orientals have fiery eyes more often than Occidentals.

1399. David Strauss calls attention to the fact that Filneck may be a reminiscence of the little castle of Filseck not far from Hohenstaufen.

ACT II. SCENE 8.

1405. **Was Saladin mir will.** Colloquialism for von mir will. The dative is the ethical dative, or dative of interest. Some consider this a Gallicism in imitation of the French *me veut.*

1410 ff. He cautions Daja not to betray his secret and seems to hint at a possible union of the Templar and Recha, which would quiet Daja's conscience.

ACT II. SCENE 9.

1428 ff. Cf. Scene 2, lines 1030-1093, where Al-Hafi did his best to avert danger from Nathan, but in vain.

1433–4. Cf. line 450. Nathan knows the way from having been there on his commercial voyages.

1435. **Des Wegs,** *along the way.* Genitive of place.

1437. **Ein Nackter** = ein Pilger, as he would become a begging Dervish once more.

1441. The gold purse contained about 30,000, the silver about 500 Turkish piasters (= about one dollar apiece). Cf. Act IV, Scene 3 and Act V, Scene 1, where the leathern purses are in Saladin's palace.

1443. **Und weiter ist es nichts?** The Sultan appears in a different light to Nathan since he has become the friend of the Templar whom Saladin had spared. He has no fear of suffering wrong at his hands. Nor is it Nathan's nature to cherish childish fears.

1444–5. **Wie er Euch von Tag zu Tag Aushöhlen wird bis auf die Zehen?** In his collection of "Proverbial Sayings" Lessing notes from Sebastian Frank: „Er ist hohl bis an die Zehen" (said of one who is insatiable). From this Lessing formed the present expression bis auf die Zehen aushöhlen = aussaugen, *to suck out one's marrow, to drain dry.*

1446–8. The prudent Nathan's riches are compared to usually never empty barns (sonst nie leeren Scheuern) of wise charity (der **weisen** Milde), which the extravagance of Saladin is to drain dry until the poor home-mice (die armen eingebornen Mäuschen, that is, those poor people whom Nathan cares for) shall starve. Cf. the Priamel noted by Lessing: „ein Scheuern ohne Mäuß = Das ist wider die natürlich Art."

1456. Eben das = eben nachdem daß. Daß in German is often used for a compound conjunction like the French *que*.

1459. Verloren glaubte, schon (verloren) **gegeben hatte.** The omission of verloren is more than poetic license.

1466. Der Roche (pr. as a German word), now called **Thurm.** It is the English *rook* (castle at chess), Persian *rokh*, said to have meant *warrior, hero.* With the ancient Germans the piece represented an elephant, with the Persians it was a camel mounted with archers. It took its name from the figure it represented.

1470. In Klumpen werfen, vulgar expression for auf (über) den Haufen werfen, *to upset everything.*

1474. Keine taube (hohle) Nuß. From the common expression: Das ist keine taube Nuß werth Lessing formed: Es galt keine taube Nuß (keine Kleinigkeit). The stakes were a thousand *dinare.* Cf. lines 804–5.

1489. Unter meinen Ghebern. Cf. lines 450, 1071. Al-Hafi had once been with them, hence he calls them meine Gheber.

1497. Plackerei, *worry and turmoil,* for placken is intensified plagen.

1498. Delk, or **Dalk,** is the Arabic for the German Kittel (smock) of a Dervish. Here it means a tattered garment such as the begging Dervishes wore.

1506. Knall und Fall is a rhyming formula taken from fireworks (sudden explosion and fall), meaning *suddenly.*

Ihm selbst leben = sich selbst leben. In earlier times **ihm, ihr, ihnen** were used as reflexives, but Mod. H. G. demands sich. The decision to live to one's self must be an inner prompting of the heart and not a deliberate act of the reason.

1508–9. Lebt wohl! wie's Euch Wohl dünkt. The Dervish sees the inconsistency of saying *farewell* (that is, live well, be well, be prosperous) to one who would not *fare well* according to his idea, and adds: *as it seems well to you.*

1513. **Bürgen** usually has the preposition für; für meine Rechnung bürgt — Ihr oder Sittah.

1514. **Die** (= Dafür) **bürge ich. Wilder** = ungebundener Naturmensch. The free, unrestrained life of a Dervish who worshipped nature was his ideal life.

1515. Critics trace this celebrated saying that the beggar is the only true king to the Persian poet Saadi, but the idea is too universal to be property of any one author.

ACT III. SCENE I.

1519. **Noch so bald** = möglichst bald, augenblicklich. Imitated from the negative noch nicht so bald.

1535. Hitherto Recha has had but one wish, **einen Wunsch aller Wünsche** (to see and speak with the Templar), which dilates her heart, and she fears that no other equally pleasant wish will come to take its place when that is satisfied.

1538 ff. Daja's desire to reveal Recha's birth to her leads her to enigmatical speeches which Recha interprets in her own way.

1546. **Als die ich,** etc. The relative sentence preceding the antecedent gives a fine effect to the whole clause. Klopstock and Goethe used the same device.

1547. **Sperre dich** = sträube dich. It is not an elegant expression, belonging rather to daily life.

1548. Cf. Is. lv, 8. Daja sees the hand of Providence at work, but is forced to speak in riddles.

1556. "Too scientific for a girl," observed Ramler. But Recha is Nathan's child and has been instructed in his philosophy, and is here merely repeating her well-learned lesson. It is true Lessing is preaching his own gospel through her, still that does not change the fact that Recha had been well instructed in regard to God.

1564. **Den Samen der Vernunft,** that is, the religion of reason. Saat would be better than Samen. Nathan had not educated Recha in any revealed religion, but in the pure religion of reason; hence she would not listen to the weeds (**Unkraut**) of other lands.

1571–4. According to Recha the Christian faith took away the power to act and the clearness of consciousness (cf. lines 360–4).

1577. **Nur schlägt er mir nicht zu** = Nur ist er mir nicht zuträglich, paßt nicht zu meinem Wesen.

1579–80. According to Nodnagel, Lessing is skillfully preparing the way for Recha's apparent coldness toward the Templar, which would otherwise appear strange to us.

1587. Deeds, not faith, interest Recha. For when faith is mere imagination (wähnen) about God it can produce no real heroism. Cf. Nathan's lesson: „Begreifst du aber, Wie viel andächtig schwärmen leichter als Gut handeln ist?" Line 360 ff.

1589–92. Religion does not depend upon any faith (confession), it is resignation to God. Schiller sees in these words the whole spiritual trend of the Nathan. It is the Age of Enlightenment speaking through Lessing.

1600. **Ob auch er** (so denkt wie du), for then he would also wish to convert her; or whether he thinks as my father, for then he will be more congenial to me.

1601. The indefinite es (Kommt es nicht an unsre Thüre?) denotes the uncertainty in the speaker's mind as to who was coming. This indefinite use of es is quite common in German and can generally be translated by the indefinite *some, some one, somebody.*

ACT III. SCENE 2.

1604. **Und doch** (säumte ich vergebens so lange).

1608. **Wassereimer.** The Templar had considered himself the mere mechanical instrument of rescue with which his free will had nothing to do, and Recha is now repaying him for his bitter words to Daja. Her bitterness is seen in „herausschmiß," which represents mere blind chance at work in a haphazard way, while Recha thinks Providence orders all things.

1610. **Mir nichts, dir nichts,** an idiomatic expression, *just so, with perfect indifference.*

1617. **Herausschmiß.** Certainly a vigorous term, which sounds strangely in Recha's mouth, but probably the strong language of the

Templar justifies its use by her. It is, however, not so vulgar as some would make it, for good poets often use it even now.

1618–19. Probably the Templar had boasted that in the Occident wine urged men to more foolish deeds than the rescue of a Jewess, so that wine may have prompted him and not his free will. The Mussulmans were prohibited the use of wine and the Jews were restricted in its use.

1619–20. Compare the Templar's cold remarks to Nathan, lines 1213–15: „Es ist der Tempelherren Pflicht, dem Ersten, dem Besten beizuspringen, dessen Not sie sehen." The too mechanical view of the Templar receives its merited rebuke from Recha, who puts his every folly (jede Thorheit, l. 1625) in its true light.

1624. **Dich übel anließ,** *gave you short replies, treated you curtly, snubbed you.*

1630. **Diese kleinen Stacheln.** The sarcastic remarks with which the Templar had sought to escape thanks for his good deed.

1633–4. It is not such an uncommon trait to be *chary of one's grief* and prodigal with one's life. Grief is sacred, while life belongs in a sense to others, which scenes of great danger prove beyond doubt. Intimate friends have a certain right to share one another's grief, but the Templar was alone in Jerusalem and was moreover melancholy. Compare his reason given to the friar: „Wenn ich nun melancholisch gern mich fühlte?" line 552. It shows the sympathetic nature of Recha, however, to be moved at his grief, and she abandons her sarcastic tone.

1640. **Zwar . . . verstellt . . . der Schreck (den Menschen, wie Euch, als ihr in Todesgefahr schwebtet).** Sight and hearing were so absorbed in Recha that speech fails him.

1641. Notice the double accusative after finden (the direct object Euch and the factitive accusative den nämlichen). Lessing also uses the verb glauben (lines 2034–35) in the same way.

Desgleichen, *the same*, that is Pause, as above, line 1640.

1648. **Auf Sinai,** where he had accompanied pilgrims. Cf. line 595.

1652. Als (er die zehn Gebote von ihm empfing).

1653. There was no superstition in Recha, she was too well educated by Nathan and knew that God was omnipresent. She had no idle curiosity to seek the place where Moses may have stood, that was indifferent to her.

1656–8. Some refer this question to the remark of Till Eulenspiegel that he always wept when descending, for he knew that another mountain would soon come, but laughed when ascending, because he would soon be descending into the next valley. Others refer it to a passage in Breuning von Buchenbach's Orientalische Reysz (Strassburg, 1612), who, after describing how he had made the ascent of Mt. Sinai on a side where there were steps, states that he descended on a side where there were no steps, for which reason the descent was the more difficult and troublesome.

This naive and rather childish question seems very odd when coming from Recha; for we expect from her only noble thoughts and great intelligence. Commentators differ as to the exact significance of the question. During the crusades the air was full of just such absurd superstitions, and Lessing may have wished to ridicule them. But why put the words in Recha's mouth and not in Daja's, where they would be appropriate? Recha had just rebuked the Templar for his rude behavior, and may now wish to give a lighter turn to the conversation; possibly there was also just a shade of mischief in her question. In line 1600 she says: „mir liegt daran unendlich, ob auch er (so denkt wie du), and here she is testing the Templar to see whether he is superstitious like Daja. In his turn he recognizes in Recha a congenial soul, hence his reference to Nathan's words: „Kennt sie nur erst!“ She is not a fanatic, and therefore worthy of his esteem, friendship, nay even his love. She has solved her doubts also, but the angel theory and her father's thorough cure have completely removed every sentiment of love in her breast.

1663. **Meiner Einfalt,** genitive after lächeln, which, in higher diction, governs this case. Recha was conscious of the absurdity of her question, but it was only by such a question that she could discover whether the Templar was bigoted or one of nature's noblemen.

1672. **Mir sagt . . . verschweigt?** Recha's tone, her remarks about her question, her silence had clearly shown the Templar that she considered such superstitions only follies. For there were higher questions to discuss and greater problems to solve which would ennoble man and not degrade him to a mere seeker after wonders.

1683. They had not made any such appointment. He only wishes to leave Recha because he shows his love too plainly, as Daja observes after his departure.

1687. **Dazu** = Noch dazu, *moreover.*

ACT III. SCENE 3.

1694. **Was kömmt ihm an?** This verb usually requires the accusative, but cf. Schiller, Jungfrau von Orleans: „Mir kommt ein eigen Grauen an bei diesem Segen." It is equivalent to von Gutem oder Bösem befallen werden.

1708–9. Daja firmly believes that Recha's calmness rests upon the belief that the Templar's distraction and anxiety assure her of his passion for her, but Recha herself is quite unconscious of its cause.

1718. That would mar Daja's plans, as she hopes to save Recha to the Church and get back to Europe with her.

ACT III. SCENE 4.

1734. It must be remembered that Nathan was conversing with the Templar and had to be called by Daja. Then the Dervish detained him a while.

1735. It was the sister who set the trap to catch Nathan, hence the reproachful tone in Schwester! Schwester!

1739–42. „Fallen legen," „auf Glatteis führen," „Geld fischen" are all idiomatic phrases of common life; *set traps, lead one on the ice, bait the hook for money.*

1743. **Abbangen** is a very unusual word taken by Lessing from the colloquial language. In his remarks on Adelung's Dict. he says: Abbangen, durch Bangemachen einem etwas ablisten, abpressen. Ich weiß keine gedruckte Autorität; aber ich habe sagen hören: Er hat mir mein Haus mehr abgebangt als gekauft. *Extort by intimidation.*

1745. **Der Kleinigkeiten kleinste.** That is, money. So thought Lessing, and the trait repeats itself in all his great characters. Cf. Major von Tellheim, Nathan, Saladin, Werner, the Dervish, etc.

1756. **Sich ausred't** = sich ausredet = se excusare, *how he gets out of the trap set for him.*

1759–60. **Die Netze vorbei sich windet** = an den Netzen vorbei sich windet. When no other preposition accompanies the noun, vorbei governs the accusative and stands after the noun.

1774. **Beschönen** = beschönigen. The former is the historically correct form, but beschönigen, formed after the analogy of other verbs in –g, has superseded it.

1779. **Ich tanze, wie ich kann.** He thinks of the awkward bear dancing to the public, and would prefer to have it worse rather than better.

1783–5. History confirms Sittah; for Saladin's prudence and foresight contributed as much as his sword to his success.

1786–7. There seems to be no definite source for this fable-like illustration. Lessing's fable (Fabeln II, 7) of the Lion and the Ass does not apply well to the passage, nor that of the Lion and the Jackal. It hardly needs any source. It is correct in form and true in its nature and needs no authority to give it currency.

1794. **Bestehen** = die Prüfung der Lection bestehen, *stand the test.*

1795. **Der Vorhang,** of the antechamber. **Rauscht,** *rustles.*

ACT III. SCENE 5.

1778. **Nur ohne Furcht.** Saladin thinks of a crouching Jew as he knew them. Sittah thinks Nathan may be „ein furchtsamer, besorglicher" Jude.

Die = die Furcht. The idea of cursing the enemy with fear, etc., is frequent in the Old Testament and in antiquity; it is therefore very appropriate in the mouth of a Jew.

1801. Nathan does not admit the competency of the people to call him *the Wise* and modestly declines the title.

1801–2. Perhaps the Latin proverb *Vox populi, vòx dei* was in Lessing's mind when he wrote these lines. Cf. Schiller's Maria Stuart, Act IV, Scene 8, where Burleigh says to the queen: „Gehorche der Stimme des Volkes, sie ist die Stimme Gottes."

1806–7. Cf. the Templar's remark, lines 741–2: „Seinem (Nathan's) Volke ist reich und weise vielleicht das nämliche."

1811. **Ich höre dich beweisen, was du widersprechen willst.** Widersprechen with the accusative is found in Mid. H. German. Nathan's proof shows his wisdom.

1819. **Trockene Vernunft,** *sober reason.*

1821. **Aufrichtig,** etc. Saladin is thinking of the religious problem that he is going to propose to Nathan while Nathan applies it to business matters. Nathan has already learned from the Dervish that Saladin wants money, but he prudently pretends to know nothing about it.

1827. **Schachern** = handeln = here *haggle.* It is borrowed from the Hebrew and means to *haggle, to jew.* Saladin uses the word as referring to Sittah and Nathan.

1832. **Reget.** The Templars had broken the truce.

1835. **Gesteuert** = gezielt, hinausgewollt. Auch **die** Absicht habe ich nicht gehabt.

1837. **Heischen** is stronger than either begehren or fordern, for it means that what one desires must come.

1841. **Einleuchten** = mit dem Verstande als wahr erkannt werden.

1842. **Ich bin ein Jud'.** Cf. Introd. p. xxv ff. and lines 1312, 2156. He seeks thus to avoid hazardous discussions which might get him into difficulty.

1843. Although chronologically between Jew and Mussulman, Christians here form a third party merely in the controversy of the best religion.

1848. **Einsicht, Gründen, Wahl des Bessern.** Saladin had really studied his lesson. Die Einsicht beruht auf Gründen, die zur Wahl des Bessern, zum Vorzug des einen vor dem andern, führen (Düntzer). But if Einsicht rests upon Gründen it is rather strange why it should precede and not follow.

1850–2. The historical Saladin had decided this question for himself, as he was a strict Mussulman; but he was liberal, and, if tradition speaks the truth, did discuss these questions with Christians and Jews.

1855. **Wägst mich mit dem Auge?** = mißest mich mit den Augen.

1862. **Belauschen** = behorchen, darauf lauschen, um es wahr zu nehmen.

ACT III. SCENE 6.

1868. **So bar, so blank** denote *bare, blank,* that is, the truth entirely free from error.

1870. In ancient times the metals were merely weighed, not coined, therefore **Münze** does not apply well here to ancient means of payment. Nathan means simply that the truth must first be maturely weighed, tested and proved, as coins are weighed, tested and proved.

1872. **Stempel** = Prägkeule; **Brett** = Zahlbrett, *counter.* The official stamp guarantees against fraud.

1873. **Darf** = nötig hat, braucht.

1874. The omission of the article before Sack and **Kopf** is taken from common life, unless we look upon this as a contraction of the preposition in and the acc. den; **in'n** = in. That seems, however, far-fetched. Cf. also Goethe in Götz and Werther (an Kopf, in Statt, in Sack).

1875. Saladin demands the truth without testing it himself, as usurers are accustomed to get their money without too much trouble, hence Nathan considers him more a Jew than he is himself.

1878–9. It is the truth. Saladin did yield to Sittah's suggestion to set a trap for the Jew. Cf. Act III, Scene 4. Nathan's noble heart struggles against such a suspicion, but experience tells him that princes have few scruples. Lessing had also found that out in his own dealings with princes.

1881–2. **Mit der Thüre ins Haus stürzen** (fahren, fallen), an idiomatic expression meaning *to blurt out.* Nathan means that Saladin's question is a blunt one. The simile of the door is continued in the following lines.

1885. **Stockjude,** *Simon pure jew.* Stock in such compounds is merely strengthening.

1888–9. **Das war's! das kann mich retten!** Nathan is now ready to meet Saladin with the Tale of the Three Rings which will help him out of his dilemma. He sees that Saladin is setting a trap for him and he will satisfy him with a tale, as children are satisfied. But we must remember that it is only a parable to illustrate the truth, not the truth itself.

ACT III. SCENE 7.

1891. **So ist das Feld rein,** *The coast is clear.* But das Feld ist frei is more common. Sittah was not listening.

1892. **Du bist zu Rande** = zu Ende, am Ende.

1899. **Leib und Leben,** an alliterative formula like the English *life and limb.*

Gut und Blut is a rhyming formula, such as we often find in German.

1900. Lessing was against martyrdom merely for the sake of gaining a name. Hence Nathan is too wise to choose a course that would lead to unnecessary danger, but yet wishes to be true to himself and his God.

1901. **Einen meiner Titel.** The sultans of the East were accustomed to have pompous titles, and one of Saladin's titles was Besserer der Welt und des Gesetzes (= des Glaubens, the Moral Law).

1908–9. **Ja, gut erzählt.** Cf. Lessing in a letter to Ramler (Feb., 1779): „Mich verlangt, wie Sie mit der Erzählung zufrieden sein werden, die mir wirklich am sauersten geworden ist."

1911. **In Osten,** now im Osten. Earlier usage omitted the article.

1913–14. The opal of the East is noted for its play of colors and is highly prized for settings in rings, etc.

Farben spielte = in Farben spielte.

1915–16. The superstition of the Middle Ages supposed that the precious stones possessed magic virtues and they were worn as amulets. Cf. the story of Benedict Arnold's precious stone that lost its bright color when failure was to attend his steps just before his betrayal.

Vor Gott und Menschen, etc. is Biblical. Cf. Luke ii, 52. Lessing found this feature in the Latin versions. See Intr., pp. xxi, xxii.

1917. This is an addition of Lessing which gives a rational turn to a superstition.

1926. **In Kraft,** now Kraft alone is used.

1933. **Entbrechen,** cf. line 1293, note.

1945. **In Geheim** = now insgeheim.

1965–6. Nathan had not yet told the whole truth, but wants to see how far he can venture.

1970. **Ich dächte.** Saladin now speaks and gives Nathan the desired opportunity to open more of the truth to him. He also begins to feel an interest in the question.

1973. Confessors of positive religions wear different clothing, eat different kinds of food, drink different drinks. The Jews eat no pork, the Mussulmans drink no wine, etc.

1974. The argument used here is similar to that used by Reimarus, in the fourth Wolfenbüttel Contribution, in the first Fragment: „**Von der Verschreiung der Vernunft auf den Kanzeln.**" Cf. also Introd., p. xxiv.

1992–3. The rest of this is Lessing's addition. Boccaccio's story ended with the question who can distinguish between the three religions.

2006. **Bezeihen** is the older form from which we have **bezicht, bezichten, bezichtigen.** At present only **zeihen** is admissible in the sense of accuse.

2024. **Betrogene Betrieger,** *deluded deluders.* Each maintained that he had the genuine ring, which, according to Nathan, was lost, and the father had substituted three false ones. All three had lost confidence in the virtue of his ring to make himself beloved of God and man, or rather, they had forgotten that that was the true test of the ring. Hence the ring acted only inwardly and not outwardly.

2041–48. This passage is said to contain the whole idea of the drama. Unprejudiced thought, love of mankind, gentleness, these are the true tests of humanity. In a review Lessing says: "It is fortunate that here and there a divine thinks of the practical side of Christianity at a time when the most lose themselves in fruitless disputations; now they condemn a simple Moravian, now they give by their so-called refutations a much simpler religious mocker new material for mockery; now they quarrel over impossible agreements before they have laid the foundation for them by purification of the heart from bitterness, quarrelsomeness, calumniation, oppression, and by the spread of that love which alone marks the Christian. To patch up a universal religion before they strive to lead men to the unanimous practice of their duties is nonsense. Can we make two bad dogs good by shutting them up together? Not agreement in opinions, but agreement in virtuous acts will make the world calm and happy." It is an indirect plea for religious tolerance, but falls short of Lessing's standard of his *third stage*. It is the best epitome that the Age of Enlightenment ever made and can well be studied by Christians. See Introd., p. xxiv.

2053. **Sprechen** = das Urtheil sprechen, *pronounce judgment*.

2060. **Aber sei mein Freund.** In Boccaccio we have the same ending of the tale; Saladin wishes the Jew to become his friend. Cf. Introd., p. xxi ff.

2063–4. Lessing's sources let Saladin relate his distress to Nathan, but Lessing has shown great delicacy in allowing Nathan to offer his services to Saladin. It shows Nathan's nobility of soul and relieves Saladin from great embarrassment.

2074–5. We know that Al-Hafi had been to Nathan and warned him, but the interest the latter takes in the Templar had produced a change in him.

2077. **Freierdings.** Cf. allerdings, schlechterdings, platterdings, neuerdings, which are all false formations licensed by usage. Freierdings has been condemned, as well as frischerdings, both of which Lessing coined.

2080–1. **Das Nämliche an mich zu suchen** = das nämliche Ansuchen an mich zu stellen, das Nämliche mich anzusuchen. An is here the real preposition and not the separable prefix. Cf. Goethe: Wer etwas an ihn zu suchen habe; and Schiller: Sucht ihr etwas an ihn?

2083. Notice the great delicacy of Nathan in the use of the verb schicken instead of leihen or borgen. In the next line he skillfully calls Saladin's attention to the Templar as he had promised him, lines 1269–70.

2085. **Eine große Post.** Literally, *item in an account*, here *obligation*. Now der Posten is used for the older die Post. The Templar had refused every reward, still Nathan felt in duty bound to reward him.

2087. The order of Templars was founded for fighting against the Saracens; they had broken the truce; they were opposed to the marriage of Sittah with Richard's brother and of Melek with Richard's sister. Saladin's hostility to them was well known. Cf. lines 231–2.

2090. **Das Leben Spartest** = Das Leben schontest. Cf. line 1346

2091–2. Saladin had not really given him his freedom, nor did he have him watched. He could naturally think, therefore, that the Templar had taken advantage of his carelessness and gone away. It seems improbable that Saladin had entirely forgotten him, yet this inconsistency is hardly noticeable here.

2105. Bloße Leidenschaft = here „tiefe Sehnsucht nach seinem Bruder, welche des Tempelherrn Anblick in ihm geweckt hat" (Düntzer). Cf. Schiller's verses:

> Das eben ist der Fluch der bösen That,
> Daß sie fortzeugend immer muß gebären.

2107–8. Und bei dem andern Bleibt es doch auch? refers to the financial aid he has promised Saladin.

ACT III. SCENE 8.

2111. Niemeyer interprets this line as if the Templar were a wounded victim escaping from the block. The stroke causing the wound is his growing love for Recha, whose presence he had fled to escape danger. He is at least a weary victim fleeing from danger.

2112–3. Cf. lines 1696–8, which explain his condition in Daja's words.

2117. Ihm auszubeugen, d. h. durch eine Wendung sich entziehen. The form beugen for biegen came from the imperative singular and the second and third persons singular indicative, which formerly had eu. In the figurative sense we should expect biegen, but as early as Luther the two forms became interchangeable.

2118. War der Streich zu schnell Gefallen. The impression made by Recha was quick and decisive; foreseeing this his refusal to see her again had been long and stubborn. And yet, as already expressed, it is probable that his reason for refusing to see her at first was because of his prejudice against Jews and his fear that she might belong to the fanatics of that time, though this is not inconsistent with the idea that she did make an impression upon him when he rescued her from the fire.

2123–4. With the Templar there could be no question of a resolution formed by free and deliberate consideration, by active participation of the will; he simply suffered under the impression made. Niemeyer refers it to the dramatic motive of "passion."

The form litt', litte, is the older lengthened form of the imperfect indicative, as in sahe, schiene, etc., now obsolete.

2125. **An sie verstrickt** = mit ihr verknüpft.

2130. This was contrary to the rules of the order to which he belonged, and the fact that the object of his love was a Jewess made it all the worse.

2132–3. **In dem gelobten Land.** He uses the word gelobt in a double sense. Line 2132, Das gelobte Land is the land which Jehovah promised (gelobte, imperfect from geloben; in the text past part.) the Israelites, while the Templar, line 2133, praised (gelobt, past participle from loben) the land in which he had already overcome so many prejudices. Cf. Act II, Scene 5. The following arguments are rather specious ones to free his conscience while breaking away from his order.

2139–41. The Templars were sworn to everlasting hatred of Mussulmans, they took the oath to fight against Saracens; but the Templar must love Saladin for sparing his life, and contemplated breaking all the other rules to which he was bound by oath.

2141–2. That is, oriental sky, as his father Assad was born there.

2144–5. Assad the Mussulman had married a Christian.

2149. **Straucheln.** Stumbling precedes falling. The father had broken his covenanted faith, but the Templar was only contemplating it.

2154. **Ermuntrung.** The Templar feels that Nathan, the unprejudiced Jew, will not only approve but even encourage his love to Recha. But Nathan suspects a more serious obstacle than creeds.

2157. **Glüht heitre Freude.** The intransitive verb is used transitively. Verräth durch sein Glühen heitre Freude. Cf. line 1914, der hundert schöne Farben spielte. We should expect sein Antlitz instead of er. Cf. further Zorn or Liebe blicken.

2158. Historically true of Saladin, who sent all away pleased with him.

ACT III. SCENE 9.

2162–3. Der Mann steht seinen Ruhm = hält seinen Ruhm aus. Cf. seinen Mann stehen = ihn aushalten. The dative is also used with stehen: einem stehen, *to be equal to one.*

2175. Zur Stelle = auf der Stelle.

2180–2. The Templar conjures Nathan by the holiest bonds of nature to forget the bonds of religion (spätere Fesseln) and give him his daughter. The appeal is made in recollection of their former conversation (lines 1310–13), where Nathan maintains that the higher law makes one a man before it makes him a Jew, a Mussulman, or a Christian.

2184. Lieber, lieber Freund! Notice the gradation. Nathan begins with Junger Mann, then Junger Freund, lastly Lieber Freund, which shows his sympathetic pity for the Templar.

2189. Beide, that is, Erkenntlichkeit und Liebe.

2191–2. As Nathan was unprejudiced in regard to religion he could have no objection to the Templar on that score, and this was the only objection that the Templar could possibly see.

2194–6. Nathan is feeling his way carefully to the solution of the mystery about the Templar's birth, which is the real hindrance to their union. If the Templar had told him the truth, there would have been no difficulty. But the Templar interprets Nathan's cautious inquiry as *curiosity* (line 2198, Neubegier, now Neugier), when it is merely the desire to prevent a mistake.

2202–3. Curd ist Conrad. Curd and Kunze are diminutive forms to Conrad (Mid. H. G. Kuonrat), as Götz to Gottfried, Seiz to Siegfried, Heinz to Heinrich, Fritz to Friedrich, Uz to Ulrich.

2209. Bastard oder Bankert. The former denotes the illegitimate child whose father is of nobler rank than the mother. **Bankert** = Bankart, belongs to the vulgar language.

2210. Der Schlag ist nicht zu verachten. Cf. Philip Faulconbridge in King John and Edmond in King Lear, Schiller's Bastart von Orleans in Der Jungfrau von Orleans, Sterne's Tristam Shandy Wieland, etc. — **Schlag** = Menschenschlag = Menschenart, Art.

2211. The Templar now believes that it is a test of nobility which

Nathan desires him to stand before he will give him the hand of his daughter. According to the law of **Ahnenprobe** he must show his descent from a certain number of nobles in succession.

2213–15. The bitterness and irony show manifestly that he has not yet overcome his prejudice against the Jews, nor has he reached the higher standard of nobility. He does not doubt the genuineness of Nathan's ancestral tree, as such records are always infallible, and when Nathan gets to the end of his list at Abraham he (the Templar) can continue it to Adam. His own lack of honesty in giving his own family puts him in all the worse light. He has a long road to travel before he reaches Nathan's plane.

2219. Ich will Euch ja nur bei dem Worte nicht den Augenblick so fassen = Ich will Euch nicht gleich beim Worte nehmen (or fassen), nicht den Augenblick der Hitze benutzen. Nathan knows that he will be understood when reason asserts itself once more and he has cleared up the mystery of Curd's birth. The Templar sees his wrong and asks pardon.

ACT III. SCENE 10.

2228. Schon mehr als g'nug, continuation of the Templar's speech, so sah ich sie Schon viel zuviel, above.

2230. Von einer Kleinigkeit, that is, his love to Recha, which, in his efforts at self-mastery, appears to him as a mere trifle. In his monologue the white heat of passion wrought up his soul to its profoundest depths and now the cold wave of reason is congealing all feeling. So he ever fluctuates between violent extremes, never stable, never rational and thoughtful.

2233. Den aufgedunsn'nen Stoff. Lessing took his figure from baking; der aufgedunsene Teig is kneaded together by the mind and brings order and light into the soul.

2253. Denn versichert = Denn seid versichert. The omission of the auxiliary here is rather bold, but Lessing is fond of such omissions. Daja will not betray Nathan unless she is sure the Templar loves Recha; for otherwise it would avail her nothing.

2259. Armer Ritter; pitiful because he thought to conceal from a woman that he was in love.

2261–2. Das wir zu haben Oft selbst nicht wissen = quod nos habere ipsi sæpe nescimus. It is contrary to the spirit of the German language to use the accusative with the infinitive, but it found defenders in Lessing, Goethe, and Wieland.

2266–7. Sich aus dem Staube machen and **eine sitzen lassen** are both colloquial, idiomatic expressions. *To decamp, cut sticks; to abandon, forsake.*

2271. Geflattre = Geflatter. The older form with final e as in Geräusche, Gemüthe, Geschicke, etc. The double accusative with lehren . . . kennen is quite proper.

2285–6. The Templar speaks as Deist, not as Christian.

2288–9. Christ and his disciples performed miracles on that very soil, and now the love of the Templar is to bring Recha into the bosom of the Church again, which, in Daja's eyes, is a miracle. The Templar, who dislikes miracles, only admits that wonderful things do happen there.

2303. Der Vater soll schon müssen. Daja wishes to say that by the disclosure of the secret Nathan will be only too glad to escape further punishment by renouncing all claim to Recha, but the Templar understands her to mean the employment of force. That is, she uses müssen in the sense of necessity imposed upon Nathan by the force of circumstances, and he understands it in the sense of actual force applied by others, and he will not listen to force in that sense.

2304. Cf. Luke x, 30.

2305. Er muß nicht müssen. Cf. line 385, Kein Mensch muß müssen. As father of Recha he has the absolute right to dispose of her as he will and no one can force him to give her to any one. Daja changes her muß müssen to muß wollen, as she knows that Nathan is only the foster-father and has no legal right to Recha. Having brought her up as Jewess when she was a Christian would subject him to severe punishment.

2309. Daja keeps up the musical figure which the Templar had employed; for Einfallen is used in music to denote that one instrument joins in accord with another, and is stronger than einstimmen, also used in the same sense. The Templar continues the figure in his *discordant note* (Mißlaut).

2320. **Daß er doch gar nicht hören will!** For Daja had troubled him often enough with her scruples on that subject, and he would not listen to her.

2330–1. **Laßt Euch nicht die Wehen schrecken.** The Templar thinks that Daja has converted Recha to Christianity, hence his taunts, Hat's schwer gehalten? etc. The pains of childbirth (Recha's spiritual birth) are not to frighten her from her good work; for, having discarded all belief, he can see no difference between Jew, Mussulman, or Christian. He is emancipated from the thralldom of creeds, like the Deists, but not yet purified from prejudice and bigotry so as to become a representative of the pure religion of God like Nathan and Saladin.

2338. **Von Eurer Mache** = von Eurer, der bigotten Christin, Fabrik, aus Eurer Werkstatt. Mache is an expression taken from common life, as in der Mache sein, haben, in die Mache nehmen. Cf. the English *of your make.*

2339. **Ah! so versteht Ihr's? So mag's gelten.** She sees the natural mistake of the Templar and understands the taunt and overlooks it.

2343–4. Assad is said to have become a Christian when he married a Christian wife.

2347. Supply hat before weinen machen.

2352. According to an older custom als is omitted in connection with the participle geboren. We should expect Als was sie geboren sei, als eine Christin geboren sei.

2359–61. **Die Stimme der Natur so zu verfälschen,** etc. Nature pronounced Recha a Christian at birth. In the Templar's mind, however, Nathan had turned aside (verlenken) the natural impulses of her heart from Christianity, her natural state, to himself, as if he were her real father. He had thus falsified nature in bringing her up as a Jewess when she was a Christian.

Sich selbst gelassen = sich selbst überlassen, a quite common use with Lessing.

2374. **Dem Dinge** = der Angelegenheit der Befreiung und Heimführung Recha's; his love affair with Recha and its happy conclusion. She appears to ignore the Templar's vows of celibacy, which would be a natural hindrance to any contemplated secret flight which she seems to imply.

ACT IV. SCENE 1.

* **Scene: in den Kreuzgängen des Klosters.** The cloisters enclosed a court or garden. The archways opening into this court and encircling this space were called Kreuzgänge (crossways) because they were intended for the procession following the cross of Christ, the object of these solemn processions.

2379. **Er hat schon recht, der Patriarch.** The Patriarch must have been scolding the poor friar for his lack of success in his commissions. Cf. Act I, Scene 5, where he seems glad to have failed with the Templar.

2384–6. He expresses his indignation at the worldliness of the clergy who wish to have a hand in everything. Die Nase in Alles stecken, die Hand in Allem haben are idiomatic expressions and the diminutive forms only add force to his indignation.

2396. **Wie sauer mir der Antrag war.** He repeats here his words, Ich geh', und geh' vergnügter als ich kam, line 712. But he fears he rejoiced too soon and shows his indignation at the after effect of his message, if it prove that the Templar has changed his mind.

2400–2. **Rund . . . von Euch wies't,** *flatly refused.*

2409. **Unser Engel.** In saving the Templar's life Saladin became his *guardian angel.*

2411. **Mit Fleisch und Blut.** The fleshly lusts, worldly motives have overcome the ethical reason which induced the Templar at first to refuse the Patriarch's proposal.

2412. The wieder seems to be entirely forceless, as the Templar had neither been there before nor offered his services to the Patriarch at all. It is probably used to fill out the line, but selber would be better for that purpose.

2423–4. **Die Sache ist ziemlich pfäffisch,** as it refers to a born Christian being brought up as a Jewess. Since the Reformation Pfaffe is in ill-repute and there seems to be just a shade of irony in this remark, for the Templar is in the transition stage from emancipation from creeds to the higher religion, and scoffs at all religion.

2426–7. **Weil er das Vorrecht hat, sich zu vergehen.** This seems to be the old Jesuitical rule that the end justifies the means. Absolution is in the hands of the priests and they are in a sense responsible to themselves alone.

He feels a responsibility to the Church now that he knows of a Christian who has been taken from the bosom of the Church.

2432. The Templar is blindly seeking for counsel, but finds none in himself. He also wishes to throw off on some one else the responsibility imposed upon him by this secret.

2435. **Religion ist Partei.** The higher religion of Nathan is above the partisan spirit, but sectarianism is very partisan. The Templar is only partisan because he is selfish and piqued at Nathan. As unpartisan as he believes himself to be, he still finds the partisan spirit influencing his actions.

2437–8. **Hält, ohn' es selbst zu wissen, doch nur seiner Die Stange** = nimmt sich nur seiner Religion als einer Parteisache an. Einem die Stange halten = einen beschützen, seine Partei nehmen. It is a wrestling term. The judge gave each wrestler a *second* who bore a pole (Stange) and held it over the fallen man for protection.

2440. The simple friar is rather bewildered than enlightened by this specious argument, and wisely remains discreet.

2441–3. He does not wish for a dogmatical sentence against Nathan, so far has he not fallen that he would call down the powers that be upon his friend. He now begins to discuss whether he wants *simple* or *learned* advice and decides for the former. Notice the fine choice of words; lauter (pure) belongs to simple and not to learned advice. The advice of the friar would be lauter, that of the Patriarch would be gelehrt. Hence he asked the brother to be his Patriarch (seid ihr mein Patriarch).

2449–51. Cf. Luke x, 41–2.

ACT IV. SCENE 2.

* **Scene, Der Patriarch.** See Introd., p. xxxii ff.

2455. **Dick und rot** refer to high living, **freundlich** to his inner satisfaction. The description exactly suits Heraclius.

2457. **Nach Hofe sich erheben** = Nach Hofe sich aufmachen.

2458. Saladin was noted for his simplicity. Cf. note to lines 989–99.

2469. **Blühen und grünen,** *may flourish like a green bay tree.* The style of the Patriarch is sanctimonious enough.

2473. **Dem Herrn.** Polite form of address used by the Patriarch for effect, and not in submission as with the friar.

2476. **Doch blindlings nicht.** Blind obedience was demanded of all members of orders, which the Templar contests. Lessing combats this opinion in the Fragments.

2479. Goeze preached the same doctrine in his controversy with Lessing.

2481. Cf. Matt. ii, 7, and the story of Abraham and Lot entertaining angels unawares, that is, messengers, for prophets and priests are angels of the Lord. So thought the Patriarch.

Ist zu sagen, imitation of the French *C'est-à-dire.*

2487. **Die Wilkür** = den freien Entschluß, *free will.* Kant uses it in the same sense.

2490–2. Cf. line 655.

2511. **Eine Hypotes'** = erdichteter Rechtsfall. Mere hypothetical cases have no interest for the Patriarch; he deals in facts alone. A similar incident occurred in the Goeze controversy, where Goeze objected to a purely hypothetical case. See Boxberger's footnote to this line.

2515. **Meinung.** The Templar has not yet made up his mind what to do, as he told the friar (Ihr wißt es schon, warum ich komme? Kaum weiß ich es selbst). He is seeking for light to guide him and only wants the Patriarch's opinion.

2517–18. Cf. the first Fragment published by Lessing entitled: Von der Verschreiung der Vernunft auf den Kanzeln.

2522. There is a certain difficulty about the interpretation of this passage. In antiquity such themes for dissertations and orations were common in the schools of the rhetoricians, and all through the Middle Ages they were favorite topics for discussion on the rostrums. But the reference to the theater reminds us of Goeze's controversy with Pastor Schlosser on the theater, with which Lessing had nothing to do. But Goeze was constantly stigmatizing Lessing for his theater logic, and this is probably an allusion to that part of their controversy. See Boxberger on this passage.

2526. **Schnurre** = Posse, possenhafter Einfall.

2527. **Einen zum Besten haben,** *to make game of one.* Das Beste was the prize at shooting-matches, ninepins and other games of skill, hence Etwas zum Besten haben was to make it the prize; figuratively Einen zum Besten haben is to make one the aim of all derisive remarks, to make one the butt of ridicule.

2531. **Förderſamſt** = sogleich. The word is now obsolete except in official style, which Lessing intentionally makes the Patriarch use.

2532–3. **Päpstliches und kaiserliches Recht** = jus canonicum and jus romanum. Ecclesiastical and civil right.

2535. **Obbesagte** = oben besagte.

2538. **Holzstoß.** Stoß is a heap of things laid over one another. Holzstoß is a heap of wood = here Scheiterhaufen, *the stake.*

2543–5. The Templar knew nothing of this though it is literally true. It was a chance shot with him. Daja had only told him the bare fact that Recha was a Christian.

2546. This passage shows fanaticism in its true light, in all its glaring hideousness. *No matter, the Jew is to be burned,* regardless of the fact that he has shown true love to his neighbor.

2554 ff. The Templar now assumes it as a real case and not hypothetical. But where did he get the information given here? Daja told him nothing of the kind. He can only have conjectured it from the knowledge he has of Nathan and the few words that Daja said to him. Cf. lines 1307, 2340.

2558. **Der Vernunft.** Religion of reason which the Deists advocated.

2560. **Dieserwegen** = propterea. Now obsolescent and official style.

2562–3. With Christians belief is considered very essential, but the Deists look upon the life, the moral rectitude, as the essential thing. Cf. lines 1583–9 for Recha's belief.

2570. **Ich geh' sogleich zum Sultan.** So Goeze did to Lessing when overcome in the controversy. Cf. Introd., p. x.

2571–7. The historical capitulation contains no such conditions, but rather even the Patriarch had to leave the city. Jerusalem was to remain uninjured; every Christian could leave on payment of a ransom; the Holy Sepulchre was to be spared, and every Christian could visit it on payment of a certain fee.

2574. **Zu unser allerheiligsten Religion.** This expression was very common with Goeze in his controversy against Lessing. See Boxberger's footnote to this line.

2578–82. Again we have Goeze's tactics with the duke of Brunswick in his efforts to bring Lessing into disrepute. Goeze employed almost the same words.

2584. **Sermon** = geistliche Rede; it usually means a dry and tedious sermon.

2589. **Funden.** The use of the particle ge– in the formation of the past participle did not become a fixed rule until the Mid. and Mod. H.G. periods. Even in the Mid. H.G. period some participles rarely took ge– (e. g. komen, worden, funden, etc.), and in Mod. H.G., in the language of the poets, the past participle is often formed without ge–, especially funden and worden.

The changed tone of the Patriarch is quite characteristic of him, and his historical prototype used the same tactics.

2598. **Auf den Grund kommen,** *thoroughly investigate, trace to its source.*

2600. **Mein Sohn.** As superior to inferior this accords with ecclesiastical custom. The brother is well named Bonafides, *good faith.*

ACT IV. SCENE 3.

2602. **Des Dings** (*trash*) expresses Lessing's contempt for money, which he has transferred to Saladin's character, though the great Saladin also had little regard for money.

2607. There is a traditional saying of Saladin that the hands of a king should be like a sieve, so that money would slip through them. Saladin's were so.

2609. **Abzwacken** = abzupfen, abzerren (*squeeze*). It is used of money, property, and services.

2611. **Das Armut,** now die Armut. In the preceding century, the neuter gender of Armut was employed in the collective sense for *the poor*.

2612. Die Spenden bei dem Grabe. The tribute levied on every Christian to visit the grave of the Saviour had been abolished. Marin (ii, 72) says: *Personne ne se présente devant lui sans recevoir de l'argent ou des provisions* when the inhabitants were leaving Jerusalem at the time of its capture. The generosity of Saladin to the citizens of Jerusalem is celebrated by all historians. Lessing could justly make him say that he would be glad if the alms for the poor pilgrims should not be interrupted and thus cause them to go away empty-handed.

2615. Wenn nur... Just what Lessing had in mind in writing this Wenn nur, is doubtful, but probably it was some act of generosity to to which he wished to refer.

2627. Lilla, in Arabic Leila (night), a common name for girls.

2633–5. Blieb weg . . . Einmal bleiben wir alle Weg. Euphemistic expression for sterben. Our *he passed away . . . we shall all pass away*, comes the nearest to it.

2638. Er hat der Feinde mehr (partitive gen.). Saladin indulgently refers to the passion of love which unsettled (verrückt) Assad's life-plans.

2647. Läßt den Schleier fallen. For Muhammedan women cannot appear unveiled before men.

2648–9. Und nun sein Ton. Saladin had not yet heard the voice of the Templar, for after being pardoned, the Templar was so astounded that he could not speak and Saladin was so affected that he went away in silence (lines 587–9). Nathan had immediately recognized Wolf von Filneck's (Assad's) voice, and Saladin would certainly do the same.

ACT IV. SCENE 4.

2667. Like the *Seven Sleepers*, a well-known oriental tale.

2668–9. In a letter to his brother Karl (April, 1779), Lessing writes: „Ginnistan so viel als Feenland (oder eigentlich Genienland, von dschin, dem lateinischen genius). Div so viel als Fee." Div is the name of the *evil spirit*, hence the adjective gut to qualify it; and Ginnistan really signifies the *desert of the genii*.

Blume refers to the bloom of youth as among the ancients and keeps up the oriental coloring of the simile.

2673–4. He refers to the secret love affair with the Christian lady von Stauffen, which finally led him to become a Christian in order to marry her.

2684. **Um mir**? In the last century um, especially when another preposition with the dative preceded it, governed the dative. See examples in Boxberger's footnote to this passage.

2685–6. **Im weißen Mantel,** of the Templars. **Jamerlonk** = the broad mantel of the Arabs. **Tulban** = Turban. **Filze** = **Filzhut,** *felt hat*, worn by the Templars who are said to have brought it into Europe.

2687–8. **Ich habe nie verlangt, Daß allen Bäumen Eine Rinde wachse.** Absolutely true of Saladin; for confessors of every faith lived quietly under his scepter and he had Christians in his household.

2690. Continuation of Saladin's simile. This comparison of the different barks of trees well represents Lessing's opinion that religion (i. e. creed) is only the shell after all. Saladin was peacefully disposed and would have preferred to be God's gardener and allow all trees to grow in their special way than to be his champion on the field of battle.

2693–4. **Ein Wort?** *you give me your word of honor?* **Ein Mann,** *As a man of honor I do.* Cf. the proverb: „Ein Mann, ein Wort, ein Wort, ein Mann," or „ein Wort ein Wort, ein Mann ein Mann." That is, *His word's the man.*

2694–5. The bond of friendship between them is sealed. Cf. the friendship between the Templar and Nathan, and Nathan and Saladin, so we now have a close bond between Christian, Jew, and Mussulman.

2699. **Das eine That . . . ausschlug** = daß eine That . . . gereichen, werden ließ. We must either consider ausschlagen as transitive here, contrary to its usual meaning, or change das into daß.

2700–2. Cf. Recha's remarks, lines 1604–6.

2709. **Schwierig** = empfindlich.

2712. Said to be historically true of Saladin, though in general his character was regular and well-ordered.

2715. Es mit einem haben = (in colloquial style) es mit einem zu thun haben, im Hader stehen, *to be out with one.*

2732. Von heitern Fernen. Cf. lines 1321–2.

2733. Beschwatzen, *wheedle, flatter with soft words.*

2740. Ins Feuer. Cf. line 2224, da brennt's. This time it is the flames of love. We remember his hasty entry into Nathan's house when he visited Recha.

2743. Platterdings, *flatly.* Cf. line 2077, freierdings.

2755–8. The Templar, having discarded revealed religion, calls all creeds and beliefs superstitions. He is now in the transition stage, but will soon pass to the advanced stage of Saladin and Nathan.

Es sind nicht all frei, die ihrer Ketten spotten. These words have become a proverb in German. Rückert, Erl. Ausg. II. 450, says:

Mancher wähnt sich frei, und siehet
Nicht die Bande, die ihn schnüren.

The Templar also speaks of „den Fesseln, welche die Religion den Menschen anlegt" (line 2182). He calls the doctrines of positive religion chains (lines 2434–8).

2760. Aberglauben, like Glauben, is not generally used in the plural.

2762–4. To be connected with the preceding speech of the Templar.

Blöde primarily means dim-sighted, but it is here used in the figurative sense of weak-minded. The idea is that *the worst superstition is to consider one's own superstition the more tolerable, to entrust feeble mankind to it till it grows used to the brighter light of truth.*

Gewöhne, instead of gewohne = gewohnt werden. In religious matters mankind is compared to weak-eyed people who cannot bear the full light of day.

2767. Dieser Ausbund aller Menschen = dieser Ausgezeichnetste aller Menschen. Ausbund is really the front end of a piece of cloth which lies exposed to view and is therefore the best. In Mid. H.G. also called „Schaufalt," later „Schauende." In English, *sample.*

2769–70. The Templar is again calumniating Nathan as with the Patriarch (Act IV, Scene 2). He knows nothing about the way

Nathan obtained Recha, and should not hastily conclude that he had used unfair means. Now Nathan had brought her up as a Jewess, before in no religion whatever.

2772. **Körnt** = lockt, as one does birds by scattering kernels of corn.

2773. **Schiene** = schien. Cf. litte for litt in Act III, Scene 8.

2776. **Ist ein verzettelt Christenkind.** Verzetteln = verstreuen, with the additional idea of being lost. *Is a stray Christian child.*

2780–3. Wolves in sheeps' clothing. Sehet euch vor vor den falschen Propheten, die in Schafskleidern zu euch kommen, inwendig aber sind sie reißende Wölfe.

The hounds which he is to let loose upon Nathan are the same as those that Saladin afterwards calls fanatics of the Christian mob (line 2799).

2789–90. **Sich . . . genommen hätte** = sich . . . benommen hätte. sich nehmen is sometimes used for sich benehmen.

2791. **Brausend** = leidenschaftlich, feurig.

2799. **Den Schwärmern deines (Christlichen) Pöbels.** Saladin hated fanatics of all kinds, but honored the noble-minded, though enthusiastic, believers of all creeds. So he does not want Nathan given over to the fanatical mob.

2802–3. *Be not a Christian to spite a Jew or a Mussulman.*

2804. **Blutbegier** = Blutgier. Cf. Neubegier for Neugier, line 2198.

2810–11. Ashamed of his conduct, the Templar confesses his fault and fears that he is different from Saladin's Assad. But this very fear betrays Assad's true character, which gladly showed repentance for faults committed.

2812. Impetuosity, misdirected, ungoverned by a strong will, is a a fault, but under proper control and well directed it becomes a virtue.

Lessing had the irascibility of his father, and yet he spoke in the following true words of him: „Du warst so ein guter und zugleich so ein hitziger Mann."

2819–21. Saladin ironically remarks to the Templar that the great fault in Recha's education is that she has eaten no pork, a possible thrust at those Christians who consider the eating of pork a sign of superiority over the Jews and Turks. The Templar feels the sting, as we see in his monologue (Act V, Scene 3).

ACT IV. SCENE 5.

2829–30. Lessing had the intention of letting Saladin ask the Templar this question, and wrote out the passage, but Mendelssohn objected to it, as it reminded too closely of a similar well-known scene unworthy of a Lessing; therefore Lessing omitted it. The passage has never been found. See Boxberger's footnote to the passage.

2842. The one that saves the life of a person has the same rights as the one who gives life, which is not at all true; the analogy is false. All the more would the Templar (says Saladin) have a better right to Recha than Nathan, who is not even her father. False again.

2848. **Die liebe Neubegier.** Neugier, Neugierde are now more common. Sittah softens the harshness of her curiosity by the adjective liebe, *my fond curiosity.*

2850–2. Cf. the remark of Hermann's father in Goethe's *Hermann und Dorothea :*

„Denn an der Braut, die der Mann sich erwählt, läßt gleich sich erkennen
Welches Geistes er sei, und ob er sich eigentlich Werth fühlt."

Sittah's interest in the Templar has been awakened, and she wishes to know whether he has chosen wisely or not.

ACT IV. SCENE 6.

2860. Silver groundwork inwrought with golden vines, later called „goldne, den weißen Grund durchschlängelnde Ströme" ; purchased in Babylon for Daja. Cf. lines 44–5.

2868. **Bild** is used here as throughout this passage in the sense of Sinnbild, *emblem, symbol,* and sinnbilderst, line 2872, means *symbolizest.*

2879. **Deine Siebensachen.** *Be off with the whole kit and boodle.* Siebensachen really denotes a gripsack which contains only the most necessary things.

2879–81. This passage has been explained by reference to Matt iv, 1–10, where the Saviour is tempted by Satan. There is but slight similarity, still the pious Daja would naturally think of her Bible, as she is represented as very conversant with it throughout the play, though probably an anachronism, for the crusaders knew little and cared less for the Bible than for the priest's word.

2881. Nicht rühr an! Supply ich as subject and es as object, nicht rühr' ich es an. In her passionate excitement Daja uses a forcible expression picked up from the language of the street.

2886. O stellt Euch nicht so fremd. *Do not feign to be so surprised, you know what I mean.*

2894. Nicht Feuerkohlen, etc. Cf. Rom. xii, 20, so wirst du feurige Kohlen auf sein Haupt sammeln. For the whole passage cf. lines 54–6; 165; 742–4; 2318–9. Daja misconstrues the Biblical passage in thinking of the pains of conscience which Nathan must have in spite of his good deeds; for, if he were to give Recha back to her faith, he might rejoice in real earnest for having done a good deed.

2895. Doch die alte Leier wieder? *Harping on the same string again?* We use *story* or *song* instead of *lyre*.

2896–7. Mit einer neuen Saite, that is, the love of the Templar. But it's out of tune (weder stimmt) or snaps (noch hält). For when the mystery about the Templar is cleared up, he will prove to be Recha's brother, if Nathan's fear is realized.

2904. Was wird er wollen? Like the Templar, Daja thinks the friar can have but one wish (to beg.) Hence Nathan's directions to give before he asks. Boxberger quotes Matt. v, 42: „Gib dem, der bittet," but Nathan a Jew would hardly think of the New Testament command. He gives to all and wisely, and merely wishes to spare the brother the pain and humility of asking.

ACT IV. SCENE 7.

2912ff. If the Templar, as Nathan suspects, is the son of Wolf von Filneck, then he is Recha's brother, but if not, then Nathan would betray to the Templar that he is not Recha's father without there being any necessity for it.

2916. Geh! Said to Daja, whose curiosity caused her to linger.

2918. **Herr Nathan,** formal address, which he drops when he becomes more intimately engaged in conversation with Nathan.

2919. **Annoch** = noch. Cf. the official forms of anbei, anhero, anjetzo, annoch, etc., which are still in use in official documents and often borrowed by the poets.

2920–22. Cf. for the same testimony from Al-Hafi line 1066–9.

Je nu = Nun wohl.

2930. **Buße** = Entschädigung, Vergütung, *amends.* Siebenfach, sevenfold was not the Mosaic law of restitution, but fourfold. Cf. Ex. xxii, 1; 1 Sam. xii, 6; Luke xix, 8.

2935–6. **Saß** = wohnte. Quarantana, or more accurately Quarantania, Lat. Quarantena, is the name of the desert land between Jericho and Jerusalem, but a high, rugged mountain in this region is now especially called by this name. Here the Saviour is said to have passed the forty days of his temptation (hence the name), for which reason many hermits had their cells in the various caverns during the Middle Ages. Here the man fell among thieves and was tended by the Good Samaritan.

2942. **Allwo** = wo. Cf. annoch above. These particles (an–, all–) are simply strengthening.

2944. **Ich stehe auf Kohlen;** generally auf glühenden Kohlen stehen, *to sit upon thorns*, is used here by Lessing to denote not only great impatience, but also that he is sorely pressed for time; for he wishes to find the Templar and clear up the mystery of his birth.

2947. **Siedelei auf Thabor,** *hermitage on Mt. Tabor*, between six or eight miles from Nazareth, where Christ was transfigured. In the sixth and seventh centuries there were churches and a cloister on it. At the time of the crusades there was a Latin church and a cloister built there, but destroyed by the Muhammedans and rebuilt later. In 1187 Saladin laid everything there waste.

2955. **Ins Ohr gesetzt,** comes from the proverb einen Floh ins Ohr setzen, *to put a flea in one's ear.* Cf. In den Kopf setzen, which probably led Lessing to the use of the above expression. Cf. also einem in den Ohren liegen, etc.

2958–9. The Patriarch did not believe that the Templar's hypothesis was a hypothesis, but a real case, so he had nothing better to do than to send out the good Bonafides to find the Jew.

2961. **Ob** governs the genitive when casual, the dative when local or temporal.

2962–5. The reference is to Matt. xii, 31. This is a thrust at the theologians of that time, who understood by the sin against the Holy Ghost, now blasphemy of Christ's person, now the peculiar sins of malice, etc. But the controversy was endless and bitter.

2979. **Gazza** = Gaza, a fortified seaport where formerly the Philistines dwelt. Saladin attacked and took it in 1170, but abandoned it again because important matters called him to Egypt. It is now known under the name of Ghuzzeh.

2982. **Darun** had been built not long before by a king of Jerusalem upon a height of the same name not far from Gaza.

2986. **Er blieb bald darauf bei Askalon** = er fiel, etc. Ascalon was a fortified seaport in the south of Palestine and bore a conspicuous part in the wars of the crusades.

2987. **Wohl sonst.** The friar did not know Wolf von Filneck well, but in his personal relations (wohl sonst), in contradistinction to war, where he met an honorable death, he was a dear lord.

2995–6. **So hat es gute Wege,** proverbial for *there is no haste, there is no fear; If no one else knows about the matter, there is then no fear.*

Traut mir. Nathan does not seem to trust him as he ought, hence this peculiar plea to inspire confidence. He prefers to leave the good undone rather than that it should produce evil. Surmising that Nathan had naturally brought up the child as his own, he tells him that there is no fear, for he will not betray him.

3007–8. **Und müßtet so belohnet werden?** The Patriarch's sentence was: der Jude wird verbrannt.

3008. **Das will mir nicht ein** = das will mir nicht in den Kopf, einleuchten, *I cannot understand it.*

3013–14. **Und Kinder brauchen Liebe,** alludes to the well-known stories of children nursed by wild animals, where they lack a mother's love but do have the love of animals.

3020–4. Lessing looked upon Christianity as upon ennobled Judaism, not a new religion, and this was the mistake of many and is so still. In one of the Fragments, „Von dem Zwecke Jesu und seiner

Jünger," this idea is dwelt upon. Cf. Boxberger's note to this passage. It is true that Jesus never broke with Judaism, but the doctrines he taught were so diametrically opposed to it that the Christian religion has become a new religion, has become universal. Christians, however, should learn tolerance, and that is all the friar means here. The Jews are also God's children.

3025. **Fürsprach** = Mid. H.G. Fürsprech. Now they say Wortführer, Sprecher, Vertreter bei Gericht, Fürsprecher, *intercessor*, *advocate*. See Schiller, Turandot (Act V, Scene 1). Weigand derives it from Low German Vorsprake.

3026. **Wenn Haß und Gleißnerei.** The fanaticism and hypocritical piety of the Patriarch are meant.

3032–5. Lessing often praised the simple-hearted and poor in spirit. The simple, trusting faith of the poor in heart is a better guide to pious deeds than the great knowledge of the theologians. Resignation in God also received constant praise from our poet.

Abgewinnen is a very significant word, as it portrays the inner struggle in Nathan's soul when he received the Christian child as his own. It was the battle of resignation to God's will.

3036. **Voll Wasser** = voll Thränen, is a Biblical expression.

3038–40. Gath is one of the five royal cities of Philistia lying northwest of Jerusalem, but at this time long since destroyed. The many persecutions of the Jews, even then and in our day, not for the praise of God as they claim, but for political reasons and for personal gain, warrant this heart-rending tale describing Nathan's ordeal and victory over self. This tale also has a direct bearing on Lessing's own life. For after a marriage of only one short year, the only happy year of his life, he lost a wife and child. It was a bitter struggle for the poet, and he wrestled long in anguish of soul, but came out resigned in spirit though broken in body, for he never recovered his health again. Nathan's struggle of soul was written with the heart's blood of the poet.

3046–7. A Biblical description. Cf. Job, the king and inhabitants of Ninevah.

3048. **Beiher** = **nebenher, mit Gott auch wohl gerechtet.** Just as Job wished to bring his cause with God before a judge and plead it. Job also accused God of injustice.

3050. **Und doch ist Gott.** Like Job Nathan never denied God, however much he might accuse him of injustice. Returning reason made him realize this and see that all happens through God's decrees. Therefore he must practice what he had long ago understood. Faith in God and resignation to his decrees, love to man, both friend and foe, good deeds, charity, tolerance, these are God-given virtues and must be exercised by God's children. Their practice had made Nathan wise. The decision to do so was made at this critical moment of his life and God sent him the desired opportunity immediately.

3059. **Indem** = indessen.

3068–70. This passage corresponds exactly to Lessing's idea of religion. It is his third stage. Cf. Introd. pp. xii–xiii. All religions contain the germs out of which the higher religion can be developed. Nicodemus, the Good Samaritan, the Centurion, etc., all possessed those qualities which class them as professors of that universal religion, and their mere outward conformity to their peculiar modes of worship do not exclude them from the higher rank of perfect sons of God. So Nathan and the friar meet on a common plain. The Jew is no longer a Jew, nor the Christian a Christian, but both are true sons of God.

3072. **Siebenfache Liebe.** The love for his seven sons had been transferred to the foundling. The same idea occurs in line 3075.

3078. **Nun vollends.** This last proof of Nathan's resignation to the will of God that he will obey, even if he must give up his adopted daughter whom he loves with a sevenfold love, convinces the friar completely (nun vollends) that Nathan is a true Christian.

3081. **Der erste beste.** The first one who comes along, whether his claim be good or not. It is a German idiomatic phrase meaning any one.

3084. **Minsten** = **mindesten**, the earlier and formerly very common form of the word.

3088. **Sipp (Sippe)**, masc., now obsolescent; *kinsman.*

3093. **Und dem Geschlechte dessen** = Und dessen Geschlechte.

3101. **Triegt** = trügt.

3104. **Verscharrten** = **begruben.** **Verscharren** is not elegant and is used to denote the hasty burial after a battle. It means literally to *scrape into a hole*, as animals bury their dead.

3108. **Ich kann nicht lesen.** When we remember that the knights themselves could rarely read in the Middle Ages, it will not appear strange that a poor laybrother could not read.

3112. **Ihr** = der Mutter Recha's.

3119. **Eidam** = Schwiegersohn ; naturally the Templar.

3124–5. The suspicion against Daja is unjust in one sense and correct in another. She is the only one who knew the secret and it could have been divulged only by her. However she had not divulged it to the Patriarch, but to the Templar.

ACT IV. SCENE 8.

3135. **Auch ihm nichts gesteckt,** that is, angebracht. Einem etwas stecken is to tell some one something secretly, and is taken from every-day life.

3142. **Hui** expresses how quickly the Templar will lose Recha. Synonymous, yet different from husch, flugs, nu.

3143. **Der Tempelherr ist drum.** Supply gekommen. Um etwas kommen = etwas verlieren, einbüßen, um etwas gebracht werden, *to lose.*

3150. **Unterwegens** = unterwegen or unterwegs. Unterwegen is the dative plural (unter wegen). Unterwegs is falsely formed like vormals, nachmals, etc., according to the analogy of adverbial genitives. Unter, however, never governs the genitive, so that it would be wrong here.

ACT V. SCENE I.

* **Mamalucken,** that is, slaves. They were either bought as children or were the children of the concubines of the Turkish nobles and were carefully brought up. Lessing cites from Marin: "The Mamelukes or the body guard of Saladin wore a kind of yellow livery; for this was the color of the body guard of his whole house, and all who wished to appear attached to him sought to gain credit by wearing this color. Saladin kept a thousand Mamelukes who were very much attached to him and fought bravely."

3158. **Kahira,** the Arabic form of Cairo, which latter form comes from the Italian pronunciation. The full name is Musr el Kahira, *the victorious capital.* It lies in Middle Egypt on the Nile.

3160. **Ibrahim,** Arabic form for Abraham.

3162–3. **Habe Dank der guten Zeitung.** This construction obtained in Middle H.G. *Edel riter Gunther, des Schuzzes habe danc*... It is more energetic than the usual construction, Habe Dank für die gute Zeitung. Zeitung = Nachricht.

3165–6. **Dem guten Boten Kein Botenbrot?** Botenbrot denoted first the three slices of bread given to a messenger for good news, then any reward for a message. The expression is now obsolete and Botenlohn is used instead.

3176. **So kurz vor meinem Abtritt,** euphemistic for death. They now say Abgang or Hintritt. Saladin died of a hot fever the 4th of March, 1193, in his 57th year. According to Marin, II, 320, Saladin had a presentiment of an early death. In sending his son El Dhaher, in 1192, to Upper Syria he said: "My son, you are going to reign over the states which I have given you. My infirmities make me fear that I shall never see you again."

3190. **Sprengte** = das Pferd springen ließ, *dashed off at full speed.*

3193. **Lecker** = Tellerlecker. It usually denotes a green young man, then Schelm, Spitzbube. Here it means *the rascal.*

3201. **Daß sie mein Beispiel (hat) bilden helfen.**

3202. **Zu guter Letzt,** *at the last.* Letze denotes the fortress on the boundary, then the end, leave-taking, then parting gift, or cup; it then became confounded with Mid. H.G., sich letzen = sich ergötzen, *to entertain, rejoice.* Letze (*refreshment, amusement, parting cup*) passed out of use except in several expressions, and finally became confounded with Letzt(e), the end.

ACT V. SCENE 2.

3210. **Abulkassem** is a common enough name, but the whole event here narrated is fictitious and only introduced to account for the delay of the transport.

3211. **Thebais,** the country about Thebes in Upper Egypt. There had been no revolt there.

3226. **Ihr! ich bin,** etc., addressed to the slaves in the background.

ACT V. SCENE 3.

3237 ff. The Templar begins to realize that the fanatical Christian in him is more firmly seated than the bigoted Jew in Nathan and advances one step farther in his transition stage.

3244–9. The figure is from the plastic art. The unknown father is like the slave who brings the artist the rough block, while Nathan is like the artist who chisels it into a beautiful statue.

The **Öden Strand des Lebens** is the ordinary, stupid education which the ordinary person gives to a child, while Nathan had given Recha the best that could be had. Hence Nathan is the real father.

3252. Als Christendirne. Dirne formerly had a noble meaning. but now it mostly expresses contempt, which was the Templar's intention in using it.

3254. So ein Jude, that is, a Jew like Nathan who had won the Templar's profound respect.

3256. Selbst ihr Lächeln. Not even her smile, which had enchanted him, would be valued by him without the charm of character and intellect as its priceless setting.

3265. Verflattern, taken from the butterfly which passes its time *fluttering* in the sun.

3266. Launisch. Before he was **ärgerlich** (*angry*), now he is only **launisch** (*moody, cross*).

3268–9. Wenn ich den Spott verdiente, etc., *what if,* etc. Cf lines 2819–21, where Saladin was justly quite sarcastic.

3274. Vorgeplaudert. Daja may after all have been merely gossiping and knew nothing of what she was saying. He should have been wiser than to have given heed to her words.

3282. It was not a single spark, the whole being was on fire.

3285. Ihrer warten. Warten with the genitive means *to watch, to mind, to pay attention to.*

ACT V. SCENE 4.

3292. Wanting nothing the friar was richer than Nathan with all his wealth; for the self-sufficient (genugsam) is rich.

3317. Graden Wegs = grades wegs. For the sake of euphony the weak form of the masc. and neut. adj. is used in adverbial expressions like this, but with this particular word the strong form has been retained.

3326. **Mir bange machte.** In the expression einem bange machen, bange is an adverb and the whole idea is to cause anxiety to any one. The dative is alone correct, but some look upon bange as an adjective and construe bange machen with the accusative.

3331–3. Nathan had educated a Christian child in his peculiar way and mankind would condemn him, but God knew all and had ordained all.

ACT V. SCENE 5.

3337. The Templar is not strictly truthful, for he had not waited for Nathan, but had first seen the Patriarch to get his advice in regard to Recha's case and then had hastened to Saladin to prevent any violent measures from being taken.

3346. **Stöber** = Spürhund, a kind of *setter*. Here it is used for *a spy*. Nathan is trying to find out whether the Templar has been to the Patriarch, and the Templar is trying to find out whether the friar has told Nathan anything. Hence the cautious questioning.

3350. **Die dumme — nicht die fromme.** With all his simplicity the friar was not stupid and would never lend himself as a blind tool for executing the wicked plans of the Patriarch.

3351. The Patriarch, however, considers him stupid and thinks himself shrewd enough to use his simplicity for his bad purposes.

3354. **So stellt er wenigstens sich an.** The Templar still fears that the friar may have betrayed all to the Patriarch and possibly to Nathan; he does not heartily trust him. Conscious of his own wrong he fears the result in either case.

3363. **Mit seiner Gunst** = mit seiner Erlaubniß, *begging his pardon*. The Templar had not made any complaint nor given any names.

3370. **Fehl** = Fehltritt, Fehler.

3375. **Was mich wurmisch machte** = was mich in Wuth brachte. Wurmisch = wurmig, which is the usual form now.

3381. **Auszubeugen.** Cf. line 2117.

3382. **Aus der Luft gegriffen,** an idiomatic expression meaning *unfounded, invented.* However, Nathan's questions were not unfounded, but very much to the point, for he wished to prevent any fatal mistakes.

3394–5. **Auch kurz und gut das Messer an die Kehle setzen** = einen in die äußerste Not bringen. This expression means to attack one tooth and nail, do one all the damage possible. Of course it refers to his consultation with the Patriarch.

3395–6. **Wo steckt das Gute?** The delicate thrust which Nathan aims at the Templar shows at the same time the infinite fund of humor in his character. When the Templar closes his remarks with "well and good, I determined to do all the harm possible," he asks: "Do you call that *good* then?" We see this same vein of humor and at the same time reproof in him when offering his money to Saladin.

3399. **Gehäßig,** here used in the active sense, *hates you.*

3401. **Ein junger Laffe** = ein unverständiger, unbesonnener junger Mensch.

3402. **An beiden Enden** = an Extremen. He is an extremist who always does either too much or too little.

3404–5. **Wenn ihr so mich freilich fasset.** "If you come to me condemning your own act as you do and judging yourself so severely (then I must pardon you)."

3432–4. **Ihr wähnt,** etc. The breviary had informed Nathan fully of all he wished to know about both Recha and the Templar, hence there was no longer any necessity for concealment. Cf. lines 3327–94.

3446–7. He had saved her from the fire, now he will save her from the convent.

3449. The friar had been reminded by the Patriarch's commission of his part in delivering Recha to Nathan. The discovery of the whole truth resulted from this circumstance.

3456. **Aus diesen (Händen).**

3466–7. The Templars, and most of the orders of the day, were both priests and warriors. Nathan does not yet wish to tell the secret to the Templar, hence his evasive answers.

3475–7. So Recha spoke to Daja: „was that er dir, den Samen der Vernunft Den er so rein in meine Seele streute, Mit deines Landes Unkraut oder Blume So gern zu mischen?" lines 1564–7. It is a plea for rational religion again which the Templar prefers to the *tares* of superstition. Satan sows the tares. See Matt. xiii, 25ff.

3483 ff. Lessing has skillfully brought out the character of the Templar, who inherits the impetuous temperament of Gannole in Boccaccio (see Introd. p. xxvi). Again his passion carries him away and his bitter sarcasms mar his better nature. "The shell may be bitter," says Nathan, "but the kernel is sound."

3492. **Was hattet ihr für einen Engel da gebildet** is the reading that stood in the first impression. Nathan also compares her to an angel.

3493. **Verhunzen,** *botch.* The expression comes from the works of art which are botched by bunglers. Nathan had made a noble woman of Recha, and now she should become bigoted and narrow as most religious partisans were.

3494. **Er,** that is, **der Engel** of whom the Templar had just spoken. Recha would still be worthy of their love.

3496. **Von meiner Liebe sagt das nicht.** He cannot think the distorted picture which his busy fancy creates will be loveable. He does not wish the least thing, not even her name (as Nathan's daughter) changed. The slightest change would distort the picture in his eyes.

3501. **Auch eben viel** = das ist gleich viel, einerlei, *all the same.*

3507. **Manns genug,** *to be man enough, to have the courage.* The genitive after genug was the prevailing construction at one time and is retained in this expression.

The Templar thinks that Recha is filled with the same passion as himself and will sacrifice all to follow him.

3510. **Nach Euch . . . zu fragen.** Nach einem fragen, *to mind or care for one.*

3512. The Templar is resolved to become a Mussulman in order to get Recha, and relies upon Saladin's promise to help him.

3518. **Leicht beide.** The close of the scene is rather drastic and abrupt, though the interest does not abate. It also prepares us well for the final scene.

ACT V. SCENE 6.

* **Harem.** Cf. line 1142.

3520. **Beklemmt,** for beklommen, the weak form for the strong.

3525. **Schier** = schnell, beinahe.

Fromm. This was the highest praise Lessing could give: „Ich kenne an einem unverheirateten Mädchen keine höheren Tugenden als Frömmigkeit und Gehorsam" is his saying.

3528. **Albern** = albernen, as above.

3533–6. For while reading we acquire only through the memory, but the whole soul receives by lively, oral instruction. Lessing had positive ideas on this subject: „Der aus Büchern erworbene Reichtum fremder Erfahrung heißt Gelehrsamkeit. Eigne Erfahrung ist Weisheit. Das kleinste Kapital von dieser ist mehr werth als Millionen von jener."

3528–42. Teaching by object lessons (Pestalozzi, 1745–1827) became the rage later, but earlier writers like Rousseau had turned attention to the subject of education and advocated this innovation. But perhaps the ancient method of teaching was in Lessing's mind.

3546. **So schlecht und recht** is one of those rhyme-phrases, which are so popular even in our day. Schlecht = schlicht, eben, gerade, einfältig, gut.

3547. **So ganz sich selbst nur ähnlich** = ganz original, *natural and simple.*

3550. Saladin had told her his story and Al-Hafi had often spoken to her of Nathan.

3554. **Mein Herz will Luft.** *My heart must have vent.* Overcome by the painful idea that she is to lose her father she makes a strong appeal to Sittah in her anxiety and fear, hoping that she may be able to help her.

3575. **Vergeb' . . . belohn',** forgive her for the bad (Böses) and reward her for the good (Gutes).

3579–80. Attention has already been called to this discrepancy in lines 758–62. For, if Daja's husband was drowned with the emperor Frederick in 1190 and she entered Nathan's service soon after, she could not have been Recha's nurse in childhood. Cf. Introd. p. xxxiv.

3583. **Geängstet,** now geängstiget, but Goethe also uses ängsten, Iph., Act I, Scene 2.

3586–9. Daja is one of those who believe their own way the only sure way to salvation, and she has done all in her power to convert Recha; now she has disclosed the secret of her birth. Proselyting was not in favor with Lessing.

3601. **Wem?** is here used as the dative of was, an unusual use. The was refers back to „es geht zu weit„ and wem to „Dem kann ich nichts entgegensetzen."

3612. Recha's doubt of the disclosure is expressed in the will = pretends to have disclosed.

3619. **In die Richte gehen** = geradeaus gehen, *to go straight ahead*, hence *to take the shortest cut.*

3624. **Wie ward mir (zu Mute)?**

3627. **Bei der Göttlichen (Marie).** The worship of Mary was at its highest during the crusades.

ACT V. SCENE 7.

It will be remembered that Saladin was to inspect the caravan from Egypt and see the Emir off to Lebanon and then visit Sittah.

3640. **Sie ist von sich** = sie ist außer sich, which is the more usual form.

3645. History relates many instances of Saladin's high sense of justice to friend and foe. None sought mercy or help of him in vain. Cf. Marin's summary of his character at the close of his Histoire de Saladin.

3653–4. Cf. the Templar's monologue, lines 3243ff. Not the slave who delivers the block to the artist is the author of the masterpiece into which the marble is chiseled, but the artist who plans and executes the work. There are higher, holier, closer relations than the mere authorship of one's being; viz., that of guide and wise instructor who develops the noble and pure mind and fills the soul with high and noble aspirations; he has a sacred claim to the child which far outweighs mere abstract parentage.

3656. Saladin considers the disclosure a piece of cruelty, though done with the best intentions. The Templar had told him this story, but he gives it no credence and waits for the proof.

3661. **Faselnd** = aberwitzig und wie irrig redend. The Amme (nurse) was in her dotage and may have been wandering in her mind. The question is, how did she ever find out Nathan's secret? Of course the poet is not obliged to tell us all the secrets of the play, but yet Nathan was certainly never indiscreet enough to betray his own secret to a nurse.

3674 ff. **Umgesehen** is the imperative.

Um die Wette leben will. One who would run life's race on equal terms with her; in other words, one of equal age and chances.

ACT V. LAST SCENE.

3690–2. Boccaccio also makes Saladin return the money borrowed of the Jew Melchisedec.

3691. **Bedeuten**, *inform.*

3696–9. Boccaccio also makes Saladin send away the Jew with rich presents. Lessing's skill in carrying out this motive is much greater than that of the Italian. Saladin's delicacy in his offer is extremely pleasant. Nathan, however, attends to the weightier matters first.

3706–7. Observe the strengthening double negative, like the Greek and older English; present colloquial English employs the same means of adding emphasis to the negation.

3708. **Keiner, keiner (Verlust) sonst!** Recha confesses to Daja (lines 1718–23) that she does not love the Templar, but that he would always be dear to her. Her desire to see him was the desire to be able to thank her rescuer.

3709. The thought had never entered the Templar's mind that Recha was not as passionately in love with him as he with her. Cf. line 2185f., also lines 3507–8.

3715. Cf. lines 2817–8, where Saladin promised to secure Recha for him.

3716. **Gach** = jäh. It is the impetuous Gannole of Boccaccio again. See Introd. p. xxvi. His impetuosity had led him to believe that everybody must see things just as he did without explanation or comment. He should have been sure of his affair before he spoke.

3721. **Auf irgend eine Wohlthat trotzt,** *puts overweening confidence in a good deed.* He who is too confident of the good impression a good deed will make will have to take it back.

3736. **Ist was Recht's.** *That's something remarkable, worth boasting of.*

3737. **Meines Bruders . . . nichts.** Now generally nichts von meinem Bruder, but the genitive after nichts used to be the usual construction.

3743–5. This differs from Saladin's opinion expressed to Sittah, lines 2840–44. Saladin was apparently arbitrary with Jews, as all princes have ever been.

3753–4. **Er hat ihr einen Vater aufgebunden,** *foisted himself a Jew as her father upon her a Christian, and now he is going to foist a brother upon her.*

3756. **Christ!** Once before Saladin had used this reproof with the Templar (line 2783ff.), and he deserved it.

3760. Nathan remembers the bitter disappointment the Templar has just experienced and the thoughtless passion of youth, both of which would lead him to rash and ill-considered words.

3761. Suspicion follows on the heels of distrust. If the Templar had confided in Nathan and given him his true name, he would have spared himself much trouble. But lacking the virtue of confidence in others he became suspicious and misanthropic, which led him to acts unworthy of his better self.

3770. **Das heißt Gott ihn sprechen.** Nathan's kindness in giving this excellent excuse for the Templar's apparent deception could only come from one who was guided by divine wisdom, hence the Templar says that God prompted him to say that.

3775. **Hier zu Lande kamen** = her zu Lande = **in dieses Land kamen.** After verbs of motion we should expect hierher, or in this case her, but compare lines 502, 2459, where the simple hier is used.

3785. **Er war mein Freund.** Cf. lines 2988–9, where he mentions the favors he had received from Assad.

3790–1. The Templar's eagerness to find out the brother leads him to check (nicht mehr) Nathan's story of his father and tell him of the brother, which is now of vastly greater importance to him.

3795. **Betrieger = Betrüger.** The information that he was Recha's brother produced such a revolt in the Templar that he was unable to recover from his surprise and dismay. It was a thunderclap in a clear sky to him, for he never expected to lose the woman he loved in this way. Recha and Saladin misinterpret his feeling and imagine that he considers herself and father deceivers. Saladin's bitter reproof brings him to his senses again and he makes proper amends.

3797–8. The outward resemblance to Assad finds no confirmation in the heart of the Templar who could believe Nathan and Recha capable of deception; therefore the outward resemblance is deceptive. Compare the Templar's own remark, lines 704–707. „Wie? die Natur hätt' auch nur Einen Zug Von mir in deines Bruders Form gebildet: Und dem entspräche nichts in meiner Seele? Natur, so leugst du nicht!" But the Templar's heart was as true as Assad's. Surprise, consternation, and pain at his loss, had overpowered his feelings, and he was unable to reconcile himself to the new situation.

3804–5. For the bonds of nature (the love of brother to sister and sister to brother) are stronger than the bonds that bind soul to soul. It is one of the motives of the piece. We see it in Saladin and Sittah, in Assad and Lilla. The study of the classics led Lessing to this idea; for it is the spirit of the ancient drama where we see portrayed in the Antigone and Iphigenia the tenderest brotherly and sisterly love, but conjugal love was not considered proper to be portrayed on the stage.

3808–9. The Templar remains true to his suspicious nature. He is conscious that Nathan had good reason for disowning *him* and imagines that he is going to make *Recha* suffer for his faults, but Nathan in giving the baptismal name of Recha had no intention of disowning her and dispels all suspicion by the question Und was? For what should she be made to suffer ?

3818. **Das Geschwister.** Cf. line 260.

3832. **Ah! seine Hand.** Cf. line 3109ff., where the friar says that the father had written with his own hand the family names, etc.

3833–4. Nathan had been compelled to prove the relationship between the Templar and Recha to prevent harm, but there was no reason whatever for divulging the secret of Saladin's relations to the two, unless he himself wished it. Therefore he leaves it to him, knowing that he would do what was right. It would be to mistake Lessing completely to assume that he makes Nathan guard the secret from any feeling of servility to Saladin.

3835. Erkennen = anerkennen.

3836. Meine Neffen. This expression denotes the relation existing between uncles and nephews, but when nephews and nieces are to be included, the masculine form has the preference, as including nieces.

3842. Cf. line 3669. Sittah had made the same offer in line 3524.

3844. Cf. lines 3678–9.

BIBLIOGRAPHY.

This list contains only those works bearing upon *Nathan*. For a fuller list of works upon Lessing see Minna von Barnhelm, pp. 243–4 in this same series.

Bohtz. G. E. Lessing's Protestantismus und Nathan der Weise. Erläutert von Dr. August Wilhelm Bohtz. Göttingen. Vandenhoeck und Ruprecht's Verlag. 1854.

Buchheim. Nathan der Weise, a Dramatic Poem by Lessing. Edited with English Notes, etc. By C. A. Buchheim. Second Revised Edition. Oxford. At the Clarendon Press. 1888.

Caro. Lessing und Swift. Eine Studie über Nathan der Weise. Von Dr. J. Caro. Leipzig. Verlag von Ambr. Abel.

Diesterweg. Lessing's Nathan, in Jahrbuch für Lehrer und Schulfreunde. 1865. Von Adolph Diesterweg.

Düntzer. Lessing's Nathan der Weise. Erläutert von Heinrich Düntzer. Leipzig, Ed. Wartig's Verlag. 1883.

Fischer. G. E. Lessing als Reformator der deutschen Literatur dargestellt von Kuno Fischer. Zweiter Theil. Nathan der Weise. Stuttgart. 1881.

Fürst. Lessing's Nathan der Weise. Historisch und philosophisch erläutert von Dr. Julius Fürst. Leipzig. Verlag von Wilhelm Friedrich. 1881.

Giesse. Gotth. Ephr. Lessing's Nathan der Weise. Ein Conferenzvortrag von W. Giesse, Pfarrer in Langenschwalbach. Darmstadt und Leipzig. Eduard Zernin. 1866.

Köpke. Studien zu Lessing's Nathan. Ein Vortrag von Dr. Ernst Köpke. Brandenburg a. H., 1865. Gedruckt bei Adolph Müller.

Marin. Histoire de Saladin par M. Marin. A la Haye. 1758.

Naumann. Literatur über Lessing's Nathan. Aus den Quellen. Von F. Naumann. Dresden. Königl. Hofbuchhandlung von Hermann Burbach. 1867.

Niemeyer. Lessing's Nathan der Weise, erläutert von Dr. Eduard Niemeyer. Zweite Ausgabe. Leipzig, 1887. Verlag von Siegesmund und Volkening.

Pabst. Vorlesungen über G. E. Lessing's Nathan, von Dr. C. R. Pabst. Bern. Verlag von B. F. Haller. 1881.

Rönnefahrt. Lessing's dramatisches Gedicht Nathan der Weise. Aus seinem Inhalte erklärt von J. G. Rönnefahrt. Stendal. Franzen und Grosse. 1863.

Schwarz. Gotthold Ephraim Lessing als Theologe, dargestellt von Carl Schwarz. Halle. C. E. M. Pfeffer. 1854.

Spielhagen. Faust und Nathan. Von Friedrich Spielhagen. Berlin. Verlag von Franz Duncker. 1867.

Strauss. Lessing's Nathan der Weise. Ein Vortrag von David Friedrich Strauss. Bonn. Emil Strauss. 1877.

Trosien. Lessing's Nathan der Weise. Vortrag von E. Trosien. Hamburg. Verlag von J. F. Richter.

Werder. Vorlesungen über Lessing's Nathan, von Karl Werder. Berlin. W. F. Fontane und Co. 1892.

Wünsche. Der Ursprung der Parabel von den drei Ringen. A. Wünsche. Die Grenzboten am Januar 1879.